United Nations University Series on Regionalism

Volume 15

The United Nations University Series on Regionalism, launched by UNU-CRIS and Springer, offers a platform for innovative work on (supra-national) regionalism from a global and inter-disciplinary perspective. It includes the *World Reports on Regional Integration*, published in collaboration with other UN agencies, but it is also open for theoretical, methodological and empirical contributions from academics and policy-makers worldwide.

Book proposals will be reviewed by an International Editorial Board.

The series editors are particularly interested in book proposals dealing with:

– comparative regionalism;
– comparative work on regional organizations;
– inter-regionalism;
– the role of regions in a multi-level governance context;
– the interactions between the UN and the regions;
– the regional dimensions of the reform processes of multilateral institutions;
– the dynamics of cross-border micro-regions and their interactions with supra-national regions;
– methodological issues in regionalism studies.

Accepted book proposals can receive editorial support from UNU-CRIS for the preparation of manuscripts.

Please send book proposals to: pdelombaerde@cris.unu.edu and lvanlangenhove@cris.unu.edu.

More information about this series at http://www.springer.com/series/7716

Frank Mattheis • Andréas Litsegård
Editors

Interregionalism across the Atlantic Space

 Springer

Editors
Frank Mattheis
Centre for the Study of Governance
  Innovation
University of Pretoria
Pretoria, South Africa

Andréas Litsegård
School of Global Studies
University of Gothenburg
Gothenburg, Sweden

Center for the Study of Governance
  Innovation
University of Pretoria
Pretoria, South Africa

ISSN 2214-9848   ISSN 2214-9856   (electronic)
United Nations University Series on Regionalism
ISBN 978-3-319-62907-0   ISBN 978-3-319-62908-7   (eBook)
DOI 10.1007/978-3-319-62908-7

Library of Congress Control Number: 2017951859

Printed on acid-free paper

This Springer imprint is published by Springer Nature
The registered company is Springer International Publishing AG
The registered company address is: Gewerbestrasse 11, 6330 Cham, Switzerland

Acknowledgements

This edited volume constitutes one of the many results of ATLANTIC FUTURE, a research project funded by the European Union Seventh Framework Programme under the grant agreement no. 320091. The foremost acknowledgment thus goes to the steady support of the European Commission to academic research on regionalism and interregionalism in a geographic area that has received less public and scholarly attention in the context of what has been predicted to become an 'Asian Century'.

The Barcelona Centre for International Affairs (CIDOB) coordinated the ATLANTIC FUTURE project and its consortium of 13 research institutes from all Atlantic shores. CIDOB has been a dependable and supportive partner from the initial conception of the theme to the final delivery of the contributions. In particular, Laia Tarragona, Paula de Castro and Jordi Bacaria are to be wholeheartedly thanked for their superb commitment to the project.

Crucial to the Atlantic dimension and the collaborative nature of our endeavour were three project meetings and workshop sessions that took place in 2014 and 2015 at the University of Pretoria (South Africa), at the Fundação Getulio Vargas (Brazil) and at the University of Lisbon (Portugal). The key findings were first disseminated to the public at one of the ATLANTIC FUTURE's final events in December 2015 at Johns Hopkins University (USA). All four hosting institutions excelled in organising the logistics and in facilitating an equally productive and enjoyable environment.

Special thanks go to our project leader in Pretoria, Lorenzo Fioramonti, for his persistent encouragement and acumen throughout our work, as well as to the entire team at the Centre for the Study of Governance Innovation (GovInn) for their collaboration and advice on all ends. Many thanks also need to be extended to the advisory board of the ATLANTIC FUTURE for their input at various stages and to the external and internal reviewers, who dedicated their time and expertise to providing valuable criticism on draft chapters. The editorial team at our publisher is greatly appreciated for the final work on the manuscript.

I express my personal thanks to Andréas for his diligent coediting that always took place in a context of dedicated collegiality and, more importantly, sincere friendship. Moreover, I acknowledge the support to my own work within the post-doc programme of the German Academic Exchange Service (DAAD). Finally, my greatest gratitude cannot but go to Gaia for her never-ending motivation and companionship.

Johannesburg, South Africa   Frank Mattheis
March 2017

Contents

Contributors

Riccardo Alcaro Istituto Affari Internazionali (IAI), Rome, Italy

Anna Ayuso Barcelona Centre for International Affairs (CIDOB), Barcelona, Spain

Miguel Fuentes Centro de Investigación y Docencia Económicas (CIDE), Mexico City, Mexico

Kimberly Nolan García Centro de Investigación y Docencia Económicas (CIDE), Mexico City, Mexico

Gian Luca Gardini Friedrich-Alexander-University of Erlangen-Nürnberg, Erlangen, Germany

Andréas Litsegård School of Global Studies, University of Gothenburg, Gothenburg, Sweden
Center for the Study of Governance Innovation, University of Pretoria, Pretoria, South Africa

Madeleine Goerg German Marshall Fund of the United States, Brussels, Belgium

Paul Isbell Center for Transatlantic Relations, Johns Hopkins University SAIS, Washington, DC, USA

John Kotsopoulos Centre for the Study of Governance Innovation, University of Pretoria, Pretoria, South Africa

Andrés Malamud Institute of Social Sciences of the University of Lisbon, Lisbon, Portugal

Frank Mattheis Centre for the Study of Governance Innovation, University of Pretoria, Pretoria, South Africa

Camila Pastor Centro de Investigación y Docencia Económicas (CIDE), Mexico City, Mexico

Nicoletta Pirozzi Istituto Affari Internazionali (IAI), Rome, Italy

Patrick Reilly German Marshall Fund, Washington, DC, USA

Santiago Villar Barcelona Centre for International Affairs (CIDOB), Barcelona, Spain

Chapter 1
The Atlantic Space – A Region in the Making

Andréas Litsegård and Frank Mattheis

Abstract In this introductory chapter, the field of interregionalism studies is introduced and the relation to the Atlantic region is presented. The study of interregionalism faces various challenges: firstly, interregionalism research is (still) Eurocentric; secondly, the agency of the various actors involved is often overlooked; thirdly, there is a need for more comparison between regions; and fourthly, the connection between regionalism and interregionalism is poorly understood. We propose to address these shortcomings by recalibrating the theoretical lens in order to analyse the diversity of contemporary interregionalism. The chapter thus discusses established categories of analysis as well as the post-revisionist approach to interregionalism, and outlines the contribution to the endeavour of balancing the case of the EU in the study of regionalism and interregionalism. Furthermore, we provide an overview of the context in which interregional relations across the Atlantic takes place and contextualise the most relevant regional-building processes in all Atlantic regions. The chapter ends by explaining the structure of the volume and by presenting the individual conceptual and empirical contributions of the book,, which provide state of the art and innovative analysis of interregionalism.

Keywords Atlantic • Interregionalism • Regional organisations • Regionalism • Regions

1.1 Introduction

Within the field of regionalism studies the interdependence and outreach of regional projects have gained notable importance since the early 1990s (e.g. Baert et al. 2014a; de Lombaerde and Schulz 2010, Doidge 2007; Hänggi et al. 2006; van Langenhove 2011). Interregionalism in its purest form concerns relations between

A. Litsegård (✉)
School of Global Studies, University of Gothenburg, Gothenburg, Sweden

Center for the Study of Governance Innovation, University of Pretoria, Pretoria, South Africa
e-mail: andreas.litsegard@globalstudies.gu.se

F. Mattheis
Centre for the Study of Governance Innovation, University of Pretoria, Pretoria, South Africa
e-mail: Frank.Mattheis@governanceinnovation.org

© Springer International Publishing AG 2018   1
F. Mattheis, A. Litsegård (eds.), *Interregionalism across the Atlantic Space*,
United Nations University Series on Regionalism 15,
DOI 10.1007/978-3-319-62908-7_1

two clearly identifiable regional organizations within an institutional framework (Baert et al. 2014a). However, in spite of the increasing volume of research related to interregionalism, scholars argue that interregionalism as a specific type of international relations is losing strength or being replaced by other forms of relations, most notably bilateralism and multilateralism due to the geopolitical shift from a unipolar to a multipolar world (Baert et al. 2014a; Söderbaum 2016). Some scholars have therefore come to the conclusion that interregionalism is a thing of the past (cf. Hardacre 2010; Robles 2008; Camroux 2010). Rather than ruling out interregionalism as outdated it is important to conceptualize this phenomenon in new ways, considering that interregionalism can seldom be seen in its purest form. Instead, it is necessary to recalibrate the theoretical lens in order to see the diversity of contemporary interregionalism. Interregional relations are encapsulated with other forms of cooperation such as bilateralism, regionalism and multilateralism within a multi-layered governance framework (Söderbaum 2016). The interrelationship between interregionalism and regionalism warrants some extra attention here, considering their close connection. A common proposition in regionalism research is that regionalism spawns interregionalism (Söderbaum 2016: 191). For example, Hettne argues that regionalism is a precondition for interregionalism. For two regions to establish a functioning relationship, both should have achieved a certain degree of actorness This implies, firstly, that both regions have some kind of external presence, i.e. that they make some kind of impact (economic, political, ideological etc.) on other parts of the world. Secondly, the engagement in interregional relations requires a scope of action and room for manoeuvre, in some cases even a legal personality. Actorness follows from the external presence in different contexts (Hettne 2014: 70–72). What is less studied, but not necessarily less common in world politics, is the reverse relationship; that interregionalism reinforces regionalism. Engaging in interregional frameworks creates a need for further consolidation by the participating regional actors. For example, Söderbaum argues that by supporting various forms of interregionalism in Latin America, the EU has strengthened the perception of its actorness In a similar vein, the example of the Asia-Europe Meeting (ASEM) shows that participation in interregional forums strengthens region-building "at home" by acting towards what are perceived as other, different regions. In this way, interregionalism constitutes the formation of regions (2016: 188). In this volume, the various studies will further illustrate the complex relationships between regionalism and interregionalism.

Interregionalism is conceptually and analytically rather underdeveloped, struggling to grasp the complexity of interregional relations, which explains the common perception that interregionalism has lost significance in the global arena (Baert et al. 2014b; Söderbaum 2016). This book will contribute to the conceptual and theoretical understanding of interregionalism, acknowledging and analysing the complexity of various forms of interregional relations based on new empirical data. It should be read as a contribution to endeavours of revising the case of the EU in the study of regionalism and interregionalism, as has been advocated by the post-revisionist approach of Fawcett, Ponjaert and Teló (2015). This approach encompasses the endeavour to acknowledge the pivotal empirical role of the EU in global interregionalism and to embed it in a methodological reciprocity with its counterparts.

Aiming to neither exclude nor overemphasise the EU in our research, we include as many chapters involving the EU as Latin America or Africa. We thereby aim to push the post-revisionist approach further, as we do not only create a balanced approach in studying both ends of interregionalism, but in addition contextualising all Atlantic actors, including the EU, within a broader network of entangled interregionalism. The main thread of this volume – and at the same time its main contribution to the field – stems from normalising the EU in a broader context. This implies an understanding of interregionalism in the Atlantic as a complex of overlapping and interwoven layers of relationships, which cannot be neatly dissected, as it simultaneously carries elements of competition and complementarity. This book does not assemble a collection of independent (or even isolated) bi-regional relations but considers their amalgamation as constitutive to a regional order of the Atlantic in the making.

In line with the challenges of many bilateralism, regionalism and multilateralism studies, the study of interregionalism faces similar challenges, of which four are highlighted here. Firstly, interregionalism research is (still) highly Eurocentric, even if this is increasingly challenged as discussed above, thus overlooking much of the entanglements among the rest of the world. Most studies are indeed primarily interested in the processes of the EU's external relations (Rüland 2014: 27–28). This often creates ignorance of the 'other', stemming from a general lack of sufficient data about non-EU counterparts (Söderbaum 2016: 175). Secondly, much of the literature focuses on a systemic perspective, often overlooking the agency of the various actors involved. The agency of the various state and non-state actors involved in interregional processes is far from being sufficiently studied (Rüland 2014: 27–28). According to two scholars, '[a]lthough it has almost been ten years since Neumann (2003) identified the question of agency in region-building as a blind spot in earlier studies on regions, thorough knowledge of the question of 'who' still remains incomplete' (Lorenz-Carl and Rempe 2013: 1). Thirdly, there is a great need for more comparative studies of interregionalism (Baert et al. 2014b, 188). Up to date, most interregional studies take place in isolation without a comparison of interregional processes in order to discern overarching trends. Rüland argues that '[d]eveloping a research framework and methodological tools facilitating the comparative study of interregional dialogue forums is thus an urgent task' (2014: 41). Fourthly, in the current literature many important points have indeed been raised about the relationship between regionalism and interregionalism, as shown above, but often in a rather speculative, sweeping manner without considering the specificity of individual cases based on empirical data. More research is needed into how regionalism and interregionalism relate to and impact on each other (Söderbaum 2016: 192).

In order to explicitly engage with these four shortcomings in the interregional literature we focus on relations criss-crossing the Atlantic and their contribution to a distinctive Atlantic space, characterised by a high density of interregionalism. The link between North America and Europe continues to be the strongest of any continental relationships, even if being matched by the rise of Africa, Latin America and also the Arab region. The latter are increasing their interregional links but also influence in global affairs. This book provides a comprehensive insight into these trends, studying the overlapping linkages of interregionalism in the wider Atlantic space. Such focus on the Atlantic is unique as it allows going beyond conventional antagonisms between North and South by contextualising interregionalism within a denser set of transregional interactions. This book provides new insights into the study of interregionalism, based on new empirical data and an inclusion of the generally under-researched linkages within the Global South. Interregionalism often tends to be highly asymmetrical due the high variety of regional institutionalisation, actorness and outreach. As a consequence, the linkages tend to be driven unilaterally and can produce structures of dependence.

Regions are constantly in flux, expanding or contracting in their delineation and scope. Geographical boundaries increasingly succumb to political, economic or social ideas of desired cohesion. The Atlantic space is no exception, as it is currently characterised by fragmentation rather than unity. Emerging developing countries are crafting strategies that challenge the traditional Western powers through regional and interregional initiatives. Established North-South cooperation retains an important place in this reconfiguration but contestation has become an equally defining element. At the same time, much of this contestation has exhibited a volatile character that depends chiefly on the financial and ideational investment of regional leaders and on the perception of a common external other. Positive integration factors such as identity, ideology, transfers and entanglement are not necessarily the main drivers, though they tend to provide a more durable basis for region-building than external actors, be they funders or perceived opponents.

1.2   Mapping the Variable Geometry of Regionalism and the Rise of Geopolitical Spaces in the Atlantic

1.2.1   Regionalisms Across the Atlantic Space

Before proceeding to the detailed analysis of interregionalism in the chapters to follow, the remainder of this chapter will provide an overview of their context and their preconditions: the most relevant regional-building processes in all Atlantic regions. Most projects to form regions across national borders (i.e. regionalisms) in the Atlantic Space have evolved within continental boundaries. Territorial contingency and proximity have determined the shape of most projects, and only a few organisations, such as the North Atlantic Treaty Organization (NATO), have cut across the Atlantic Ocean. Thus, different types and logics of region-building have emerged within Africa, Latin America, North America and Europe.

Regionalism in Africa unfolds between pan-African ideals of uniting the continent in an anti-colonial legacy on one side and the role of the European Union (EU) as the main funder on the other side (cf. Godsäter and Pirozzi in this volume). Both the strong normative stance of exclusion and the influence of an external actor are unparalleled among the other regionalisms across the Atlantic. Most regionalisms have materialised in regional organisations with their own centralised but powerless bureaucracies. The African Union (AU) represents the continental framework that aims to coordinate the most relevant pan-African sub-regional projects, the Regional Economic Communities (REC) (cf. Goerg and Kotsopoulos in this volume). At the same time some imperial regional constructs such as the South Africa-dominated Southern African Customs Union (SACU) and the French legacy of the African Financial Community (CFA) persist.

Regionalism in Latin America is chiefly characterised by a proliferation of regional organisations along internal political and economic rather than geographic divides (cf. Ayuso and Gardini in this volume). Regional projects thus accumulate and they represent a break-away from previous or competing projects. The recent Pacific Alliance represents liberal economic policies and an alignment with the United States of America (US), thus contrasting with the more structured Common Market of the South (Mercosur), while the Union of South American Nations (Unasur) is designed to foster regional hegemony at the expense of North American influence. Regional organisations tend to be shallow, with most policymaking concentrated in national ministries.

Regionalism in North America has been dominated by trade agreements and securitisation accompanied by little institutionalisation (cf. Alcaro and Reilly in this volume). The North American Free Trade Agreement (NAFTA) has been the only major organisation founded and it has not faced internal competition. However, differentiation has occurred in terms of an antagonism between US-led pan-Americanism and a North-South divide of the Americas. NAFTA was conceived as a core agreement to expand throughout the whole Western Hemisphere into a "Free Trade Area of the Americas" (FTAA), but it faced resistance in South America, thus limiting its outreach into parts of Central America.

Europe is undoubtedly home to the most sophisticated institutionalisation of regionalism in the Atlantic. Since overcoming the antagonism with the European Free Trade Area (EFTA) the EU has established itself as the dominant actor of integration on the continent. The EU is not only an exceptional regionalism due to its strong supranational elements but also in terms of being the only regional actor in the Atlantic that has developed a notable presence and influence in the other regions.

1.2.2 The Evolution of Contemporary Regionalisms Across the Atlantic Space – Synchronisation and Fragmentation

For most of the twentieth century, regionalisms in the Atlantic Space have been chiefly shaped by domestic factors, albeit with reference to the external framework. The driving forces after World War II included the peace-building process in Europe under the aegis of the US, the quest for economic autonomy and favourable terms for trade in Latin America, and the attempts at convergence between the newly created states in post-colonial Africa. As a result, most regionalisms of the Cold War period were characterised by a focus on clearly confined projects, such as industrialisation policies, the pooling of resources or mediation between conflicting states. Although there was a recurrent exchange of ideas between regional projects, such as developmental regional policies from Latin America to Africa, most regionalisms maintained their inward-oriented outlook.

The end of the Cold War triggered the creation of new regionalisms across the Atlantic Space. Major projects that were to play a crucial role in shaping the regional configurations, such as NAFTA or Mercosur, were set up in the early 1990s. Other key regionalisms such as the Southern African Development Community (SADC) and the EU emerged as new organisations, representing important changes from their predecessors – the Southern African Development Coordination Conference (SADCC) and the European Communities (EC). As opposed to the more inward-oriented previous regional projects, the emergence of this new generation of regionalisms was primarily influenced by three changes in the global order (Mattheis 2014). Firstly, the liberal economic paradigm established itself as a dominant prescriptive guideline, thus paving the way for regionalism as a vehicle for free trade agreements (FTA). Secondly, the democratic political paradigm also established itself as a guiding principle, forming an understanding of regionalism as a framework to support and stabilise democratic transitions. Thirdly, the end of global bipolarity between the US and the Soviet Union offered new options for regions to be formed, while for Latin America and Africa the fear of marginalisation could be countered by region-building.

While there was a sense of synchrony in the Atlantic Space about the beginning of a new wave of regionalism after the Cold War, the subsequent evolution of the various projects has been characterised by fragmentation. Latin America and the Arab world have become arenas of contesting regionalisms and aspiring regional leaders (cf. Ayuso et al. in this volume). No clear pattern of regionalism has emerged, as both the underlying norms and the delineations are being negotiated. Africa is still in a process of reconfiguration with several sub-regions that are constantly changing shape and outlook. Competition is less evident than in the Latin American case but the widespread phenomenon of overlapping membership and external funding has hampered a process of consolidation. By contrast, Europe and the North Atlantic have dominant, consolidated and expanding regionalisms. The EU and NATO have extended their reach far beyond their own region and face no internal competing project, except the possibility of a return to nationalism. North America has a consolidated project whose functional and territorial expansion has been stalled due to resistance in South America and a lack of institutional identity. The negotiations of trade agreements with the Asia-Pacific region and with Europe have not fostered a common position, thus further reducing the capacity of NAFTA to become a regional actor.

1.2.3 The Spreading of Region-Building Ideas Across the Atlantic

Regionalisms in the Atlantic Space draw their set-ups and objectives from various sources of ideas. An important source is internal and stems from the accumulated experiences with region-building in the past, including failed attempts at integration and institutional memory. Many contemporary regional organisations can be traced back to previous projects, either as a continuation or a rupture. And yet, across the Atlantic, the main source of institutional elements as well as geographical expansion is the European Union. Many other projects such as the AU or the Andean Community (CAN) make direct references to the EU and adapt elements of its modus operandi or at least of its symbolism, including regional parliaments and courts (Jetschke and Lenz 2013). The EU also functions as an anti-model when it is perceived as an undesired form of integration. NAFTA and Mercosur have rejected supranational logics and a centralised bureaucracy.

The main ideas for economic objectives chiefly stem from a liberal paradigm and the global institutions representing them, such as the World Trade Organisation (WTO) and its predecessor, the General Agreement on Tariffs and Trade (GATT) (Duina 2006). With few exceptions, such as the Bolivarian Alliance for the Peoples of Our America (ALBA), Atlantic regionalisms are generally designed to facilitate free trade and investment between their members and, in most cases, also with third parties through external agreements. Implementation, however, varies greatly between actual common markets such as the EU and SACU, on one side, and liberal schemes that primarily exist on paper as in most African REC, on the other (Jovanovic 2006). By contrast, the liberal idea of free movement of labour and of people is not readily taken up as an objective of regionalism and has only been implemented in a few projects such as the EU and the Economic Community of West African States (ECOWAS). The same is valid for common currencies, which are only found in the eurozone and the euro-dependent CFA Franc *(Franc de la Communauté Financière d'Afrique)*, even if notable parts of Latin America and Africa are effectively dollarized (Kenen and Meade 2008).

The main sources of ideas to effectively define the boundaries of a region in the Atlantic Space have often been based on identity foundations. The influence of "pan-" movements is still relevant in contemporary regionalisms in Africa and Latin America, while the legal identity of the *acquis communautaire* has provided the foundation for the EU (Fioramonti and Mattheis 2016).

1.2.4 The Atlantic Divide and the Role of Regional Powers

The major division of regionalism in the Atlantic Space remains along the North-South axis. Several projects to bridge this gap, such as the FTAA or the Union for the Mediterranean have failed to generate integrative momentum. The Organisation of American States (OAS) has increasingly been challenged by the Unasur project, which is composed only of South American states and aims to monopolise regional security governance, and more recently by the Community of Latin American and Caribbean States (CELAC), grouping 33 American states together without the US and Canada. While convergence has occurred between Western countries under NATO, the antagonism between projects in the Atlantic North and South has increased. Mercosur and NAFTA have further diverged and so have the two Atlantic Ocean-centred alliances – NATO and the Zone of Peace and Cooperation of the South Atlantic (ZOPACAS) (Cf. Alcaro and Reilly as well as Mattheis in this volume). Meanwhile, the EU's trade negotiations with Mercosur or via Economic Partnership Agreements (EPA) with the Africa, Caribbean and Pacific (ACP) groupings have faced a rocky path. Countries with the potential to overcome the North-South divides, such as Mexico, Egypt and Turkey, have acted more as buffer states than as bridge states.

By contrast, the emergence of regional powers such as Brazil, South Africa and Nigeria is closely interwoven with their membership of regional projects (Stolte 2015). Regionalisms such as Mercosur, Unasur, SADC, ECOWAS and the AU have been instrumental to their leadership and their global visibility. These countries' approaches to establishing appropriate regionalisms has not been uniform, ranging from stepping up as paymaster in order to establish hegemony to more tacit cooperative strategies. Even though the presence of a regional power has triggered opposition from smaller members, regions without clear leaders, such as Central Africa, have struggled even more to come up with active projects. However, as regional powers have increasingly been perceived as global powers, they have shifted more attention to forums such as the G-20 or the BRICS (Brazil, Russia, India, China, South Africa). In combination with the recurrent volatility of their economies, this shifting interest makes it difficult to sustain their role as constant, active leaders, given the fact that they have generally been opposed to autonomous or even supranational regional bodies.

1.3   Overview of the Chapters

The book will conduct an analysis of seven cases of interregional relations across the Atlantic space, which will allow for a much needed comprehensive approach. The chapters in the book provide state of the art and innovative analysis of interregionalism, comparing various interregional processes. This includes engaging with the issue of agency in interregional relations, arguing that interregional processes and agendas are always driven and constructed by certain actors for certain purposes. In more detail, firstly, the geographic focus on the Atlantic is unique. The book studies, in depth, interregional relations across the Atlantic in a way that has never been done before. Considering the growing interest of actors on all shores of the Atlantic in transregional relations (especially the EU, as examplified by the Atlantic Future programme which this book stems from), the book can provide important insights into the trends of both convergence and divergence, which characterise the complex entanglements of interregionalism. We point out that the relevant delineations do not necessarily correspond to the continental boundaries that are commonly assumed. Secondly, and related to the previous point, the empirical contribution is important in terms of digging deeper into both North-South as well as South-South relations. We build on previous literature and provide new insights into how a variety of different state and non-state actors shape these processes. In terms of North-South relations, we take the inherent power dynamics seriously, stemming from the colonial history, asymmetrical trade relations and development co-operation. In terms of South-South relations, African-Latin American and especially Arab-Latin American linkages are greatly under-researched so far. Mapping out and discussing various dimensions of these relations, including interregional civil society networks, is a major contribution to the field of interregionalism. Thirdly, the book provides new theoretical insights into the study of interregionalism. The first step is an agency-oriented approach, increasing the theoretical understanding of how the agency of various state and non-state actors construct and shape interregional cooperation, and how interregional institutions and structures affect the behavior of these actors. This volume also proposes a new framework for studying patterns of formal region-to-region relations. Based on the various case studies, the framework will show the emergence of four ideal-typical patterns of interregional relations: leadership, emulation, cooperation, and exchange. Also, more generally, the book shifts the theoretical perspectives towards South-South relations and non-state actors. Lastly, this book dwells into the relationship between regionalism and interregionalism, arguing that the nature of interlinkage between regionalism and interregionalism depends on the case; regionalism can either be a springboard to interregional connections or conversely interregionalism can spur regionalism, though this is not an automatism. Case-sensitive empirical evidence of different types of relationships along this continuum will be provided in the empirical chapters.

In Chap. 2, *Debunking Interregionalism: Concepts, Types and Critique – With a Pan-Atlantic Focus*, Gian Luca Gardini and Andrés Malamud lays the conceptual and theoretical foundation for the empirical chapters to come. Their starting point is the claim that the relevance of Interregionalism lies on two assumptions: that regionalism is a significant mechanism of governance and that regions are outward looking. The fact that both assumptions are contested confers the concept of interregionalism a structural fuzziness. The chapter seeks to grasp the phenomenon by following a sequential path: first dealing with definitions, types and theory, only then to look into the empirical evidence in search of correspondence between names and facts. By looking into transatlantic interregionalism and comparing various cases of interregionalism, the chapter concludes that a large umbrella often brings together very diverse groupings of countries under a same, moderately inconsequential, working mechanism: summitry.

The empirical, main section of the book starts off by two chapters discussing South-South interregional relations. In Chap. 3, *Volatile interregionalism: the case of South Atlantic relations*, Frank Mattheis argues that in their extra-regional outreach Latin America and Sub-Saharan Africa rarely make each other a priority. However, since the end of the Cold War there has been an increasing amount of political efforts to strengthen ties on a region-to-region basis. This rapprochement has been facilitated by the emergence of two regional projects following a similar logic in a post-Cold War context: the Southern African Development Community and the Common Market of the Southern Cone. At the same time, both projects face serious limitations of actorness that are illustrative of the confined space for inter-regionalism across the South Atlantic. An analysis of the formalised initiatives on political, economic and security issues between the two regions reveals that these are characterised by transregional and partly pure forms of interregionalism and that most initiatives are heavily shaped by the leading role of Brazil.

This is followed by a discussion of the relationship between Latin American and the Caribbean (LAC) and Arab countries in Chap. 4: *Actors and opportunities: Interregional processes in the Arab region and Latin America and the Caribbean*, by Anna Ayuso, Santiago Villar, Camila Pastor and Miguel Fuentes. The authors argue that the relations between regional organisations in LAC and their peers in North Africa and the Arab world are still fairly nascent and represent a much under-studied area of interregionalism in the global order. The re-launching of South-South cooperation in recent decades in a multipolar context has favoured rapprochement between LAC and the Arab world. Despite the fact that both regions are not a priority for each other, relations and exchanges have grown constantly over the last decade, accompanied by a progressive institutionalisation of high-level political dialogue. This chapter identifies and analyses the main drivers behind this multi-layered interregionalism as well as the obstacles in its way by examining how it is fostered by political, economic and social state and non-state actors.

Andréas Litsegård and Nicoletta Pirozzi start off the subsection on North-South interregionalism by discussing EU-Africa interregional relations in Chap 5: *The EU and Africa: Regionalism and interregionalism beyond institutions*. The chapter maps relevant trends of interregionalism between Europe and Africa by looking at the historical evolution and in light of recent developments. The analysis focuses on institutionalized interregionalism between the EU and the AU, as well as regional organizations in Southern, West and East Africa in the three sectors of trade, security and environment. It also goes beyond by addressing and comparing formal and informal, state and non-state, patterns of integration at the transnational level. In the chapter, the authors argue that it appears that the EU has heavily influenced the development of regionalism in Africa mainly through teaching and support. The relationship between the EU and African regions is fundamentally characterized by the former influencing regional policy of, and providing funds and capacity building to the latter.

In Chap. 6, *Interregional Relations between North America and Africa*, John Kotsopoulos and Madeleine Goerg explore the extent of interregional cooperation between North America and Africa in the area of development co-operation. Given the relative lack of relations between regional organisations on the two continents, the chapter uses quasi-interregionalism as a framework to instead explore relations of African regional organisations and with the United States and Canada respectively.

The chapter also explores where and if cooperation between the U.S. and Canada is evident in interactions with African regional entities. The results are marginal at this stage, but do point to the continuing rise in importance of African regional organisations like the African Union as increasingly prominent interlocutors.

The last part on North-South interregionalism and Chap. 7 is *EU-Latin America and Caribbean Inter-regional relations: complexity and change* by Gian Luca Gardini and Anna Ayuso. The authors analyse interregionalism between Latin America and the Caribbean and the European Union. The complexities and overlapping of LAC regionalisms are reflected in the several interregional mechanisms that the European Union has with Latin American and Caribbean countries and regional organisations. The chapter argues that different political and economic interests in Latin America have given rise to overlapping regionalist projects. Also, Latin American regionalisms have constantly evolved in terms of strategies and organisations. This has generated a number of interregional institutionalized mechanisms between the EU and Latin America and the Caribbean, which exacerbates the complexity of interactions.

Chapter 8 discusses North-North interregionalism. In *Interregional Interactions in Europe, North America and across the North Atlantic,* Riccardo Alcaro and Patrick Reilly argue that if regionalism is figured as a continuum from rudimental regional interaction to very sophisticated forms of it. Europe stands on this latter end while North America barely makes it to the middle point. The imbalance in the degree of regionalization on the two northern shores of the Atlantic explains the scarcity of region-to-region interactions. Interregionalism has thus little to say about Europe and North America, although 'quasi-interregionalism' (i.e. country-region relations) has here some of its most advanced manifestations. The case of Europe-US relations actually goes beyond quasi-interregionalism and displays traits that are more characteristic of regionalism than anything else. The chapter concludes that a comparison of regionalism in Europe and North America is therefore invariably destined to be an exercise involving a third, bi-continental region: the West.

The very last Chap. 9 of this book addresses the fundamental question of how to find appropriate delineations for regionalisms and interregionalisms. In *Latin America's Interregional Reconfiguration: The Beginning or the End of Latin America's Continental Integration?*, Paul Isbell and Kimberly Nolan García investigate the relevance of continental regional categories for Latin and South America. Their trade analysis provides qualitative evidence that the ocean basins of the Atlantic and the Pacific offer more relevant maps to understand the current evolution of regionalism and interregionalism. The chapter concludes that new 'ocean basin regionalisms' offer alternative options for regional trade agreements and interregional trade integration which, while remaining complementary to the current sub-continental and continental regionalisms, could become a new guiding frame for Latin American regionalism.

1.4   Concluding Remarks

While the novel quality of mapping regionalism and interregionalism within a broader – in this case Atlantic – order, helps to outline institutions, ideas and identities that are distinguishable from other context, there are also important limitations. As any other region in the making, the Atlantic space remains volatile and porous. Its delineation is to a large degree arbitrary and the high amount of overlapping relations poses a challenge to identifying broader trends in terms of contraction versus expansion, or of convergence versus divergence. Even though the collection of the empirical articles in this volume shows that the lens of the Atlantic does have an important analytical value, fragmentation within that space prevails, especially on the North-South axis but also between Africa and Latin America. However, alternative framings cutting across the Atlantic pose similar limitations and as for any other meaningful lens, acknowledging the plurality of regionalism and interregionalism within the Atlantic Space also provides insights for regionalism at large. These insights chiefly relate to the relevance of mutual entanglements, of ideational borders, and of institutional asymmetries. To conclude, this book has taken an important step towards opening up the interregionalism agenda outside the EU, in line with the post-revisionist approach, so as to include cases from South-South interregionalism and actors other than states. However, this research area still provides ample room for further research. The gaps both concern the lack of empirical data about non-EU interregional processes and the design of new concepts and frameworks for understanding interregionalism that are not directly derived from and biased towards the EU as a model. As the field of regionalism studies has considerably matured in terms of comparative work lately (Börzel and Risse 2016), the research on interregionalism would equally benefit from an expansion in terms of cases and methods. The role of actors other than states also remains a weak spot in current work, though this volume points out that transregionalism might be the form of interregionalism that is most prominent and thus in most need of further research, incorporating the increasing role civil society, illicit networks and businesses play in such processes. Lastly, the lens of the Atlantic has also been an endeavour to challenge conventional notions of regional borders, which are predominantly associated with terra-centric limitations. A similar re-focusing may be meaningfully applied to other maritime spaces, such as the Indian Ocean, but also to new grounds such as the understanding of diasporas and buffer areas (Russo and Rainieri 2015) as both a regional and interregional phenomenon.

References

Baert, F., Scaramagli, T., & Söderbaum, F. (2014a). Introduction: Intersecting interregionalism. In F. Baert, T. Scaramagli, & F. Söderbaum (Eds.), *Intersecting interregionalism* (pp. 12–23). New York: Springer.

Baert, F., Scaramagli, T., & Söderbaum, F. (2014b). Conclusion: Interregionalism in the 21st century. In F. Baert, T. Scaramagli, & F. Söderbaum (Eds.), *Intersecting interregionalism* (pp. 183–197). New York: Springer.

Börzel, T. A., & Risse, T. (Eds.). (2016). *The Oxford handbook of comparative regionalism.* Oxford: Oxford University Press.

Camroux, D. (2010). Interregionalism or mererly a fourth-level game? An examination of the EU-ASEAN relationship. *East Asia, 27*(1), 57–77.

De Lombaerde, P., & Schulz, M. (2010). *The EU and world regionalism. The makability of regions in the 21st century.* Farnham: Ashgate.

Doidge, M. (2007). Joined at the hip: Regionalism and interregionalism. *Journal of European Integration, 29*(2), 229–248.

Duina, F. (2006). *The social construction of free trade.* Princeton: Princeton University Press.

Fawcett, L., Ponjaert, F., & Teló, M. (2015). Introduction. In M. Teló, L. Fawcett, & F. Ponjaert (Eds.), *Interregionalism and the European Union: A post-revisionist approach to Europe's place in a changing world* (pp. 1–15). Farnham: Ashgate.

Fioramonti, L., & Mattheis, F. (2016). Is Africa really following Europe? An integrated framework for comparative regionalism. *Journal of Common Market Studies, 54*(3), 674–690.

Hänggi, H., Roloff, R., & Rüland, J. (2006). *Interregionalism and international relations.* London: Routledge.

Hardacre, A. (2010). *The rise and fall of interregionalism in EU external relations.* Dordrecht: Republic of Letters Publishing.

Hettne, B. (2014). Regional actorship: A comparative approach to interregionalism. In F. Baert, T. Scaramagli, & F. Söderbaum (Eds.), *Intersecting interregionalism* (pp. 66–82). New York: Springer.

Jetschke, A., & Lenz, T. (2013). Does regionalism diffuse? A new research agenda for the study of regional organizations. *Journal of European Public Policy, 20*(4), 626–637.

Jovanovíc, M. (2006). *The economics of international integration.* Cheltenham: Edward Elgar.

Kenen, P., & Meade, E. (2008). *Regional monetary integration.* Cambridge: Cambridge University Press.

Lorenz-Carl, U., & Rempe, M. (2013). Bringing agency (back) into African regionalism. In U. Lorenz-Carl & M. Rempe (Eds.), *Mapping agency: Comparing regionalisms in Africa* (pp. 1–13). Farnham: Ashgate.

Mattheis, F. (2014). *New regionalism in the south: Mercosur and SADC in a comparative and interregional perspective.* Leipzig: Universitätsverlag Leipzig.

Robles, A. C., Jr. (2008). *The Asia-Europe meeting: The theory and practice of interregionalism.* London: Routledge.

Rüland, J. (2014). Interregionalism and international relations: Reanimating an obsolescent research agenda? In F. Baert, T. Scaramagli, & F. Söderbaum (Eds.), *Intersecting interregionalism* (pp. 24–46). New York: Springer.

Russo, A., & Rainieri, L. (2015). *Buffer areas as spaces of connections and identification: The centrality of regional borderlands in the Sahara and the Caucasus.* Paper prepared for the ISA annual convention "global IR and regional worlds: A new agenda for international studies" February 18–21, 2015.

Söderbaum, F. (2016). *Rethinking regionalism.* New York: Palgrave.

Stolte, C. (2015). *Brazil's Africa strategy. Role conception and drive for international status.* New York: Palgrave Macmillan.

Van Langenhove, L. (2011). *Building regions – The regionalization of the world order.* Farnham: Ashgate.

Chapter 2
Debunking Interregionalism: Concepts, Types and Critique – With a Pan-Atlantic Focus

Gian Luca Gardini and Andrés Malamud

Abstract Interregionalism means region-to-region relations. Its relevance lies on two assumptions: that regionalism is a significant mechanism of governance and that regions are outward looking. The fact that both assumptions are contested confers the concept of interregionalism a structural fuzziness. In this chapter we seek to grasp the phenomenon by following a sequential path: we first deal with definitions, types and theory, only then to look into the empirical evidence in search of correspondence between names and facts. By looking into transatlantic interregionalism, we find it as a large umbrella that brings together very diverse groupings of countries under a same, moderately inconsequential, working mechanism: summitry.

Keywords Atlantic • Interregionalism • Regional organisations • Regionalism • Regions

2.1 Introduction

On 11 June 2015, 61 chiefs of states or their representatives plus the highest EU officials met in Brussels. The occasion brought together one third of the world countries and was the second EU-CELAC (or 8th EU-LAC) summit, the largest gathering of world regions ever. Yet the standing of the two partners could not be more asymmetric. The European Union (EU) is a treaty-based regional organization that makes binding decisions, adjudicates conflicts through legal procedures, commands a billionaire budget, boasts huge headquarters in several countries and employs thousands of people. In contrast, the Community of Latin American and Caribbean States (CELAC) lacks legal personality, decision-making capacities, headquarters,

G.L. Gardini (✉)
Friedrich-Alexander-University of Erlangen-Nürnberg, Erlangen, Germany
e-mail: gian.luca.gardini@fau.de

A. Malamud
Institute of Social Sciences of the University of Lisbon, Lisbon, Portugal
e-mail: amalamud@ics.ul.pt

© Springer International Publishing AG 2018
F. Mattheis, A. Litsegård (eds.), *Interregionalism across the Atlantic Space*,
United Nations University Series on Regionalism 15,
DOI 10.1007/978-3-319-62908-7_2

a budget, and any staff. While the EU has a single trade policy and advances towards bringing borders down and unifying its currency, the Latin American countries are fierce defenders of national sovereignty. The fact that this meeting is considered the pinnacle of interregionalism testifies to the elusiveness of the concept.

Interregional relations differ from conventional interstate relations in two respects. First, the nature of the actors cannot be taken for granted. Not just states but also regional organizations and civil society generally participate in the process. Issues of representation and coordination are problematic too. Whereas states need to refer to their internal structures and proceedings only sporadically and mainly through established procedures when negotiating a deal internationally, regional organizations need to have recourse to internal consultation frequently and through tortuous and less than formalized mechanisms. Furthermore, as interregional relations are usually asymmetric – since they tend to involve regions with different degrees of complexity such as the EU vis-à-vis most developing regional groupings – explicit support for further integration and the transfer of integration technologies tend to be a key part of the agreements.

Second, the scope of interregionalism is usually limited to 'low politics:' regional organizations typically engage in negotiations on economic or social issues rather than security or military matters. This said, most interregional agreements do proclaim larger political goals and are garnished with verbose rhetoric. Some interregional summits end up by issuing presidential communiqués that mention geopolitical issues and envisage the establishment of 'strategic alliances,' whatever that means. However, these statements rarely reflect or produce concrete results.

Several studies have analyzed the nature, types and prospects of interregional relations (*América Latina Hoy* 2005; Baert et al. 2014; Doidge 2011; Hänggi 2000; Hänggi et al. 2006; Hettne and Söderbaum 2000). Their conclusions are tentative, mostly agreeing on that the multidimensionality of the phenomenon requires the combination of different analytical approaches. Initially, interregionalism – as regionalism before it (Fawcett and Hurrell 1995; Gamble and Payne 1996) – was amply regarded as a step towards global governance. Lately, however, arguments have been raised that consider regionalism and interregionalism as a hindrance for global governance (Higgott and Phillips 2000; Kacowicz 2015). Although interregionalism has been defined as "institutionalized relations between world regions" (Hänggi et al. 2006: 3), all the elements in this description remain controversial. Some authors deem interregionalism unavoidable and irreversible (Kupchan 2006: 147), as some do with regional integration itself, while others are more skeptical (Aggarwal and Fogarty 2005). Few, such as Doidge (2011, 2014), go beyond mostly descriptive or normative accounts. This chapter takes critical stock of the debate before diving into the shape that interregionalism has assumed across the Atlantic Ocean. By resorting to participant observation and original interviewing with diplomats that participated in the organization of the 2013 EU-Latin America and the Caribbean Summit in Santiago de Chile, we map the real world of trans-Atlantic relations as defined by its most discernible manifestation – summitry. We further argue that, as regionalism recedes and multipolarity consolidates, there is little more to expect from interregionalism.

2.2   Identifying, Classifying and Theorizing Interregionalism

Region-to-region relations, albeit in a loose form, can be traced back to the Lomé Convention, a trade and aid agreement between the European Community and 71 African, Caribbean, and Pacific (ACP) countries signed in 1975 in Togo (Söderbaum 2012). It was replaced by the Cotonou Agreement, signed in 2000 in Benin by the EU with 78 ACP countries. Although its principles stated the equality of partners and the ownership of development strategies, an ironic reminiscence of later day South-South cooperation, fact is that the ACP countries never constituted a region per se but an artificial grouping brought and kept together by an external organization. Later on, the EU engaged in interregional cooperation with independent regional organizations, beginning with the Association of Southeast Asian Nations (ASEAN) and gradually spreading towards most regional blocs in the developing world.

Interregionalism is thus a fuzzy concept. This should not come unexpected given interregionalism's root concept – regionalism (Laursen 2003; Malamud 2013; Schulz et al. 2001). Unlike pioneering masterpieces on regionalism such as those by Nye (1968), Claude (1971) or Lindberg (1963), too many contemporary studies suffer from conceptual stretching or fuzziness or both. Although authors usually provide some kind of definition for the phenomenon they analyze, few do so in a satisfactory manner. Most definitions are either vague or ambiguous. Take, for example, the influential characterization by Hettne and Söderbaum (1998:7):

> "New regionalism is a comprehensive, multifaceted and multidimensional process, implying the change of a particular region from relative heterogeneity to increased homogeneity with regard to a number of dimensions, the most important being culture, security, economic policies and political regimes".

In this definition, analytical categories are explicitly non-exhaustive, implicitly non-exclusive, and lacking on precedence or hierarchy. This cannot plausibly produce measurable indicators and testable hypotheses. Hettne and Söderbaum (1998: 9) further define regionalization as

> "increasing levels of 'regionness', namely the process whereby a geographical *region* is transformed from a passive object to a subject with a capacity to articulate the interests of the emerging *region*" (emphasis added).

Here, the word *region* is used simultaneously to connote objective geography and subjective interests, as well as an existing object and an emerging entity.

A way out of conceptual stretching consists of understanding contemporary regionalism as an umbrella expression that covers a multiplicity of phenomena. Andrew Hurrell (1995) enumerates five of these, arguing that none should be given the exclusive rights to use the term: (a) regionalization, (b) regional awareness and identity, (c) regional interstate cooperation, (d) state-promoted regional integration, and (e) regional cohesion. The first – regionalization – can be understood as social or economic interdependence, which is usually the outcome of market-driven processes. The second – regional identity – conveys a cultural rather than a political or economic notion. The common feature of both phenomena is that neither is necessarily purposeful but is brought about by decentered factors – such as increasing trade flows or common historical roots. The following three subtypes respond to a different logic: they are either the outcome of formal state decisions – cooperation and integration – or a consequence of such decisions – regional cohesion. While cooperation entails voluntary compliance, integration requires some degree of sovereignty transfer, which discourages unilateral withdrawal and raises the costs of process reversion. In these subtypes, Hurrell (1995: 44) claims, "the *region* plays a defining role in the relations between the states (and other major actors) of that *region* and the rest of the world", while constituting "the organizing basis for policy within the *region* across a range of issues" (emphasis added). This definition uses the same concept simultaneously for an actor and an arena. Tautologically, the *region* "plays a role" regarding "policy within the *region*". Confusing wording is arguably rooted in the nominalization of the adjective *regional*. The latter should rather be conveyed by a noun, which can either be a process (integration) or an entity (organization). To give an example, *Europe* is an intelligibly but highly ambiguous noun that should not be collapsed with European integration or with the European Union. In these two expressions, "integration" and "union" are nouns while "European" becomes an adjective that delimits the particular range of an otherwise general phenomenon. Yet, most literature on regionalism uses "Europe" and "the EU" interchangeably. This is a source of contagious confusion, as similar interchangeability between a geographic area and an international organization is assumed everywhere else – wrongly.

The confusion between regional geography – a set of contiguous countries – and regional politics – an organization of contiguous countries – is not just conceptual. Real existing cases of interregionalism also come in different configurations. This is the reason why the world of interregionalism cannot be understood without splitting it into subtypes.

In a pioneering article, Hänggi (2000) developed a typology of interregional arrangements to account for existing cases. He distinguished three types:

(a) pure interregionalism, that is relations between regional groupings (such as EU-ASEAN or EU-Mercosur);
(b) transregionalism, that is arrangements where states participate in an individual capacity, as in APEC, the Trans-Pacific Partnership or EU-Latin America and the Caribbean before the establishment of CELAC (this label is also applied to more informal relations including non-state actors); and.
(c) hybrid interregionalism, that is relations between regional groupings and single powers (such as the so-called strategic partnerships of the EU with several regional powers, including the Transatlantic Trade and Investment Partnership currently under negotiation).

Hänggi's types have been dissected, and applied empirically, in a special issue of the *Journal of European Integration* devoted to the EU as a global actor and the role of interregionalism (Söderbaum and Van Langenhove 2005).

Hänggi's second type merits special analysis. Take the case of the South Atlantic Zone of Peace and Cooperation (ZOPACAS). This organization was created in 1986 through a UN general assembly resolution – after a Brazilian initiative – and brings together three Latin American and twenty-one African states. Although it may look like a bi-regional phenomenon, in practice it is not an agreement between two pre-existent organizations but between individual states (see Mattheis in this volume). Such transregional character is even more apparent in the case of the Trans-Pacific Partnership, which brings together countries from North America, South America, Asia and Oceania. In fact, these basin-based agreements erode existing land-based regional organizations rather than bringing them together. This centrifugal dynamics has been labeled cross-regionalism and is retaken below.

A bizarre but ever more frequent type of interregionalism is the one developed between overlapping regions, that is, regional organizations that share members. In these cases, some states sit at both sides of the table. An illustrative case is the relationship between Mercosur and UNASUR, whose summit meetings are sometimes conflated thus making it difficult to disentangle whose logic or regulations apply. We have discussed this issue elsewhere (Malamud and Gardini 2012; Gardini and Ayuso in this volume) and will not develop it further here, but the articulation of segmented and overlapping regionalism has multiplied to the extent that it now falls into the folder of interregionalism (Malamud 2013; Hulse et al. 2015). It resembles a multidimensional chessboard, with intra- and inter-level interactions, rather than a matrioska, in which inner objects just fit into but do not interact with outer objects.

If overlapping interregionalism becomes a fourth type within Hänggi's typology, we suggest that stealth interregionalism might become the fifth one. The paramount case is currency integration between several African states and the Euro zone. As it happens, the West African CFA franc (the official currency in eight countries), the Central African CFA franc (likewise for six other countries), the Comorian franc, the Cape Verdean escudo and the São Tomé and Príncipe dobra are all pegged to the Euro through bilateral agreements, totaling seventeen independent African states whose monetary policy is decided in Paris and Frankfurt (http://ec.europa.eu/economy_finance/euro/world/other_currencies/index_en.htm, last accessed 4 November 2014). This makes for one third of the African continent! Studies of interregionalism have very rarely included this phenomenon as worth analyzing (for an exception see Mattheis 2014), although it also takes place in other regions such as the Caribbean.

2.2.1 A Modest Typological Proposal

Formal region-to-region relations, Hänggi's first type, are a logical and chronological aftermath of prior regional integration. Afterwards, they can be supportive of regional integration along two dimensions. The first one regards the type of involvement of the senior partner – provided there is one, which occurs in most cases studied in this volume, with the Europe-North America linkage being an exception (see

Table 2.1 Patterns of formal region-to-region relations

		Senior partner's role	
		Active	Passive (or equal)
Main dimension of interaction	Politico-institutional (polity-related)	Leadership	Emulation
	Socio-economic (policy-related)	Cooperation (aid)	Exchange (trade)

Alcaro and Reilly in this volume). Involvement may be active and focused or passive and dispersed. The second criterion concerns the dimension in which the interaction takes place. This may be either politico-institutional or socio-economic. By combining the two criteria, four ideal-typical patterns of interregional relations emerge: leadership, emulation, cooperation, and exchange (Table 2.1).

Leadership means that the senior region (usually a regional organization, sometimes a regional hegemon) takes most of the responsibility for establishing the goals, monitoring the course, and supporting the instruments required by the junior region (not always an organization) to carry out the undertakings agreed upon. A historical example is the role played by the United States in the reconstruction of Europe after World War II and its support to the processes of cooperation, coordination and integration – albeit, in this case, the United States was a single country and not a regional bloc. The US also fostered the creation and early institutionalization of the Central American Common Market (CACM) through financial and institutional support; the crisis of the bloc started precisely when the US lost interest in its development and ceased to supply leadership. A different kind of leadership may be exerted through conditioned inclusion, whereby a regional bloc offers full or limited access to neighboring countries (which may until then have belonged to another bloc) in exchange for domestic reform. The EU provides the best example of this mechanism through its enlargement policies towards EFTA first, Southern and Northern European countries later, and Eastern European and Mediterranean countries more recently.

Emulation is the strategy by which an emergent regional bloc replicates the institutional structure or the integrating strategy of successful brethren. This was the path initially followed by the Andean Community, as it undertook the creation of an early supranational structure that reproduced the EU's (Saldías 2010). Some authors contend that mimicry was also at the roots of Mercosur and its institutional evolution (Medeiros 2000; Rüland and Bechle 2014).

Cooperation stands usually as a euphemism for economic aid. Under this label, the senior region does not necessarily participate in the establishment of the junior region's goals, but instead provides it with technological, financial, or economic assistance. This is the type of relationship that links the EU to poorer regions such as the one bringing together the ACP (Africa-Caribbean-Pacific) countries.

Lastly, *exchange* is arguably the least demanding type of relationship, as it involves mostly negative policies – thus easier to pass and implement – such as tariff removal and free access to regional markets. This is the case of the ongoing

EU-Mercosur negotiations. The negotiation of this kind of agreements is being progressively upgraded by additional requirements such as investment guarantees, intellectual property rights, environmental and labor regulations, and common standards. Yet, free trade agreements (FTAs) concern chiefly economic matters, and trade partners are formally on an equal footing – in contrast to cooperation agreements.

The role of the EU in the development of interregionalism has been studied as a case of diffusion. In exploring the extent to which the EU has sought to promote regional integration beyond its borders, Börzel and Risse (2009) analyzed what

> "the EU seeks to export and how it has used its external relations and foreign policy to foster cooperation between regions (inter-regionalism), on the one hand, and regional cooperation among third countries, on the other."

While it is conceivable that other world regions might spontaneously imitate the EU institutions, argues Schmitter (2010), the EU "has dedicated considerable resources and efforts to clone itself and meets regularly with its 'counter-parts' in Asia, Latin America and Africa." In these approaches, the EU acts as external federator (Santander 2010) and interregionalism is considered a driver of further regionalism rather than its consequence.

This book has produced six chapters dealing with different interregional interactions in the Atlantic area. Most of them arrive to similar diagnosis: "serious limitations of actorness" on the part of the engaging regions (Mattheis in this volume), large asymmetries or "imbalance in the degree of regionalization"/institutionalization (Alcaro and Reilly in this volume; Pirozzi and Godsäter in this volume), and low priority conferred to interregional relations (Ayuso et al. in this volume; Kotsopoulos and Goerg in this volume). They also classify most cases into Hänggi's hybrid or quasi-interregional category, and those that deal with the EU accept that it has led a leading role (our left column on Table 2.1) except when dealing with the North American region (lower right cell on Table 2.1). More distressing are the conclusions by Isbell and Nolan García (2015), who claim that "new ocean basin regionalisms" are substituting traditional land-based regions, therefore changing the nature of interregional relations. The focus on the Atlantic space adopted in this book is consistent with the emerging phenomenon of cross-regionalism, which defines the simultaneous participation in various trade agreements irrespective of geographic location. Tovias (2008: 4) argues that, by engaging in this strategy, states "strive to escape their initial uncomfortable status of so-called 'spoke' by signing agreements with more than one 'hub'". The ascendancy of cross-regionalism – and the parallel decay of regionalism – stems from the emergence of multipolarity in the international system and does not bode well for the standard types of interregionalism.

Regardless of the form, purpose and organizational feature that interregionalism may assume, most varieties tend to reach a pinnacle in interregional summits. Whether relations take place between two regional intergovernmental organizations or between "two or more regions that are dispersed and porous, and where neither region negotiates as a region" (Söderbaum 2012:1200), exchange and dialogue at the highest political level are defining moments. Thus, interregionalism can be understood – at least largely – as an exercise in summitry. This is the focus of the following sections of this chapter.

2.3 Interregionalism as Summitry Exercise

Interregionalism across the Atlantic is characterized by an increasing number of summits between national and regional leaders. Only in the last 3 years, heads of state and/or government, diplomatic corps, and business and civil society representatives from the four shores of the Atlantic engaged in a multitude of events, including – among the most significant – two Summits of the Americas (2012 and 2015); a South American-Arab Countries Summit (2012); two EU-Latin America and Caribbean Summits (2013 and 2015); an Africa-South America Summit (2013); an Africa-EU Summit (2014); an Arab-US Policymakers Conference (2014); and a US-Africa Leaders Summit (2014). Regardless the interest, value, and results of each of these events, proliferation tends to decrease the marginal returns for all stakeholders of huge international assemblies. There is a risk that "too many summits kill the summits" (Gahr Store 2012: 11).

The "summit fatigue" is by now a well-documented problem in all fields and at all latitudes of international activity. For instance, the intensity of the G-20 process since the beginning of the crisis in 2008 pushed the Obama administration to call for a rationalization of the process and to reject hosting candidatures and new proposals for more and more events (Cooper 2010). If the argument is valid for major gatherings on topical issues, it is even stronger for specialized events, such as the World Summit on Information Society or the World Summit on Sustainable Development. In these cases the required presence and use of specific technical expertise as well as political representativeness cause strain on state leadership and bureaucracies as well as on civil society stakeholders who intend to attend the summit or to participate in the process before, during or after the core event (O'Siochru 2004; Peake 2002).

This overcrowded scenario inevitably affects regionalism and interregionalism too in their summitry dimension. The increase in the number of summits at the European level has raised concern and brought about a number of critiques of summit inflation in regionalist processes (Melissen 2003). Interregional summits are obviously affected too. They have to compete for human and financial resources against a large and expanding number of other international – including regional – and national commitments. As an illustrative example, it is worth remembering how one EU-Latin American and Caribbean Summit had to be postponed for over six months because of the congested international agenda. Initially scheduled for June 2012, it clashed with another three high-profile international meetings the same month: the G-20 in Mexico, the Rio + 20 UN Conference on Sustainable Development and the Euro Area Summit in Brussels. The summit was eventually celebrated at the end of January 2013.

2.3.1 Problems and Challenges of Interregional Summitry

So what are the key problems of interregionalism as a summitry exercise caused by the excessive use of this instrument and the congestion of the international agenda? What kind of difficulties and challenges characterize the process? And why, in spite of these acknowledged limitations, do interregional summits remain widely used in international diplomacy? The type of shortcomings can be understood with reference firstly to the nature of the problem and secondly to the categories of actors affected. The resilience of interregional summits can be explained with arguments stemming from both theory and practice of international affairs.

The first problem affecting interregionalism in its summit form is the clarity of their aims and purposes. This refers to the expectations and the benefits it generates. This in turn leads to a discussion of the parameters used to assess success or failure. What are interregional summits for? What outcomes is it legitimate and realistic to expect? Whose expectations count most? It seems that significant doubts and uncertainties about the process exist (Caetano 2010). This is valid both for the direct participants and the stakeholders broadly understood. Interregional summits more than anything else are about dialogue and whether or not they are successful is perhaps not the right way to pose the question (FCO 1 2013). Instead it would be more useful to identify what their purpose and benefits are, and to realize that most of the benefits are difficult to measure and quantify and they are to be found at the margins of the summits (ibid.). This is a case in which exclusion costs are higher than participation's.

A particular aspect of this discussion on purpose concerns the involvement of civil society. Its participation in interregional summits is more and more common and it often involves the presentation of position papers to ministerial or head of states assemblies. Now, it is quite difficult to assess the exact expectations of governments and state actors in these mega events. It is even more difficult to evaluate civil society's, because of the varied nature of its components but also for the limited understanding stakeholders seem to have of summit procedures and outcomes. In these cases, clarity of roles and expectations is problematic. This is also true for a number of civil society consultation mechanisms at the international level. As the EU DG Trade-Civil Society Dialogue suggests, while the objectives of consultation and transparency can be satisfactorily met, more uncertainty exists about policy improvement. Similar developments have been registered in the EU-Africa Forum (Pirozzi and Godsäter in this volume) and in the Council for Arab Relations with Latin America and the Caribbean (CARLAC; Ayuso et al. in this volume). After all, civil society's role is to participate, not to deliberate, and engagement is based on the principle "one voice not one vote", which is often blurred or misunderstood (Ecorys 2006).

Another problem that affects interregional summits is time. The organization of such high-profile events requires a large amount of time and dedicated teams. This is true for the host country, of which a massive logistic and organizational effort is required. It is also true for participant countries, which have to contribute to the drafting of the final declaration, discuss and agree on the agenda of the summit itself and that of their delegations. The latter always engage in other activities and visits on the fringes of the summit in order to maximize the use of time. There is also the issue of timing in the calendar year to avoid congested periods or clashes with other international or national events where leaders and technical and support teams, not least the security ones, may have to participate. Finally, the generally short duration of the summit itself gives in fact little time for substantial discussion, and most of the work has to be prepared by state bureaucracies in advance.

A related problem is the opportunity cost. Participation in an interregional summit means that leaders and key state officials, as well as civil society delegations, cannot deal with other issues for a few days. With the increasing density of international forums and commitments, the decision to send top leaders or high-level representatives to interregional summits is a delicate one, precisely because returns may not be immediately obvious. Other events and activities may in fact gain more political reward or media exposure, and national priorities may just prevail over loose international commitments and lengthy speeches and travels. Only 34 heads of State out of possible 61 made it to the 2013 EU-Latin American and Caribbean summit, which "was met with almost total indifference in Latin America as well as in Europe" (Sberro 2013:1). Conversely a failure or a scandal at the summit may give unwanted media exposure to leaders. The UK delegation considered a success that the same event was not hijacked by radical Latin American leaders and that the Falkland-Malvinas issue was not raised at any stage (FCO 1 2013). But the UK had not sent either the Head of State or Government or the Foreign Minister, which indicates a quite low political interest in the interregional summit. Where a strategic value is clearly detectable participation of leaders is high. This was the case at the 2009 5th Summit of the Americas where President Obama for the first time introduced himself to the other leaders of the Americas. These saw the advantage of participation and no country sent representatives of lower status than Head of State or Government. In the absence of clear gains or strategic priorities, interregional summits struggle to attract top participants, who may find other venues and activities more convenient according to political or economic calculation.

Interregional summits are expensive exercises. The organization, logistics, communication, transportation and accommodation involved are a burden for taxpayers and state finance. Indeed the high cost of interregional summits is particularly evident when measured against the uncertainty or even the paucity of the results and benefits produced (Whitehead and Barahona de Brito 2005). If one considers that most of the costs are often bore by the host country, and that for the duty of reciprocity these kind of events often take place in developing countries, one may wonder if that money could be better spent otherwise. It is estimated that the 2012 Summit of the Americas held in Cartagena, Colombia, cost about 30 million USD, that the 2008 EU-Latin America and the Caribbean Summit in Lima, Peru, cost around 35 million USD, and that, by comparison, the 2012 G-20 in Mexico cost 80 million USD (MinRel 1 2012). To this, one has to add the costs for the participants. In times of crisis and media watch of public expenses, significant investments in interregional summits organization and participation ought to be subject to scrutiny and rethinking.

Swollen and diluted agendas also constitute a limitation of interregional summits. A final declaration of countless points and observations is hardly a credible commitment and doubtfully a selection of real priorities for cooperation, action or even discussion. It certainly presents significant challenges for follow-up and implementation. As an example the final declaration of the 2014 EU-Africa Summit counted on 63 items, while the 2013 final declaration of the EU-Latin America and the Caribbean Summit was composed of 48 points, a significant reduction when compared to the record 104 points of the 2004 Guadalajara Declaration (see corresponding chapters in this book). Furthermore, at times the contents and provisions of interregional summit declarations and action plans "can at best be regarded as optimistic assumptions" (Eyinla 2004:176). Yet, understandably, agendas and final declarations are a compromise between a large number of countries, even if the summit is supposedly between two regional organizations. In addition, with a view to interregional summits, coordination mechanisms within regional organizations are at times cumbersome, little efficient, or non-existent. This results in the host country having to deal with an accumulation of items to be added to the agenda so that this can be acceptable to all participants. While this may ensure a level of consensus, it makes the achievement of tangible results, and their communication to stakeholders, extremely difficult.

The most problematic aspect of interregional summits is their limited capacity to produce practical results. While a specific definition of what practical results means may be elusive, there seems to be a quite widespread dissatisfaction at policy decision and implementation as well as at the paucity of common actions undertaken as a direct result of these summits. This is a preoccupation for both policy-makers and academics (MinRel 2 2012 and MinRel 3 2012; MAE 2012; Maihold 2010; Whitehead and Barahona de Brito 2005). A first difficulty is the limited capacity of follow-up and implementation of the decisions taken (?) and the priorities identified during the summits (Maihold 2010). In interregional summits where the EU is involved this aspect generally falls under the competence of the EU Commission but the results have been perceived as dissatisfactory (FCO 2 2012; MAE 2012). A second aspect concerns the inability of these interregional summits to produce actual effects on the international system, and in particular to promote or advance the international position of the participants, especially the party perceived as the weaker (Maihold 2010). Thirdly, one may wonder if this instrument is in fact inadequate to the new global context (Peña 2010). Recent changes at the regional level too, such as the creation of new regional groupings or the emergence of new international powers and aggregations, make the rethinking of the current interregionalist schemes a necessity.

The final point to discuss is who is affected by the proliferation of interregional summits. Obviously political leaders have to select between competing commitments. They have to justify and balance their choices about participation in national and international events in front of the demands and pressure from government branches, political parties, opposition, the media, lobby groups, and civil society.

State bureaucracies are also highly affected as they have to prepare the travels, assess and draft documents, liaise with partners and the organizers, and they often struggle with shortage of staff, especially in less advanced countries. Also civil society and business who intend to participate in interregional summits find proliferation problematic due to their limited resources and expertise, costs and opportunity costs. Sometimes the real hope for civil society is to have a few minutes with key politicians to campaign for their cause rather than give a substantive contribution to the summit itself or to one of the collateral events (MAE 2012). Both national and transnational civil society organizations require increasing funding and expertise to contribute proactively to these processes.

2.3.2 Explaining the Resilience and Proliferation of Interregional Summits

In spite of these critiques and apparent lack of tangible results, interregional summits are inescapable instruments of international diplomacy. A number of theoretical and empirical reasons have been proposed to explain this resilience. From a theoretical perspective, a first explanation is offered by the very processes of regionalization and globalization, which by limiting the control of nation states on their own policy choices in fact encourage states to engage in regional and interregional cooperation (Roloff 1998). This reasoning is broadly adaptable to fit major International Relations theories. It fits realist and neo-realist approaches as nation states attempt to balance-off regionalist challenges from and alliances of other world regions through interregionalism; and it also fits a liberal-institutionalist approach as interregionalism can be understood as a joint attempt by nation states to manage the complexity of global interdependence (Hänggi 2000).

Another theoretical approach may explain more specifically why, in spite of all documented shortcomings and skepticism by policy-makers, interregionalism survives and in fact proliferates. Rhetorical action (Schimmelfennig 2003) suggests that rhetorical commitments produce actual effects. That is to say that when a rhetoric and narrative exercise is repeated through time and widely accepted, this shapes political interests, values and legitimacy and therefore it determines policy actions and choices too. Applied to interregionalism, this means that commitment to the process expressed in final declarations and convenient political statements and media coverage end up perpetuating a system in which few actually do believe. This is consistent with the observation that in international affairs the institutionalisation of norms produces patterns of behaviour that are hard to alter in the absence of significantly changed circumstances (Goldstein and Keohane 1993).

Perhaps the most convincing theoretical explanation is provided by the multi-bilateralism approach (Hill and Smith 2011: 401; Le Gloannec 2004). The proliferation of international forums and gatherings at least makes multilateral events convenient venues to take forward bilateral affairs and agendas. Participants have the opportunity to meet the partners in which they are interested and to conduct bilateral talks as well as to form ad hoc alliances, not necessarily related to the topic under discussion in the multilateral venue. Policy-makers too embrace this explanation (MAE 2012). They see in interregional summits an opportunity to maximize time to meet with their key bilateral partners in certain geographic or issue areas. In fact, according to a participant in the 2013 EU-Latin America and Caribbean Summit, this occasioned good personal links, a chance to take forward the national agenda in the region and to be seen by strategic partners (FCO 1 2013). It seems that conceptual distinctions between pure interregionalism and more hybrid forms (Hänggi 2000) are in fact blurring in the diplomatic practice and the hectic pace of today's international summitry.

In addition to theoretical explanations, there are very practical and pragmatic reasons for the resilience and flourishing of interregional summits. Firstly, they provide a forum for discussion and political direction in interregional relations. This top-level dialogue seems not only indispensable but also genuinely functional to the process if this has to have any meaningful purpose. Furthermore, change and results in these cases are not to be assessed in the short period but over the long run. Secondly, with the increase and diversification of regional organizations and the reconfiguration of regional spaces and aggregations, as well as power dynamics and distribution in various parts of the world, interregionalism is a logical step to connect new regional actors, powers and agendas. Thirdly, most of the shortcomings identified by the literature and the policy-makers can be addressed. For instance time and money, as well as human resources, can be saved by the use of "virtual summits". The summitry process is perhaps not ideal but it is perfectible and no obvious alternative is available. Fourthly, in spite of constant complains at exclusion and at the waste of resources, civil society demand for more weight in international decision-making often materializes in the quest for more summits, with more space for social actors and NGOs within them. For all these reasons, the summitry exercise is a resilient aspect of regionalism and interregionalism. These processes can take many forms and evolve institutionally, but dialogue and direction at the highest political level remain key to any international political process.

2.4 Conclusions

The analysis of interregionalism varies widely from studies that focus on causes through those that highlight processes to those that investigate effects. This variation sometimes hinders comparison and should be taken into account when conducting further research. Additionally, it raises the question of relevance: is interregionalism important because it brings about novel developments or is it simply a (perhaps unavoidable but) inconsequential by-product of regionalism? Furthermore, could it simply be a product of EU foreign policy activism that might fade away together with the EU? After all, "theorizing on interregionalism has always been intrinsically linked to, and indeed dominated by, the study of the

European Union" (Doidge 2014:37).This is one of the issues this book is set to elucidate. The conclusion is that the theoretical focus on the EU does not denote eurocentrism as much as the real developments on the ground: were it not for the EU, we would most probably not be talking of interregionalism as much as we do.

Although there has been progress regarding conceptualization, identification of cases and typologies of actors that engage in interregional relations, there is still a long way ahead before sound theorizing can take off. In order to define the substance of what constitutes an actor of an interregional relation, we could paraphrase Kissinger and ask, say, what's the phone number of Latin America? (for that matter, Asia, the ACP or UNASUR). Phone number may stand for an autonomous secretariat or any other manifestation of regional institutionalization, without which it is conceivable to speak of a forum or arena but not of an international actor (Fabbrini and Malamud 2013). The threshold between one and the other has not yet been clearly drawn – but it should eventually. An alternative could be not to think of thresholds but of degrees of actorness, in a similar vein to what has been proposed for regionness. Measuring degrees may provide a better description of empirical variation; on the other hand, setting thresholds would allow for the formulation of explicative hypotheses, e.g. accounting for spillover effects.

In the available literature, the link between regionalism and interregionalism is often unclear – apart from the logic assumption that the latter is somehow derived from the former. But, contrary to inter-state relations, regions engage in interregional relations sometimes and with some selected others, though not all the time or with all other regions. So, what pushes a region to relate to some – but not all – others, or to sometimes relate to states instead of regions? What defines the timing? Looking from the reverse angle, is interregionalism able to promote regionalism? If such were the case, how far and under what conditions? Finally, there is the question of mimicry, resemblance and emulation, which are categories usually utilized to describe regionalism: do they also apply to interregionalism? To varying degrees, these questions are addressed in several chapters of this book.

There has also been growing interest regarding the relation between culture and identity, on the one hand, and regional and interregional processes on the other. Neofunctionalism as much as liberal intergovernmentalism contends that interests rather than identity drive regional integration, although identity conflicts may hinder it. However, cultural variables are sometimes used in order to explain the differential performance of diverse interregional processes. Embryonic knowledge and imprecise connections ask for more research in this area.

Throughout the recent literature on regional and interregional affairs, and due to much ado about informal processes, there is less and less questioning about the centrality of the state. Earlier analyses predicting the demise (or at least definitive decline) of the state have lost the argument against more 'realistic', empirically-grounded approaches that bring the state back in. As welcome as this outcome may be for political scientists, this news could backfire into our subject matter: if states do not matter less, regions might not matter more – and neither might interregionalism.

Acknowledgments We are grateful to Benjamin Faude, Andréas Litsegård, Frank Mattheis and Fredrik Söderbaum for very generous advice.

References

Aggarwal, V., & Fogarty, E. A. (2005). The limits of interregionalism: The EU and North America. *Journal of European Integration, 27*(3), 327–346.

América Latina Hoy. (2005). Issue #40 on "Presidential Summits". University of Salamanca.

Baert, F., Scaramagli, T., & Söderbaum, F. (Eds.). (2014). *Intersecting interregionalism. Regions, global governance and the EU*. New York: Springer.

Börzel, T. A., & Risse, T. (2009). Diffusing (Inter-) Regionalism: The EU as a Model of Regional Integration. *KFG working paper Series*, No. 7, Kolleg-Forschergruppe (KFG) "The Transformative Power of Europe". Free University Berlin.

Caetano, G. (2010). Introducción. In G. Caetano (Ed.), *Las Negociaciones entre América Latina y el Caribe con la Unión Europea*. Ediciones Trilce: Montevideo.

Claude, I. L. (1971). *Swords into plowshares. The problems and progress of international organization*. New York: Random House.

Cooper, A. F. (2010). The G20 as an improvised crisis committee and/or a contested 'steering committee'. *International Affairs, 86*(3), 741–757.

de Medeiros, M. A. (2000). *La Genèse du Mercosud. Dynamisme Interne, Influence de l'Union Européenne et Insertion Internationale*. Paris: L'Harmattan.

Doidge, M. (2011). *The European Union and interregionalism. Patterns of engagement*. Ashgate.

Doidge, M. (2014). Interregionalism and the European Union: Conceptualising group-to-group relations. In F. Baert, T. Scaramagli, & F. Söderbaum (Eds.), *Intersecting interregionalism. Regions, global governance and the EU*. New York: Springer.

Ecorys. (2006). Evaluation of the civil society dialogue at DG trade. Assessment of relevance, effectiveness and efficiency of CSD policy and procedures. *Report commissioned by the EU Dg Trade*. Rotterdam 9th October.

Eyinla, B. M. (2004). Beyond Cairo: Emerging pattern of Euro-African relationship. *Africa: Rivista trimestrale di studi e documentazione dell'Istituto italiano per l'Africa e l'Oriente, 59*(2), 159–178.

Fabbrini, S., & Malamud, A. (2013). Le organizzazioni regionali e l'integrazione economica. In R. Belloni, M. Moschella, & D. Sicurelli (Eds.), *Le organizzazioni internazionali: struttura, funzioni, impatto* (pp. 167–186). Il Mulino: Bologna.

Fawcett, L., & Hurrell, A. (Eds.). (1995). *Regionalism in world politics: Regional organization and international order*. Oxford/New York: Oxford University Press.

FCO 1, Foreign and Commonwealth Office. (2013). Interview with a Diplomat member of the UK delegation to the 2013 EU-Latin America and the Caribbean Summit. London, 28th February.

FCO 2, Foreign and Commonwealth Office. (2012). Interview with a Diplomat who supported the UK Government Delegation to the 2013 EU-Latin America and the Caribbean Summit. Santiago de Chile, 14th September.

Gahr Store, J. (2012). Trops de sommets tue les sommets. *Le Monde Diplomatique*. September, 11.

Gamble, A., & Payne, A. (1996). *Regionalism and world order*. London: Macmillan Press.

Goldstein, J., & Keohane, R. O. (1993). Ideas and Foreign Policy: An Analytical Framework. In J. Goldstein & R. O. Keohane (Eds.), *Ideas and foreign policy. Beliefs, institutions, and political change* (pp. 3–30). Ithaca/London: Cornell University Press.

Hänggi, H. (2000). Interregionalism: Empirical and theoretical perspectives. Paper prepared for the *Workshop "Dollars, Democracy and Trade. External Influence on Economic Integration in the Americas"*. Los Angeles, May 18.

Hänggi, H., Rüland, J., & Roloff, R. (Eds.). (2006). *Interregionalism and international relations*. London/New York: Routledge.

Hettne, B., & Söderbaum, F. (1998). The new regionalism Approach. *Politeia, 17*(3), 6–21.

Hettne, B., & Söderbaum, F. (2000). Theorizing the rise of 'Regionness'. *New Political Economy, 5*(3), 457–473.

Higgott, R., & Phillips, N. (2000). Challenging triumphalism and convergence: The limits of global liberalization in Asia and Latin America. *Review of International Studies, 26*(3), 359–379.

Hill, C., & Smith, M. (2011). *International relations and the European Union*. Oxford/New York: Oxford University Press.

Hulse, M., Stapel, S. & Striebinger, K. (2015). Conceptualizing and theorizing the drivers, interactions, and effects of overlapping regionalism. Paper prepared for the *workshop overlapping regionalism: Drivers, interactions, effects*, ISA Annual Convention. New Orleans, 17 February.

Hurrell, A. (1995). Regionalism in theoretical perspective. In L. Fawcett & A. Hurrell (Eds.), *Regionalism in world politics. Regional organization and international order*. Oxford: Oxford University Press.

Isbell, P., & Nolan García, K. A. (2015). Regionalism and interregionalism in Latin America: The beginning or the end of Latin America's 'Continental Integration'? *Atlantic Future Scientific Paper 20*.

Kacowicz, A. (2015). Regional governance and global governance: Possible links, alternative explanations, and the Latin American case, 1991–2015. Submitted for publication.

Kupchan, C. A. (2006). The new Transatlantic interregionalism and the end of the Atlantic Alliance. In H. Hänggi, J. Rüland, & R. Roloff (Eds.), *Interregionalism and international relations*. London/New York: Routledge.

Laursen, F. (2003). Theoretical perspectives on comparative regional integration. In F. Laursen (Ed.), *Comparative regional integration: Theoretical perspectives* (pp. 3–28). Aldershot: Ashgate.

Le Gloannec, A.-M. (2004). The unilateralist temptation Germany's foreign policy after the Cold War. *Internationale Politik und Gesellschaft, 1*, 27–39.

Lindberg, L. N. (1963). *The political dynamics of European economic integration*. Stanford: Stanford University Press.

MAE, Ministero degli Affari Esteri. (2012). Interview with a Diplomat who supported the Italian government delegation to the 2013 EU-Latin America and the Caribbean Summit. Santiago de Chile, 14th September.

Maihold, G. (2010). La productividad del proceso de cumbres euro-latinoamericanas. Una evaluación a diez años de rio. In G. Caetano (Ed.), *Las Negociaciones entre América Latina y el Caribe con la Unión Europea* (pp. 21–60). Montevideo: Ediciones Trilce.

Malamud, A. (2013). Overlapping regionalism, no integration: Conceptual issues and the Latin American experience. *EUI Working Papers, RSCAS 2013/20*.

Malamud, A., & Gardini, G. L. (2012). Has regionalism peaked? the Latin American quagmire and its lessons. *The International Spectator, 47*(1), 123–140.

Mattheis, F. (2014). *New regionalism in the South: Mercosur and SADC in a comparative and interregional perspective*. Leipzig: Universitätsverlag Leipzig.

Melissen, J. (2003). Summit diplomacy coming of age. Discussion papers in diplomacy, Netherlands Institute of International relations "Clingendael".

MinRel 1, Ministerio de Asuntos Exteriores de la Republica de Chile. (2012). Interview with a Diplomat responsible for the logistics of the 2013 EU-Latin America and the Caribbean Summit. Santiago de Chile, 13th September.

MinRel 2, Ministerio de Asuntos Exteriores de la Republica de Chile. (2012). Interview with a Diplomat responsible for the organisation of the 2013 EU-Latin America and the Caribbean Summit. Santiago de Chile, 20th September.

MinRel 3, Ministerio de Asuntos Exteriores de la Republica de Chile. (2012). Interview with a Diplomat responsible for the organisation of the 2013 EU-Latin America and the Caribbean Summit. Santiago de Chile, 19th September.

Nye, J. N. (1968). *International regionalism.* Boston: Little, Brown & Co.

O'Siochru, S. (2004). Civil society participation in the WSIS process: Promises and reality. *Continuum: Journal of Media and Cultural Studies, 18*(3), 330–344.

Peake, S. (2002). The Jo'Burg Summit: What did it really mean for renewables? *Refocus, 3*(6), 46–49.

Peña, F. (2010). Ante las nuevas circunstancias internacionales: experiencias y futuro de las relaciones América Latina y Caribe con la Unión Europea. In G. Caetano (Ed.), *Las Negociaciones entre América Latina y el Caribe con la Unión Europea* (pp. 61–70). Montevideo: Ediciones Trilce.

Roloff, R. (1998). Globalisierung, Regionalisierung und Gleichgewicht. In C. Masala & R. Roloff (Eds.), *Herausforderungen der Realpolitik* (pp. 61–94). Koln: SYH-Verlag.

Rüland, J., & Bechle, K. (2014). Defending state-centric regionalism through mimicry and localisation: regional parliamentary bodies in the Association of Southeast Asian Nations (ASEAN) and Mercosur. *Journal of International Relations and Development, 17*(1), 61–88.

Saldías, O. (2010). Networks, courts and regional integration. Explaining the establishment of the Andean Court of Justice. *KFG working paper,* 20, Free University of Berlin.

Santander, S. (2010). EU-LA relations: from interregionalism to bilateralism? *Working paper* # 29, CAEI – Centro Argentino de Estudios Internacionales.

Sberro, S. (2013). After the first EU-CELAC summit in Santiago: A new beginning for the biregional strategic association? *Paper presented at the European Union Studies Association (EUSA) Conference.* Baltimore, May 9–11.

Schimmelfennig, F. (2003). *The EU, NATO and the integration of Europe. Rules and Rhetoric.* Cambridge: Cambridge University Press.

Schmitter, P. C. (2010). Governance arrangements for sustainability: A regional perspective. *Corporate Governance: The International Journal of Business in Society, 10*(1), 85–96.

Schulz, M., Söderbaum, F., & Ojendal, J. (Eds.). (2001). *Regionalization in a globalizing world: A comparative perspective on forms, actors and processes.* London/New York: Zed Books.

Söderbaum, F. (2012). Interregionalism. In G. Ritzer (Ed.), *The Wiley-Blackwell encyclopedia of globalization* (pp. 1200–1202). Chichester: Wiley.

Söderbaum, F., & Van Langenhove, L. (2005). Introduction: The EU as a global actor and the role of interregionalism. *Journal of European Integration, 27*(3), 249–262.

Tovias, A. (2008). The brave new world of cross-regionalism. *CEPII Working Paper* No. 2008-03.

Whitehead, L., & Barahona de Brito, A. (2005). Las cumbres mundiales y sus versiones latinoamericanas: ¿Haciendo una montaña de un grano de arena? *América Latina Hoy, 40,* 15–27.

Chapter 3
Volatile Interregionalism: The Case of South Atlantic Relations

Frank Mattheis

Abstract In their extra-regional outreach Latin America and Sub-Saharan Africa rarely make each other a priority. However, since the end of the Cold War there has been an increasing amount of political efforts to strengthen ties on a region-to-region basis. This chapter argues that this rapprochement has been facilitated by the emergence of two regional projects following a similar logic in a post-Cold War context, in particular the Southern African Development Community and the Common Market of the Southern Cone. At the same time, both projects face serious limitations of actorness that are illustrative of the confined space for interregionalism across the South Atlantic. An analysis of the formalised initiatives on political, economic and trade issues between the two regions concludes that these are characterised by transregional and partly pure forms of interregionalism and that most initiatives are heavily shaped by the leading role of Brazil.

Keywords Atlantic • Interregionalism • Regional organisations • Regionalism • Regions

3.1 Introduction

This chapter aims to analyse the growing interregional relations between Latin America and Africa based on the most relevant regionalisms in the Atlantic context. The regionalisms of concern are located on the shores of the South Atlantic, in South America and in Southern Africa. The stimulation of interregional dialogue within the South Atlantic space mainly concerns the actors within the Common Market of the South (MERCOSUR) in South America and the Southern African Development Community (SADC) while other layers of regionalism such as the Bolivarian Alternative for the Americas, the Pacific Alliance or the Economic Community of Central African States have been less concerned with such ambitions.

F. Mattheis (✉)
Centre for the Study of Governance Innovation, University of Pretoria, Pretoria, South Africa
e-mail: Frank.Mattheis@governanceinnovation.org

© Springer International Publishing AG 2018   33
F. Mattheis, A. Litsegård (eds.), *Interregionalism across the Atlantic Space*,
United Nations University Series on Regionalism 15,
DOI 10.1007/978-3-319-62908-7_3

In a broader sense, regionalisms emerge from existing or desired interactions and interdependences (Söderbaum 2004: 16). Their regional character stems from transcending established notions of nation and community and aiming to institutionalise a new form of inclusion and exclusion. Belonging to a region can be framed in geographic, ideological, functional, historic or social terms (or a combination of those). Regionalism embraces a "series of interlinked, but distinct, phenomena" (Gardini 2012: 51) while providing an ideational sphere for projects following a region-making paradigm. The most tangible form of regionalism is its institutionalisation in a regional organisation; however, such projects can take many other forms, involving high degrees of informality, non-state actors as driving forces and imaginations rather than implementation. The underlying regionalisms in Southern Africa and South America, which have driven the process of interregionalism, largely stem from state actors that have the ambition to outgrow the traditional region. However, their limited capacity curbs the potential outreach and adds an important element of volatility.

The phenomenon of interregionalism stems from the intensification and institutionalisation of regionalisms across the globe. Before proceeding to interregionalism, the second section will therefore deal in detail with the most relevant regional-building processes in Southern Africa and South America in terms of their Atlantic dimension. The third section of this chapter will then analyse three cases of interregionalism, ranging from relations between regional organisations to variable multilateral forums. The concluding remarks will contextualise them within the typology of prevalent patterns in the Atlantic.

These processes emerged in the 1990s with MERCOSUR in South America and SADC in Southern Africa. Both incorporated an economic paradigm shift to liberalism and the fear to be left behind in a tri-polar world order between Europe, North America and East Asia. MERCOSUR and SADC played a crucial role in providing the main arenas for regionalism in their sub-regions. They include the major states such as Brazil, Argentina and later Venezuela in the first case and South Africa, Angola and Mozambique in the second one. At the time of their creation MERCOSUR and SADC made it their core task to deepen trade relations between their members, without much space for a social agenda or ambitions to developing relations with other regions (with the exception of donor relations, specifically in the case of SADC). The main state actors in the creation and process of regionalism have been the heads of states as well as ministries for economy and foreign affairs. In the course of 1990s, transnational business and civil society started to perceive MERCOSUR and SADC as relevant spaces of interaction and governance. They have contributed to certain aspects of regionalism related to their own activities but in many cases they have also shifted their attention to other arenas that are more conducive to their objectives.

The notion of different regionalist sequences triggered by crises in turn deals with the conditions for certain types of regionalism and is particularly relevant to understand the oscillations in the forms and logics of regionalisms under scrutiny (Riggirozzi and Tussie 2012; Fioramonti 2012).

3.2 The Basis for Interregionalism: Contemporary Regionalisms in South America and Southern Africa with an Atlantic Dimension

The position in the world system is crucial for the production of new spaces and it can be particularly pronounced for regionalisms in the South (Katzenstein 2005; Fawcett 2008). Accordingly, the restructuring of the bipolar world order after 1989 opened up a window of opportunity for South-South relations. One the one side, central actors of the world order such as the U.S. and multilateral organisations faced limitations in their authority and credibility. On the other side, challenges in the many areas such as climate, energy and development were acknowledged as regional and global issues that required new forms of cooperation.

Policy-makers increasingly conformed to the global paradigms of neoliberalism, democracy and ultimately regionalism. The new paradigm for regionalism was to make an offensive step towards full integration into world markets (Hettne 1999). This meant more support for the private sector and policy adjustments to attract FDI.

At the time of their creation in the early 1990s, MERCOSUR and SADC represented a rupture from previous more inward-looking projects and became the formal expression of new regionalisms by means of official declarations and legal contracts. The founding treaties defined an institutionalisation that would subsequently face several constraints in the context of different global and local changes at the end of the 1990s. In its founding treaty, the Treaty of Asunción, MERCOSUR directly referred to the changing world order and the formation of economic blocs (MERCOSUR 1991). Meanwhile, the creation of a new regional organisation reflected the enthusiasm of political elites in Southern African states to jointly take advantage of the opportunities that opened up after Apartheid. In addition, the pillar of commonly advancing donor relations became more important with the end of Cold War divisions in the region. Previous regional donor coordination had not delivered the expected rise of social and economic indicators and a weak institution was feared to play in favour of a dominant South Africa, once the political transition allowed it to join (Oosthuizen 2006).

Towards the end of the 1990s, various challenges for SADC and MERCOSUR cropped up. SADC suffered from the proliferation of projects in the decentralised sectors and did not have an established structure to deal with security issues. MERCOSUR was under pressure due to the financial crisis and the limited political will to go beyond economic integration. In both cases, the answer was an institutional reform to strengthen the secretariats and create new organs. Regional cooperation between national governments moved from punctual and informal cooperation to more institutionalised and formal meetings (Mattheis 2014).

Over the years, MERCOSUR gave way to an ever-growing expansion of tasks to coordinate. What started as an instrument for trade and investment soon became the arena of reference for numerous new issues. The modifications followed functional needs, national trends and institutional dynamics. The agenda of MERCOSUR thus changed the essence of regionalism but the institutions that were designed to fulfil the limited objectives of the original treaty lagged behind in terms of power and capacity. Multiple arenas for negotiations without decision-making power were created and attached to the three main organs. Ministerial reunions, working groups and technical commissions were each divided into dozens of commissions, forums, institutes and ad hoc groups. Hundreds of institutionalised branches covered a wide range of policy areas ranging from school libraries over biodiversity to cigarette trade.[1]

Vertical expansion had a different dynamic within SADC. The multitude of topics to be regionally coordinated reflected the interest of all member states to be in charge of one sector due to the related prestige and funding. In the 1990s, numerous protocols were negotiated and signed on various issues. Many of them dealt with the creation of a regional market, chiefly through numerous SADC agencies dealing with trade, energy and infrastructure. Despite a memorandum that was issued to stop an excessive vertical expansion, SADC inflated to 20 sectors and over 500 projects by the late 1990s but only about 20% of the projects had a regional scope (Oosthuizen 2006, 82). The required financing went far beyond the actual regional and foreign contributions. Vertical expansion thus faced major constraints regarding its purpose to generate financial income. SADC reform in 2001 rationalised the proliferation of projects. It triggered a contraction in the vertical scope. The new agenda further prioritised a neoliberal imagination of the region but also opened up to other transnational topics such as food security, natural disasters or HIV/AIDS. However, national authorities were reluctant to give up an effective or at least potential source of income. The membership in SADC consequently related to the rent-seeking of governments (Standaert and Rayp 2012). The involvement of foreign development agencies played an important role in the expansion.[2] Not only did their financing offer an incentive to apply for more funding but also were they directly involved by promoting certain topics.

The vertical expansion shifted from a catchall approach to a concentration on two issues: economic liberalisation in a linear expansion from free trade area to common market, and the containment of political instability and violent conflicts. Security threats emerged as a regional issue in 1994 in the context of the genocide in Rwanda. Regional security cooperation was however only gradually implemented (Khadiagala 2001). The first Lesotho crisis in 1994 was mediated outside of SADC. In 1998, the second Lesotho crisis, following an unconstitutional change of government, was in turn solved by the military intervention of Botswana and South Africa under a SADC mandate. In the late 1990s, the Congo conflict was regionalised and SADC became a forum for state leaders to legitimise interventions in other political crises such as in Madagascar in 2009. Conversely, SADC also served as legitimisation for the absence of interventions, such as when it repeatedly reaffirmed "the indivisibility of SADC and solidarity with the government and people

---

[1] See   http://www.mercosur.int/innovaportal/v/762/1/secretaria/acceso_autoridades_gestor (retrieved on 07.01.2015) for a complete overview.

[2] External funding still represented over 50% of the SADC budget in 2009/10 (SADC 2009).

of Zimbabwe" (SADC Summit of Heads of State and Government 2003). For each crisis, SADC installed mediation mechanisms or even coordinated interventions (van Nieuwkerk 2010). It thereby provided legitimacy for these actions and shielded off the region against external involvement.

Concerning horizontal expansion, both regionalisms emerged as incomplete territories and gave way to exclusion and inclusion on the basis of varying terms. SADC has gradually expanded by incorporating Congo-Kinshasa in 1998 and Madagascar in 2005. This expansion does not reflect clear admission criteria but primarily strategic and economic interests in energy and resources in the case of Congo as well as a claim to geographic cohesion in the case of Madagascar. On other occasions, SADC has fragmented, most visibly concerning the negotiation groups for an Economic Partnership Agreements with the EU and the overlapping membership with other regional organisations in East and Central Africa.

The aspirations of MERCOSUR towards a comprehensive South American regionalism were underlined by associating the Andean countries and Chile in the course of the 1990s. So far however, the only new inclusion was Venezuela as the fifth full member in 2012 against considerable resistance from several domestic actors in MERCOSUR questioning the fulfilment of admission criteria.

MERCOSUR had also being created as an expression of democratisation. Chile was by definition excluded due to its authoritarian regime (van Klaveren 2000). The same applied to Paraguay that was excluded from the MERCOSUR after the de facto coup d'état in 2012 on the grounds of violating democratic principles.

Democratic standards have also been an integral part of SADC discourses and principles but their enforcement was linked to internal power constellation rather than to external pressure. While SADC engaged in a military intervention in Lesotho to restore an elected government in 1998, it backed the Mugabe government in Zimbabwe despite persistent human rights violations (van der Vleuten and Ribeiro Hoffmann 2010).

The SADC treaty (article 3) and the Protocol of Ouro Preto (article 34) provided the two organisations with legal personality and thereby enabled them to turn into actors in their own right. However, the institutionalisation of a genuinely regional perception has been fragile. Both regionalisms have added new bodies over time and expanded existing organs. Some of them, such as the parliamentary commissions and the secretariats, were potentially supranational but were not vested with substantial decision-making powers. The political relevance of MERCOSUR and SADC has thus remained confined to a context marked by other actors. Instead of evolving on its own, MERCOSUR's scope was transformed from a predominantly economic scheme to a more political project. By contrast, SADC has oscillated between commercial and security priorities in accordance with sporadic agenda changes (Nathan 2002).

While state actors have been crucial in the initial conceptions, regionalisms would be difficult to sustain if private actors were consistently excluded or excluded themselves. A recurring critique has been the lack of transparency and participation in the decision-making process (Caetano et al. 2009). Nevertheless, the ascendance of a state-led regionalism has been accompanied by an expansion of activities between neighbouring administrations and businesses, often on a so-called translocal micro-level (Hettne 2006).

In its first years, MERCOSUR had fulfilled several of its ambitious goals and was thus likely to stay. Civil society organisations started to analyse the process and formulated demands (Cason 2011). In SADC, social actors also recognised the relevance of regionalism but were largely absent from the formal process during the 1990s. The SADC secretariat was unable to fulfil its coordinating role and the creation of the SADC Council of NGOs only created a limited space for participation, despite a Civil Society Forum accompanying the SADC summits. The SADC Parliamentary Forum also provided an arena for the involvement of citizens but the practical opportunities have been severally curbed by the marginal position in the institution and the influence of political leaders on the represented members (Oosthuizen 2006). A regional social space would also undermine the system of neopatrimonialism that remained a feature of many states in Southern Africa. Some civil society groups have been opposing regionalisms in its dominant form and formulated alternatives that circumvent the national states (Godsäter and Söderbaum 2010).

In South America, the regional political shift in 2003 had important implications for the way regional space was conceived. The Brazilian president Da Silva emphasised notions of MERCOSUR's "social legitimacy" and "regional citizenship" (Brazilian Ministry of External Relations 2008: 77). With progressive leaders taken over national governments, MERCOSUR's regional policies changed significantly and social norms ranging from human rights to education were adopted (Bizzozero 2011). In 2006, the Social summit of Mercosur was installed to bring together social organisations and it has been held regularly since.[3] Mercosur thus institutionalised opportunities for social actors to participate in the regional project (Serbin 2012). Nevertheless, their influence was largely based on consultation and less on decision-making. These new arenas for expression and negotiation were designed to strengthen the participation of citizens in the institutions but they have largely run in isolation to the official Mercosur process. NGO ties within global or continental networks remained more central for funding, political support and access to information.

There were numerous contestations of the dominant regionalism. While some actors would rather do without a relevant regional organisation and defended national borders, many others proposed structural changes to the regional project, in particular concerning the interpresidential and interministerial concentration of power, the neoliberal agenda and the implementation of regional policies. The forging of a regional social space chiefly occurred through transnational networks of actors that were, as in the case of Mercociudades – a network of city administrations, at least initially excluded from the dominant regionalisms. Another channel for contestation was the establishment of new institutions such as parliamentary representations and tribunals. Despite being often marginalised and curtailed, they opened up an arena for the reflection on regionalist models. Even though these

---

[3] Cf. http://es.socialmercosul.org/cupula-social/ (retrieved on 02.02.2015).

organs, just like many other parts of the regional organisations reproduced and reinforced national structures of power, they demonstrated the potential of transcending the rationale of nation states by challenging the dominance of the supreme actors.

With reference to the typology compiled by Alcaro and Reilly in this volume, the functions and drivers of the two dominant contemporary regionalisms in Southern Africa and South America have diverged considerably. However, there are important similarities with respect to their regionness and to the regionalisms' capacity to structure international relations. Those similarities in terms of their frequent lack of internal cohesion and of their marginal relevance outside of their region are subsequently structuring the interregional rapprochement. They frame the type of interregionalism that can effectively occur between the two regions.

3.3   Interregionalism Between South America and Southern Africa

3.3.1   Patterns of Interregionalism

With the proliferation of regionalisms across the globe, interregional contacts between these projects have increased, too, chiefly from the European Union (Ponjaert 2013). These initiatives encompass a wide range of forms, both concerning their institutionalisation and the topics they cover. To categorise the multitude of interregionalism scholars identifies four types of interregional relations (see Rüland 2014; Söderbaum et al. 2005; Hänggi 2006; Baert et al. 2014). The most formalised type is *pure interregionalism* between established regional organisations. This is probably the most widely analysed form concerning the EU but also the one that is less likely to find between Africa and Latin America, where regional organisations struggle to establish themselves as actors in their own right. Interactions between those two regions thus do not readily fit into this scheme. Other types of interregionalism seem more plausible. *Transregional relations*, for example, constitute a second category to capture relations between regions that lack internal cohesion. Membership in such region-to-region dialogues tends to be diffuse and is not moderated by pre-existing regional organisations. Nation-states from both regions participate on their own, even though regional powers can act as spokespersons (Rüland 2014).[4]

Hybrid interregionalism, sometimes called 'quasi interregionalism', is a third category, describing contacts between regional organisations and less institutionalised regional groupings, often delineated by the counterpart (Hänggi 2006). Some authors identify a fourth type, *bilateralism*, describing interactions between a regional organisation and individual states (Baert et al. 2014). This can be subsumed

---

[4]Aggarwal and Fogarty (2004) also point to transnational production networks and the transnational activities of non-governmental organisations and civil society actors in that context.

within the category of hybrid regionalism. However, this particular type is of the special significance to this paper, because it underlines the role of regional powers.

In the following section the different layers of interregionalism across the South Atlantic will be examined: two examples of transregional relations (the Africa-South America summit and the Zone of Peace and Cooperation in the South Atlantic (ZOPACAS), which seem to be the most prevalent form,[5] and example of pure interregionalism (between MERCOSUR and SACU/SADC). It is important to note that both cases have been preceded or facilitated by bilateral interregionalism between Brazil and Africa. Hybrid interregionalism is difficult to trace, as it seems to be mainly fit for the EU's external relations.

3.3.2 The Africa-South America Summit

The Africa-South America Summit (ASA) represents the intercontinental scale of transregionalism, encompassing the countries of both regions as a whole.[6] It was initially conceived as an extension of Brazil's Africa Forum, a form of interregional bilateralism. Brazil and Nigeria took the lead for the first event that took place in 2006 in Abuja. While the African Union was the obvious umbrella on the African side, the delineation of South America reflected the sphere of influence of Brazil, encompassing its neighbours Surinam and Guyana, which are often marginalised in region-building, but excluding its competitor Mexico.[7]

Venezuela challenged Brazil's leadership by hosting the second meeting on Isla Margarita in 2009 and strongly promoting its own foreign policy ideology. Both countries had portrayed themselves as representing the interests of the Global South and thus the competition was less about the content of the interregional cooperation but mainly about the role of the protagonist (Gobierno de Venezuela 2010). However, the interest in this format seems to have dropped, as the following summits have been postponed several times and the number of participants decreased. The second summit was scheduled for 2008 and took place the year thereafter. The third one was planned for 2011 in Libya but was eventually held in 2013 in Equatorial Guinea. Conversely, regional organisations, in particular the AU, have played an increasingly prominent role in the events,[8] pointing to the potential or pure interregionalism behind hosted in a transregional shell. However, the main actors have so far

---

[5] The Community of Portuguese Language Countries also falls in this category but due to Brazil being the only South American member and not representing its region within this organisation, it will not be covered in this paper.

[6] A similar initiative has been launched in 2005 by Brazil to bring together South American and Arab States under the Spanish acronym ASPA (South America-Arab States Summit), cf. Ayuso et al. in this volume.

[7] Cf. http://asasummit.itamaraty.gov.br/asa-ingles/summit-of-south-american-africa (retrieved on 18.04.2015).

[8] Cf. http://www.au.int/en/asa (retrieved on 18.04.2015).

been nation states and in particular the heads of state. Considering the importance of national sovereignty in both regions, the legitimising and symbolic value of such mega-events plays a recurring role. In addition, there is also a functional-rational element, given that many countries of the region face the challenge of limited public budgets. Diplomats and cabinet members are able to take advantage of the ASA summit by meeting an extensive range of high-level counterparts, including representatives from seldom-visited countries. This can provide the ground for new alliances and cooperation. As within ZOPACAS, Brazil was effective in using this opportunity. In 2006 it rallied support for its Olympic bid. Another parallel with ZOPACAS is the dependence on leading and/or hosting countries to finance and organise such meetings in a context without permanent or centralised structures.

The limits of this high-level format are also very visible, given the rise of similar events competing for the limited time and finances from its heads of government. Other exercises of summitry, such as between South America and Arab countries, and the bilateral interregionalism with China clearly compete for these resources. Given the existence of other partly overlapping venues such as ZOPACAS and the Community of Portuguese Speaking Countries, the ASA summit is prone to signs of redundancy, not least because it offers less functional or cultural grounds than its summitry competitors. The extensive partaking and the non-committing format of the ASA summit might translate into little more than rhetorical figures without a clear objective. In this sense, transregionalism exhibits even more of a temporal and punctual character than forms of interregionalism (Alden and Vieira 2005).

3.3.3 The Zone of Peace and Cooperation in the South Atlantic

ZOPACAS emerged as a new form of interregional cooperation between adjacent countries of the South Atlantic in the mid-1980s. With the support of 15 states, Brazil successfully proposed a resolution for its creation to the UN general assembly in 1986 (UNGA 1986). Its main purpose was to establish the South Atlantic as a demilitarised space free of foreign military bases, internal aggression and nuclear weapons. The Apartheid regime was explicitly mentioned as aggressor and threat to the security of the region, and was therefore excluded as a member, and so was occupied Namibia. The secondary purpose was to promote development through cooperation between member states in economic, environmental and social matters.

For its chief promoter Brazil, the ZOPACAS provided an important geopolitical means. Within an organisation that was supposed to form a legitimised guarantor for a peaceful South Atlantic, Brazil tried to institutionalise the exclusion of the two superpowers (Gamba-Stonehouse 1989).

Argentina supported the initiative because it provided support in one of its major foreign policy issues – the British occupation of the Falkland Islands/Malvinas. Argentina was actively seeking international support in its territorial dispute and had encountered major problems in gathering favourable votes for its UN petition

(Tulchin 1987). African states had been reluctant for three major reasons. Firstly, under the military anti-communist regimes, Argentina had been a strategic and ideological ally of South Africa and the U.S. Secondly, the economic and political ties of the Anglophone countries with their former metropolis were still dominant. And finally, Argentina's armed intervention was itself condemned as an act of aggression. The firm adhesion to the Western bloc was already being reconsidered in the aftermath of the war, and Africa's weight within the UN provided a considerable incentive to reassess its perception. Argentina started to reach out to the continent and engaged in a series of high level official visits to Africa. Relations with South Africa declined rapidly as Argentina underwent a democratic transition that was also expressed by an active role in the international isolation of South Africa. As a new foreign policy rationale, Argentina defined itself as still being culturally part of the West but structurally located within the Global South (Jiménez 2010). These processes were all well appreciated by most African states. ZOPACAS thus provided an ideal institution to promote all of Argentina's foreign interests. It gave the country the opportunity to escape the bipolar system, to build up relations with new allies in the Third World, and to gather support in the cause of the Malvinas/Falkland Islands.

For most African members, ZOPACAS was above all an important step towards overcoming Apartheid. The institutionalisation further cemented the isolation of South Africa bringing extra-regional members in line with the anti-Apartheid maxim. It thus complemented organisations such as the Frontline States. In addition the ZOPACAS provided additional legitimacy as it directly stemmed from the UN General Assembly.

To African countries, maintaining a zone free of armament would also stabilise the status quo. Coup d'états were common and one appeased border meant less pressure to build up an external defence on that side. After all, many states did not have one proper war naval, let alone a navy. Hegemonic ambitions in the South Atlantic were thus unattainable and ZOPACAS could prevent the expansion of any foreign power. This point of view contrasts starkly with Brazil's, as it assumes that ZOPACAS would limit the ascendance of any hegemon, including its own members.

However, the widespread support for the organisation did not bring about a leader that could count on undisputed support among its neighbours (Lechini 2007). Therefore, conflicts between Brazil and its contestants were never openly carried out but constituted a balance of powers instead. In the 1990s, the priorities for the individual countries shifted. The end of the Cold War and Apartheid had stripped ZOPACAS off some of its main ambitions and many countries turned their back on the organisation or even on South-South relations in general.

Similar to many regionalisms of the time, priorities shifted and new objectives were included to revive the ZOPACAS. It should help institutionalising democratic transitions by providing instruments to support human right, multiparty systems and racial equality. In addition, ecological issues and organised crime emerged as important policy fields.

With the end of Apartheid, South Africa joined ZOPACAS and the desire to align its foreign and defence policy gave the organisation some new impetus. At the same time, defence and security lost their importance and became an issue dealt with among the countries actually owning navies. Argentina and South Africa carried out a joint naval manoeuvre in 1993 and were subsequently joined by Brazil and Uruguay in biannually recurring military exercises under the name ATLASUR (Lechini 2006). This cooperation has been institutionalised within the national defence policies and for most navies it constitutes a prioritised pillar of alliance.

The overall heterogeneity among the members and their interests kept ZOPACAS from turning into an entrusted organisation. The biannual summits were usually closing with non-binding declarations and sometimes even postponed, often due to the lack of political will or interest in the respective host country. Some momentum surfaced in 2007, when Angola showed notable dedication in setting the agenda for the organisation. However, this did not seriously challenge the leadership of Brazil, which was revived afterwards by considerable financial commitment and political will during the Lula years.

ZOPACAS' biggest asset as an organisation is the opportunity to unite all of its members by offering a UN-framework against interventions of external powers. Another feature is the number of agreements that have been reached in several areas such as concerning the fight against illicit drug trade or mutual help in shipwreck.

ZOPACAS is chiefly built around elements of maritime security. This distinguishes it from other layers of interregionalism and explains its transregional scope. The organisation contains both a strategic and a functionalist element. Defence and disarmament provide an overarching rationale that is sidelined by technical agreements.

In sum, ZOPACAS as a transregional arena combines features of regionalism and interregionalism. It serves as an instrument to expand regional leadership both in established and in new spaces. It also enhances sovereignties vis-à-vis external forces on the one side and internal challenges on the other. However, due to its almost non-existing institutionalisation it is heavily dependent on key actors to set the agenda and to provide the means to implement it.

3.3.4 MERCOSUR and the Southern African Development Community (SADC) and the Southern African Customs Union (SACU)

Intriguingly the beginning of pure interregionalism between the Southern Cone of South America and Southern Africa were a consequence of Brazil's partial retreat from Africa in the 1990s. The own region and specifically MERCOSUR became the first priority and the strategy to engage with the whole continent was abandoned in favour of identifying strategic partners, chiefly post-Apartheid South Africa, the Portuguese speaking Angola and Mozambique, and oil-rich Nigeria. The rapprochement with SADC was thus mainly an expression of Brazil's interest to rationalise its main interests in the region by dealing with a regional body that encompassed three of those countries.

On the South American side, MERCOSUR had just been established and now bound the member states to act commonly in trade matters. From Brazil's perspective, negotiating a free trade agreement with SADC would be a first test whether MERCOSUR could effectively improve the position of its member countries in the global world order.

Starting in 1995 mutual high-level visits between Brazil and South Africa took place regularly and various bilateral accords were signed, eventually giving way to a Joint Commission Agreement in 2000. During that time Mandela also participated at a MERCOSUR summit in 1998 as the first President outside of the region.

Political commitment was thus clearly visible on both sides but engaging in direct negotiations with SADC turned out to be more complicated than anticipated. The obstacles became apparent once concrete steps needed to be taken. First of all, the institutional setting did not facilitate interregional agreements. None of the secretariats had the capacity to conduct external relations on their own, let alone an external representation. South American officials were as rare to find in Gaborone as Africans in Montevideo. Secondly, most SADC members simply lacked political interest in such an agreement. The organisation faced major internal challenges that prevented building up a common and comprehensive external agenda. Given that Apartheid had vanished, South-South coalitions lost importance for regional affairs. South America had again disappeared from the map and interregionalism was dominated by relations with its main donors in Europe. Thirdly, trade between most countries was modest and concentrated in a few volatile natural resources dependent on world market prices. Most commercial contacts and investments were weak and superficial except for a few multinational enterprises in mining and food. Lastly, with the exception of South Africa, the SADC members simply did not have resources for such an endeavour. The scarce personnel capable of negotiating such an agreement would have to be spared from the WTO rounds or SADC itself.

In contrast, relations with South Africa alone looked more promising and the country offered an entry point into the whole region. In the 1990s, the increase of South Africa's trade with Argentina and Brazil grew notably and underpinned the economic potential of an agreement. The private sectors of South Africa, Brazil and Argentina also manifested some interest and in particular the automotive industries formulated explicit demands (White 2003).

Consequently, MERCOSUR opted to start negotiating a free trade agreement with South Africa in 2000. Relations between SADC and MERCOSUR were maintained over time but still remained uncommitted. The attempt towards pure interregionalism was downsized into bilateral interregionalism.

South Africa's interest in MERCOSUR can mainly be attributed to the priorities of the post-Apartheid government. On the global level, it strived to overcome the decades of isolation, particularly in multinational forums. Former opponents had turned into potential allies. South Africa's Department of Trade and Industry developed the so-called "trade butterfly" strategy (Erwin 1999: 21). In addition to the traditional ties with Africa, Europe and the U.S., South Africa should spread out its wings to Latin America and Asia. MERCOSUR, being the most innovative and successful grouping on its continent at the time, cropped up as the natural partner. South Africa was also interested in the experiences of South America in dealing with issues of reconciliation after the military dictatorships.

Brazil and South Africa both shared the idea of exploring possibilities for South-South agreements with potential allies. But while MERCOSUR bound Brazil within the bloc, South Africa was able to start the negotiations on its own terms, as its regional framework was less constraining (Hentz 2005). SADC and SACU members were at that point free to sign individual Free Trade Agreements (FTAs). After South Africa unilaterally completed a FTA with the EU in 1999, the SACU members, who would bear its consequences without having been involved in the negotiations, called for a revision of the rules. The subsequent reform in 2002 did not reverse the hegemonic structure for that matter but it changed enough to become relevant for the South Atlantic realm.

SACU members were now required to sign new trade agreements as a single entity – much like MERCOSUR had to. The negotiations MERCOSUR had so far undertaken with South Africa were consequently being transformed into a SACU issue. An unintended side effect of the SACU reform was hence the agenda for the transformation of bilateral to pure interregionalism.

MERCOSUR found itself negotiating with four additional countries, making a potential agreement more difficult to reach and less attractive to sign. However, even though delegates from all five SACU countries were present at the negotiations, South Africa was the only spokesperson, marking in practice a return to bilateral interregionalism. This odd set-up created a number of misunderstandings as to who constituted the counterpart of MERCOSUR. Once it was clear that South Africa was handling all the matters on behalf of SACU, negotiations resumed.

However, the conditions for interregionalism changed significantly between 2001 and 2003. Even though MERCOSUR was hit by a profound economic crisis, which made external negotiations less appealing for both parties, two events notably improved the framework: Lula da Silva became President of Brazil and the WTO talks experienced a collapse that led to a languishing of multilateral trade. South-South relations became a new priority; both due to the political shift and due to the North-South divide in multilateral trade.

Consequently, Brazil carried on in the driver's seat of the SACU-MERCOSUR talks. It became a convenient instrument for Brazil to gain influence and prestige in the world while ensuring the cohesion of its own regional grouping. Brazil thus engaged in convincing the other MERCOSUR countries to pursue an agreement. Even though the SACU-MERCOSUR negotiations were still very technical, the mere fact that they took place was very political (Roberts 2004).

Within 2 years relations assumed a more formalised stage and a preferential trade agreement was agreed and signed by both parties in 2004. Due to the very limited range in terms of goods and rules, the Preferential Trade Agreement (a watered down FTA) was not ratified and negotiations towards an improved trade agreement started. Eventually, after twelve lengthy rounds of negotiations concerned with technical details, a new agreement was signed in 2008 and 2009. The initial agreement had been further developed but crucial parts such as the automotive sector were again postponed. Overall substantial changes were lacking.

From an economic point of view, the agreement contained little significance and a notable impact on trade could not be expected. In the light of the constraints affecting the budget and personnel of foreign affairs of the smaller states, this constituted a significant disappointment.

For South Africa and Brazil the immediate impact on trade was less relevant. Political elites in charge visibly gave priority to the South Atlantic negotiations even though substantial economic benefits were meagre. The PTA was not pushed in response to demand from economic actors but as a political instrument for South-South cooperation at large (Nutenko 2006), as captured by the India-Brazil-South Africa forum. It thus became a pioneer agreement between two regionalisms of the South. For both groupings it was one of the first agreements to be signed with another regional bloc, underlining the novelty of pure interregionalism. Another attempt at pure interregionalism was the proposal to establish formal relations between SADC and the newly created Union of South American Nations (UNASUR), which had a broader geographic scope. These ideas have yet to materialize but point out that the interregional potential of existing regionalisms is becoming a recognised feature.

3.4 Concluding Remarks

The South Atlantic is an important space for interregionalism both for South America and Africa, which has been particularly driven by several state-led initiatives over the past decade. However, it is far from being the main or even only avenue. The Pacific Alliance and the growing presence of India and China in Africa are reminders that not everything revolves around the Atlantic. At the same time, the well-established relationship with Europe remains paramount for both regions, despite all South-South ideology.

In addition, the South Atlantic is not the monopoly of African and South American states. Some external actors have economic interests, such as Norway and its fisheries industry. The UK remains a very present actor due to its territories and patrolling military in the region. The EU and the U.S. aim to provide security in the Gulf of Guinea.

The self-positioning of the South American and the African regionalisms in the Atlantic order and beyond also requires a differentiation. The functions of producing regional order follow distinct logics. The regional hegemony of South Africa and Brazil plays out in distinct ways, the external dependence is much more pronounced in Africa, and the institutional set-up is very different, too. Learning and transfer of ideas is very limited on the interregional level. For SADC and to lesser degree for MERCOSUR, Europe remains a main point of reference and so do previous attempts at regionalism within the region. There seems to be little room for coercion or teaching (Lenz 2013), as mutual knowledge and the extra-regional sphere of influence are still limited on both sides.

The emergence of South Atlantic interregionalism is due both to internal conditions such as foreign policy shifts in Brazil, as well as to external conditions such as the underrepresentation in global governance mechanisms. The main instruments of interregionalism appear to be formalistic, including various high-level meetings and the signing of a PTA. Summitry as identified by Gardini and Malamud in this volume plays a key role for the form interregionalism takes. Declarations and the staging of solidarity prevail over binding structures and establish a defining notion of volatility. The ratification of agreements is seldom a priority, further underlining the importance that is given by political elites from both shores of the South Atlantic to circumvent any perceived curtailing of national sovereignty. Given the comparatively weak political, economic and diplomatic ties between the two regions, summitry offers a particular convenience to gain knowledge about potential new partners for existing foreign policy priorities.

Yet, despite the fact that most interregional initiatives are developed by governmental agencies, the chain of actors involved in the processes range from transnational business (mining, agroindustry) and trade officers to foreign ministries and finally technicians. Civil society generally plays a marginal role in the dominant forms of interregionalism. Civil society has also developed interregional ties – some more long-standing such as between trade unions and other more recent such as through the social forums. However, neither have these ties produced a counter-project to the state-led forms of interregionalism, nor have they gained a relevant space inside of them.

The main categories of interregionalism (pure, transregional, hybrid and bilateral) can be meaningfully applied to the case of South America and Southern Africa. However, the analysis reveals a pattern where hybrid interregionalism does not readily figure. In addition, transregional and pure interregionalism are nested within bilateral interregionalism and thereby form a complex that follows similar logics and actors. ZOPACAS and the ASA summit underline Brazil's preponderance in interregionalism, which moves from the bilateral to the transregional stage or in the case of SACU-MERCOSUR to pure interregionalism.

Closely related to the establishment of regionalisms are the concepts of actorness and regionness, which highlight the emergence of regions as actors in their own right (Hettne 2003; Doidge 2011). By forming interregional linkages, the actorness of a regionalism can indeed be strengthened. Interregionalism has provided visibility, external recognition and ultimately legitimacy to the formal organisations MERCOSUR and SADC, and above all to the regional leadership of Brazil and South Africa as being constitutive to regional order. However, in the cases examined in this paper interregionalism has not yielded more institutionalisation on the regional level, a feature that is considered to be crucial for regional actorness (Doidge 2011). The relationship between interregionalism and regionalism is therefore only mutually reinforcing to a certain point. The most innovative feature of interregionalism might be that is serves a starting point for imagining a new regionalism, which is different from the interregional formation of mega-regions (Baert et al. 2014). ZOPACAS is the most striking example, as it proposes the South Atlantic as its own region and not as an interstitial space between regions. Under which conditions interregionalisms transform into regionalisms should therefore be considered a crucial research question, especially for scholars dealing with the potential of an emergent Atlantic space.

References

Aggarwal, V. K., & Fogarty, E. A. (Eds.). (2004). *EU trade strategies: Between regionalism and globalization*. Houndmills: Palgrave Macmillan.

Alden, C., & Vieira, M. (2005). The new diplomacy of the South: South Africa, Brazil, India and Trilateralism. *Third World Quarterly, 26*(7), 1077–1095.

Baert, F., Scaramagli, T., & Söderbaum, F. (2014). Introduction: Intersecting interregionalism. In F. Baert, T. Scaramagli, & F. Söderbaum (Eds.), *Intersecting interregionalism: Regions, global governance and the EU* (pp. 1–12). Dordrecht: Springer.

Bizzozero, L. (2011). Los primeros veinte años del MERCOSUR: Del Programa de Liberación Comercial al Plan Estratégico de Acción Social. *Densidades* (6), 23–34.

Brazilian Ministry of External Relations. (2008). *Brazilian Foreign Policy Handbook*. Brasilia: Alexandre de Gusmao Foundation.

Caetano, G., Vázquez, M., & Ventura, D. (2009). Reforma institucional del MERCOSUR: Análisis de un reto. In G. Caetano (Ed.), *La reforma institucional del MERCOSUR: Del diagnóstico a las propuestas* (pp. 21–76). Montevideo: CEFIR.

Cason, J. (2011). *The political economy of integration: The experience of Mercosur*. Abingdon: Routledge.

Doidge, M. (2011). *The European union and interregionalism: Patterns of engagement*. Farnham: Ashgate.

Erwin, A. (1999). Globalisation and regionalism in the South in the 21st century. In G. Mills & C. Mutschler (Eds.), *Exploring South-South dialogue: Mercosur in Latin America and SADC in Southern Africa* (pp. 15–21). Johannesburg: SAIIA.

Fawcett, L. (2008). Regionalism in world politics: Past and present. In A. Kösler (Ed.), *Elements of regional integration: A multidimensional approach* (pp. 15–28). Baden-Baden: Nomos.

Fioramonti, L. (Ed.). (2012). *Regions and crises: New challenges for contemporary regionalisms* (International political economy series). Houndmills/Basingstoke/Hampshire: Palgrave Macmillan.

Gamba-Stonehouse, V. (1989). *Strategy in the Southern Oceans: A South American View*. London: Pinter.

Gardini, G. L. (2012). *Latin America in the 21st century*. London: Zed Books.

Gobierno de Venezuela – Ministerio del Poder Popular para la Comunicación y la Información. (2010). *II Cumbre América del Sur – África – ASA 2009* (Colección Cuadernos para el debate). Caracas.

Godsäter, A., & Söderbaum, F. (2010). Civil society in regional governance in Eastern and Southern Africa. In D. Armstrong, V. Bello, J. Gilson, & D. Spini (Eds.), *Civil society and international governance: The role of non-state actors in the EU, Africa, Asia and Middle East* (pp. 148–165). Hoboken: Taylor & Francis.

Hänggi, H. (2006). Interregionalism as a multifaceted phenomenon: In search of a typology. In H. Hänggi, R. Roloff, & J. Rüland (Eds.), *Interregionalism and international relations* (pp. 31–62). London: Routledge.

Hentz, J. J. (2005). *South Africa and the logic of regional cooperation*. Bloomington: Indiana University Press.

Hettne, B. (1999). Globalization and the new regionalism: The second great transformation. In B. Hettne (Ed.), *Globalism and the new regionalism* (pp. 1–24). Basingstoke: Macmillan.

Hettne, B. (2003). The new regionalism revisited. In F. Söderbaum & T. M. Shaw (Eds.), *Theories of new regionalism: A Palgrave reader* (pp. 22–42). Basingstoke: Palgrave Macmillan.

Hettne, B. (2006). Beyond the "new" regionalism. In A. Payne (Ed.), *Key debates in new political economy* (pp. 128–160). London: Routledge.

Jiménez, D. M. (2010). La política exterior de Raúl Alfonsín (1983–1989): Un balance aproximativo. *Temas de historia argentina y americana* (17), 99–121.

Katzenstein, P. J. (2005). *A world of regions: Asia and Europe in the American imperium*. Ithaca: Cornell University Press.

Khadiagala, G. M. (2001). Foreign policy decisionmaking in Southern Africa's fading frontline. In G. M. Khadiagala & T. Lyons (Eds.), *African foreign policies: Power and process* (pp. 131–158). Boulder: Lynne Rienner Publishers.

Lechini, G. (2006). *Argentina y África en el espejo de Brasil: ¿política por impulsos o construcción de una política exterior?* Buenos Aires: CLACSO.

Lechini, G. (2007). Middle powers: IBSA and the new South-South cooperation. *NACLA Report on the Americas, 40*(5), 28–32.

Lenz, T. (2013). EU normative power and regionalism: Ideational diffusion and its limits. *Cooperation and Conflict, 48*(2), 211–228.

Mattheis, F. (2014). *New regionalism in the South – Mercosur and SADC in a comparative and interregional perspective*. Leipzig: Leipziger Universitätsverlag.

MERCOSUR. (1991). *Tratado de Ascunción para la Constitución de un Mercado Común*.

Nathan, L. (2002). *Community of insecurity: SADC's struggle for peace and security in Southern Africa*. Farnham: Ashgate.

Nutenko, L. (2006). MERCOSUR y los países de Asia y de África: Nueva etapa de interacción. *Iberoamérica (Trimestral desde Moscú)* (3), 103–112.

Oosthuizen, G. (2006). *The Southern African development community: The organisation, its policies and prospects*. Midrand: Institute for Global Dialogue.

Ponjaert, F. (2013). Interregionalism as a coherent and intelligible instrument in the EU foreign Policy toolbox. In M. Telò & F. Ponjaert (Eds.), *The EU's foreign policy: What kind of power and diplomatic action?* (pp. 135–158). Farnham: Ashgate.

Riggirozzi, P., & Tussie, D. (Eds.). (2012). *The rise of post-hegemonic regionalism: The case of Latin America*. Dordrecht: Springer.

Roberts, S. (2004). *Reflections on approaching an FTA negotiation with Mercosur: A review of key issues* (SAIIA Trade Policy Report 6). Johannesburg.

Rüland, J. (2014). Interregionalism and international relations: Reanimating an obsolescent research Agenda? In F. Baert, T. Scaramagli, & F. Söderbaum (Eds.), *Intersecting interregionalism: Regions, global governance and the EU* (pp. 15–35). Dordrecht: Springer.

SADC Summit of Heads of State and Government. (2003, August 26). Communiqué of the Summit of Heads of State and Government, Dar Es Salaam. http://www.sadc.int/files/3913/5292/8384/SADC_SUMMIT_COMMUNIQUES_1980-2006.pdf. Accessed 23 July 2017.

SADC. (2009). *Activity report of the SADC secreteriat: For the period August 2007–July 2008*. Gaborone.

Serbin, A. (2012). New regionalism and civil society: Bridging the democratic gap? In P. Riggirozzi & D. Tussie (Eds.), *The rise of post-hegemonic regionalism: The case of Latin America* (pp. 147–166). Dordrecht: Springer.

Söderbaum, F. (2004). *The political economy of regionalism: The case of Southern Africa*. Basingstoke: Palgrave Macmillan.

Söderbaum, F., Stalgren, P., & van Langenhove, L. (2005). The EU as a global actor and the dynamics of interregionalism: A comparative analysis. *Journal of European Integration, 27*(3), 365–380.

Standaert, S., & Rayp, G. (2012). *Regional integration agreements and rent-seeking in Africa* (Working paper series 773). Gent.

Tulchin, J. S. (1987). The Malvinas War of 1982: An inevitable conflict that never should have occurred. *Latin American Research Review, 22*(3), 123–141.

United Nations General Assembly. (1986). *Declaration of a zone of peace and co-operation in the South Atlantic.*

van der Vleuten, J. M., & Ribeiro Hoffmann, A. (2010). Explaining the enforcement of democracy by regional organizations: Comparing EU, Mercosur and SADC. *Journal of Common Market Studies, 48*(3), 737–758.

van Klaveren, A. (2000). Chile: The search for open regionalism. In B. Hettne (Ed.), *National perspectives on the new regionalism in the south* (pp. 132–156). Basingstoke: Macmillan.

van Nieuwkerk, A. (2010). SADC's common foreign policy. In C. Harvey & A. van Nieuwkerk (Eds.), *Proceedings of the 2009 FOPRISA annual conference* (pp. 97–112). Gaborone: Lightbooks.

White, L. (2003). *Driving SACU – Mercosur: Trans-Atlantic co-operation in the automotive industry* (SAIIA Reports 34). Johannesburg.

Chapter 4
Actors and Opportunities: Interregional Processes Between the Arab Region and Latin America and the Caribbean

Anna Ayuso, Santiago Villar, Camila Pastor, and Miguel Fuentes

Abstract This paper analyses interregional links between Latin America and the Caribbean (LAC) and the Arab region. The relations between regional organizations in LAC and their peers in North Africa and the Arab world are still fairly nascent and represent a much understudied area. Recent institutional rapprochement between LAC regional organizations and North African and Arab regional institutions are remarkable however. The re-launching of South-South cooperation in a multipolar context over the past decades has boosted this trend. Relations and exchanges between both regions have grown constantly over the last 10–12 years, along with a progressive institutionalization of high-level political dialogue. This study aims to identify and analyze the main drivers behind this multi-layered interregionalism as well as the obstacles in its way, by examining how it is fostered by state and non-state actors in political, economic and social formations.

Keywords Atlantic • Interregionalism • Regional organisations • Regionalism • Regions

4.1 Introduction

Decolonization fragmented former imperial polities into a global system of nation states during the second half of the twentieth century. In the wake of the collapse of the dynamics of bipolarity and nonalignment which had characterized geopolitics during the Cold War, regionalism was increasingly championed by European states as an alternative to the short-lived unipolar system dominated by the Unites States

A. Ayuso (✉) • S. Villar
Barcelona Centre for International Affairs (CIDOB), Barcelona, Spain
e-mail: aayuso@cidob.org; svillar@cidob.org

C. Pastor • M. Fuentes
Centro de Investigación y Docencia Económicas (CIDE), Mexico City, Mexico
e-mail: camila.pastor@cide.edu; mfuentescarreno@gmail.com

© Springer International Publishing AG 2018   51
F. Mattheis, A. Litsegård (eds.), *Interregionalism across the Atlantic Space*,
United Nations University Series on Regionalism 15,
DOI 10.1007/978-3-319-62908-7_4

after the fall of the Soviet Union. Regionalist initiatives have since been increasingly institutionalized.

As regions and regional institutions become consolidated as political actors, they not only develop internally, but also build external networks of relations, increasingly analyzed through the lens of interregionalism. Interregional relations result in the emergence of new governance spaces, bounded on one side by global governance institutions and on the other by regional governance. Baert et al. (2014) note that interregional relations are often nested within other forms and levels of cooperation such as bilateralism, regionalism and multilateralism. Transregionalism has also emerged as an analytic tool that allows us to investigate phenomena beyond the narrow framework of interaction between two institutionalized regions within formal and mainly inter-governmental structures.For political scientists such as Aggarwal and Fogarty (2005), transregionalism refers to interregional relations where two or more regions are dispersed, have weak actorship, and where neither region negotiates as a regional organization. It constitutes a failed or exceptional regionalism or a precursor to regionalism. The concepts of transregionalism and transnationalism have, however, also been used to account for phenomena involving increasingly relevant non-state actors, from NGOs scaffolding global humanitarian or environmental efforts to transnational networks of corporate production and the transfer of religious practice through human mobility.

We explore the institutionalization of regionalism in Latin America and the Arab world since the 1950s, focusing on political, economic and cultural processes constituting emerging interregional ties since the 1990s, when regionalism emerged as a leading form of geopolitics.

4.2 Regionalism in Latin America and the Caribbean and the Arab Region

The Latin American region is composed of 33 countries that are members of the Community of Latin American and Caribbean States (CELAC in Spanish). A complex map of overlapping regional institutions co-exists in Latin America and the Caribbean (LAC), which, historically, has been one of the regions defining an Atlantic economy. In spite of a common language, LAC does not constitute a homogeneous sphere in cultural, geographical, historical, political or economic terms. These countries share a colonial legacy and have become an institutionalized political group that defines itself in contrast to its northern neighbors. There are, however, distinct sub-regions.

Central America, South America and the Caribbean are differentiated by specific trends and this has led to political subdivisions, crystallized in several institutionalized regional actors with specific political and economic strategies. The subdivisions created by regionalist projects correspond to political criteria and shared interests rather than geography. LAC is a heterogeneous space integrated by a web of ties and a plethora of multilateral institutions. Different mechanisms configure multiple regional spaces ranging from hemispheric to sub-regional spaces. New initiatives at the beginning of the twenty-first century intended to increase the autonomy of the actors involved and to enhance sustainable development in order to overcome historical imbalances. Others have been configured by particular ideological or strategic options. All are interconnected and face global challenges.

On the other side of the Atlantic, the 22 states that are members of the League of Arab States (LAS, Jamiat ad-Duwal al-Arabia in Arabic) will be analyzed as a region. Ferabolli (2015) has made a strong case for the analytic autonomy of an Arab regionalism rather than grouping Arabic speaking countries within Middle Eastern or Mediterranean regional contexts. The political tensions between the Arabophone world and its former Ottoman colonial metropole, today's Turkey, the instrumentalization of theological differences within Islam to render linguistic distance from Farsi-speaking Iran into Sunni-Shia rivalries, and its sustained military confrontation with its political antagonist, Israel, have strengthened pan-Arabism as an ideology and political project and underlie the politics of its regionalism and interregionalisms.

As in LAC, distinct institutions overlap in the Arab region in a complex scaffolding of institutional forms and projects. LAS, active from 1945 through the present, initially focused on promoting decolonization in the Arab world and has continued to champion Arab unity as political project. Regional institutions that developed in the 1980s attempting economic integration foundered on political divergence, and the most recent wave, best exemplified by the GCC, centers on a security agenda. Though the Arab world is not geographically an Atlantic space, its historical migratory ties and growing economic interaction with the LAC region have facilitated the emergence of interregional opportunities.

The relationship between regional organizations in LAC and their peers in North Africa and the Arab world is still fairly nascent. The introspective character of the first LAC regionalism, the sustained orientation of each region to its former colonial metropole or "political North", and the scarce economic ties between these regions have been obstacles to the development of interregional relations. However, three particular LAC organizations have clearly strengthened ties with North African and Arab regional institutions: MERCOSUR, UNASUR and CELAC.

4.2.1 Evolving Regionalism in Latin America and the Caribbean

Despite the United States agenda of continental regionalism during the Cold War, governments in several LAC countries enhanced economic development through an import substitution model intended to overcome dependence on primary commodities exports in the late 1950s. Structured as a defensive strategy before extra-regional and more competitive markets, it limited exchange between the region and the world. This LAC wave of economic associations and integration was deemed a "closed" regionalism. The oil crisis in 1973, public debt accumulation and external debt crisis triggered a change in national economic models and regional projects. Regional organizations were transformed according to neoliberal economic policies based on the Washington Consensus.

In 1994, the US relaunched hemispheric relations through summitry within the OAS System with the Summit of the Americas. Latin American states deepened economic integration and aspired to sub-regional economic/monetary unions. The Treaty of Asunción (1991) created the Common Market of the South (MERCOSUR), which, according to Hurrell (1995), has increased institutionalized interaction between bureaucracies, politicians, new interest groups and entrepreneurs in an intra-regional integration process. This kind of regional integration was perceived as increasing bargaining power with industrialized countries in the context of multilateral trade negotiations leading to the creation of the World Trade Organization (WTO) in late 1994. After MERCOSUR, the Tegucigalpa Protocol (1991) renewed the Central American Integration System (SICA) and The Trujillo Protocol (1996) transformed the Andean Pact into the Andean Community (CAN).

The new millennium has favored extra-regional commerce and, thus, interregionalism, but success in establishing supranational institutions has been limited. This regionalism stresses political and social issues beyond trade. Trade-focused integration processes have not been abandoned, however as the creation (in 2012) of the Pacific Alliance by Mexico, Colombia, Peru and Chile shows. Over fifteen extant regional cooperation organizations can be classified into two main groups according to their main objectives. One set of integration processes aims to progressively establish a Free Trade Area (FTA): SICA, CAN, MERCOSUR, the Caribbean Community (CARICOM) and the Pacific Alliance. MERCOSUR and the Pacific Alliance are the main actors in the LAC region by market size. However, they represent different integration strategies. The Pacific Alliance has a liberal orientation, while MERCOSUR is more protectionist.

The second group includes a diversity of sectorial organizations, classic intergovernmental cooperation bodies and political forums without permanent institutions. Some have developed significant institutional cooperation mechanisms in the fields of security and social policies. In contrast, the newcomer CELAC, grouping all LAC countries, has neither permanent institutions nor legal personality. A common feature is the lack of supranational institutions, which often derives in the tendency to block regional decisions in defense of national interest.

4.2.1.1 The Common Market of the South (MERCOSUR)

MERCOSUR was created through a treaty signed in 1991 by Brazil, Argentina, Uruguay and Paraguay with the objective of establishing an FTA with minimal institutional framework and an intergovernmental structure. MERCOSUR aquired legal personality and established permanent – but feeble- institutions in 1994.

The MERCOSUR process has been conditioned by bilateral relations between Argentina and Brazil, the initial driver countries and the main engines of integration (Pagani and Martínez Larrechea 2005). The full implementation of a common external tariff has been repeatedly delayed. Commercial interdependence among MERCOSUR members is still low and interregional investment is also very low, with an average of 2% of total investments. The rise of leftist governments in most member states has led to a renewal of the project, increasingly focused on political and socioeconomic issues. Lacking non-intergovernmental bodies weakens MERCOSUR integration. Slow economic integration, poor implementation of common rules, and protectionist measures have prevented MERCOSUR from taking advantage of its foreign policy agenda.

MERCOSUR has signed agreements with Arab countries that align with liberalizing economic strategies: Egypt, Morocco, Jordan and the Gulf Cooperation Council (GCC), as explained in Sect. 3.3.1.

4.2.1.2   The Union of South American Nations (UNASUR)

UNASUR was discussed at the Brasilia summit (2000) and created in 2008. During this period, the project evolved, incorporating the perspectives and political interests of the different actors involved. Today, members of the Pacific Alliance, MERCOSUR, CAN and CARICOM with divergent trading strategies co-exist in the same institution. In the political arena, UNASUR, comprises the counter-hegemonic ALBA bloc led by Venezuela; a more pragmatic group of countries seeking to increase regional and extra-regional alliances without confrontation, like Chile or Colombia; and revisionist countries like Brazil and Argentina looking to rearrange their position in the multipolar global context (Garzón 2015).UNASUR promotes regional infrastructure and creates common rules on shared concerns: security, energy and financial cooperation.

UNASUR maintains an intergovernmental structure and decisions are made by consensus. The South America Defense Council (CDS in Spanish) was created in 2008. Security became the axis for a broad institutional and political framework, including the South American Council for the Fight against Drug Trafficking (2009) and the South American Council on Public Security, Justice and Coordination of Action against Transnational Organized Crime in 2012 (UNASUR 2015).

All members of UNASUR have been strengthening their ties with Arab countries through high level meetings and increasing trade, as will be analyzed in Sect. 4.3.1.

4.2.1.3   The Community of Latin American and Caribbean States (CELAC)

In 2011 CELAC emerged from the confluence of previous initiatives and the political momentum of convergent leadership across Brazil, Mexico and Venezuela. The Rio Group, a political forum created in 1986 through regional support for peace negotiations in Central America, had consolidated as a forum for reaching common positions, especially at United Nations. The Brazilian initiative convening the first

Summit of Latin America and the Caribbean on Integration and Development (CALC) in 2008 provided new political impetus.

Recently, at the third CELAC summit held in Costa Rica (2015), the Belen Declaration and the CELAC Action Plan proposed 27 fields for cooperation, including a future Latin America and the Caribbean FTA of doubtful feasibility. While Chile, Peru, Colombia and Mexico are striving to open up their markets, MERCOSUR members are reluctant to follow the same steps. There are also disagreements regarding the extent of future institutionalization. While ALBA countries work towards a stable institutional alternative to the OAS, others prefer a flexible forum that does not compromise their relationships with the US. So far, CELAC is primarily a political actor connecting South America with North America and the Caribbean. CELAC is also a privileged interregional interlocutor.

Although CELAC is the most recent LAC integration effort, relations with Arab countries, in particular with GCC, have already been launched, as will be briefly described in Sect. 3.3.2.

4.2.2   The Evolution of Regionalism in the Arab World

Two anti-imperialist regionalisms have integrated the Arab world since the close of World War II. The Arab League was founded in Cairo in 1945 by the Kingdom of Egypt, the Emirate of Transjordan, the Kingdom of Iraq, the Kingdom of Saudi Arabia, Lebanon and Syria; Yemen joined months later. Established on the secular principles of state sovereignty and Arab nationalism, LAS grew to 22 member states as North African and Gulf countries born of decolonization joined. LAS became an observer of the General Assembly at the UN in 1950 and established a Joint Defense and Economic Cooperation Treaty in 1952 to coordinate regional military cooperation after the 1948 Arab Israeli war. LAS achieved limited integration of Middle Eastern states and actors: post-colonial alliance safeguarding the sovereignty of newly established states, forum coordinating policy positions, contain conflicts such as the Lebanese crisis of 1958, settle Arab disputes and deliberate on matters of common concern.

The Cold War polarized the region into Soviet and American allies: monarchies aligned with the US, secular republics flirted with the Soviet Union or engaged with both. Concerned with Soviet access to the region's oil reserves, the United States intervened to limit the operation of LAS or provide alternatives to its leadership. The Soviet Union developed close military and political ties with Egypt, Syria, Iraq, Libya, the People's Republic of Yemen and Somalia. The attempt to create a common market between 1957 and 1967 met with limited success. Since the first summit in 1964, LAS was used by regionally hegemonic powers to redefine their regional position. Initially LAS operated as a tool to promote Egypt's leadership in the region, with headquarters in Cairo and Egyptian diplomats as Secretaries General. LAS was instrumental since 1964 in the creation of organizations representing Palestinians: the Palestinian National Council and the Palestinian Liberation

Organization. In 1968, it established the Organization of Arab Petroleum Exporting Countries (OAPEC) to protect the production of oil reserves.

Much as the OAS provides a hemispheric alternative for affiliation in the Americas, the Organization of the Islamic Conference (OIC) provides a regional alternattive on the basis of a common religious tradition. Founded with 25 member states in 1969 after the defeat of Arab states by Israel in 1967, its first high-level meeting established a permanent secretariat in Jeddah. It's three main bodies: the Islamic Summit of heads of state convenes every 3 years; the Council of Foreign Ministers, convening yearly to develop means of implementing policy; and the executive organ, the General Secretariat. In 1999, the Parliamentary Union of OIC member states was established in Tehran. With the Palestinian National Authority a member, the Palestinian struggle has been a privileged issue.

With 57 member states today and permanent delegations to the UN and the EU, the OIC cultivates Muslim solidarity, institutionalizes cooperation, defends Muslim causes in world politics and contributes to dispute settlement in Muslim countries. Important revisions to its charters in 2008 and 2011 shifted the focus towards promoting human rights, fundamental freedoms and good governance, replacing the Cairo Declaration of Human Rights in Islam created by the OIC in 1990 with endorsement of the Universal Declaration of Human Rights. In 2011, the organization was renamed the Organization of Islamic Cooperation.

4.2.2.1 The League of Arab States: New Order, New Challenges

Secular Arabism has been eroded by sub-regional projects and external pressure. The oil boom of the 1970s deepened the contrast between Arab Gulf oil-rich rentier states developing as conservative monarchies championing Islam, and Eastern Mediterranean oil-poor secular republics. Egypt and Jordan's peace negotiations with Israel in the 1980's divided the region politically. The Iraqi invasion of Kuwait and the Iraq war accentuated regional discord, with Arab states uniting again only to face American military intervention after September 11th 2001.

The terrorist attacks on New York and Washington legitimated the militarization and securitization of US foreign policy, culminating in the wars against Afghanistan (2001) and Iraq (2003). These wars triggered a new regional disorder in the Arab world characterized by escalating inter- and intra-state violence limiting regional political cooperation. The "war on terror" inspired forced democratization of states in the region. Re-emerging competition for regional hegemony has strengthened bilateral and informal diplomatic conflict management initiatives. Foreign military intervention is instrumentalized to "securitize" regional cooperation, mainly through the Arab League.

New sub-regional efforts towards cooperation and economic integration have weakened the League as a collective actor. Average tariffs applied by LAS countries to other members of the organization have not translated into greater trade. According to Decreux et al. (2012), LAS share of intra-regional trade was 11% by 2010 (excluding oil), showing the limited success of preferential agreements among its members to improve regional economic integration. Emerging economies have absorbed shares as trading partners, superseding the region's historical partnership with the European Union.

Since 2011, popular uprisings have forced regional organizations to act on what were earlier perceived to be the internal affairs of member states, while enhancing military cooperation to prevent foreign intervention. The UN demanded that both LAS and GCC take an active role in the regional security situation. At the Arab Economic Summit of 2011 shortly after uprisings began. LAS Secretary General Amr Moussa encouraged leaders to invest in sectors that might pre-empt revolts by tackling the economic burdens of popular sectors. LAS did not provide considerations on responding to uprisings forcing rulers out of power in Egypt and Yemen, or take a clear stance regarding protesters. Where state violence escalated, LAS avoided statements against the use of force to repress popular uprisings, despite the fact that LAS is composed of 13 permanent committees on issues such as relations with civil society, human rights, women and youth. After the fall of several regimes, an Arab Parliament was established at the Baghdad Summit of March 2012. LAS's newest body seeks economic, social and developmental cooperation, fostering joint mechanisms, guaranteeing national security and promoting human rights. It remains weak in reviewing treaties, unifying Arab legislation and pushing the project of an Arab Court, established in art. 20 of the League's charter.

Civil society has sought to promote agendas through LAS, calling for it to ensure effective sanctions on the Syrian government and discuss violence during the transition between Mubarak and Morsi and the recent escalation against the Muslim Brotherhood by al-Sisi's government. LAS' Arab Charter on Human Rights, effective since 2008, has not proven useful in monitoring these demands or the recent violence between Houthi militiamen and the Yemeni government. Syria has been suspended from LAS since November 2011 in response to the ongoing civil war there.

LAS policies have shaped possibilities for interregionalism since the 1950s, whether the exceptional pragmatism of Franco's Spain or third-worldist solidarity of LAC. In the past two decades LAS has been increasingly helpless before security concerns: the US invasion of Iraq in 2003, the Lebanon-Hezbollah war in 2006. With popular revolts and revolutions questioning state power since 2011, regional leadership is being reconfigured in favor of Gulf hegemony. Non-state actors increasingly mobilize non-Arab national projects based on linguistic or religious criteria: Amazigh separatism in North Africa, Kurdish nationalisms and variously imagined "Islamic" authorities in the Levant. The roles that LAS and GCC will play in relation to multiple actors engaged in the current processes and the resulting political landscapes is an open question.

4.2.2.2   The Gulf Cooperation Council: Sub-regional Alternatives for Arab Regionalism

Sub-regional cooperation developed as an alternative to the political, economic and cultural disparities between the conservative monarchies (Morocco, Jordan and Saudi Arabia) and formerly revolutionary regimes (Egypt, Syria, Iraq and Libya). With the end of the Cold War a "new regionalism" developed in the Arab world, with its three historically distinct sub-regions establishing formal intergovernmental economic and political cooperation agreements.

The Cooperation Council for the Arab States of the Gulf, GCC, composed of the six states bordering the Gulf – Bahrain, Kuwait, Qatar, Saudi Arabia, Oman and the United Arab Emirates- focuses on security and alliance formation rather than economic cooperation. Founded in 1981, it has been the most active of the three sub-regional actors. It has three main bodies: the Supreme Council – with an attached Commission for the Settlement of Disputes; the Ministerial Council; and the Secretariat General. Cooperation focuses on military and security affairs, as GCC members consider themselves the regional guarantor of stability. To this end, a Peninsula Shield Force against external aggressions was created in 1982, a collective security agreement was signed in 2001, a Joint Defense Council was formed in 2001 and a Supreme Military Committee in 2003. Despite security success, trade has faced major challenges: Bahrain and Oman signed separate free trade agreements with the US, creating gaps in the GCC common external tariff and intra-GCC exports dropped from 4.2% to 2.2% between 2000 and 2011. Economic cooperation has advanced towards joint customs regulation and a future joint currency. According to Gariup (2008), the institutionalization of the Gulf sub-regional security complex can be considered an attempt to: (1) strengthen the sovereignty of the Gulf states; and (2) balance regional powers by giving smaller states the advantage of politics of scale, strengthening the collective position of members in the sub-system and excluding unstable neighbors such as Yemen and Iraq.

The Arab Maghreb Union (AMU)–formed of Algeria, Libya, Mauritania, Morocco and Tunisia – and the Arab Cooperation Council (ACC) – of Iraq, Jordan, North Yemen and Egypt – were both established in 1989. AMU was committed to creating a common market, but political quarrels and individual states' relations with Europe have paralyzed this sub-regional project. The ACC was an Egyptian attempt to re-insert itself into Arab politics after the estrangement that followed its negotiations with Israel, themselves partly a response to being left out of the GCC. The Gulf War and the Oslo peace process revealed the limited capacities of the ACC and the continuing centrality of the security agenda despite the end of the Cold War. The ACC did not survive the Iraqi invasion of Kuwait in 1990.

The Agadir Agreement for Arab-Mediterranean economic integration signed by Morocco, Jordan, Tunisia and Egypt in 2004 to go into effect in 2007, and the GCC commitment to a common currency – foreseen for 2010–can be understood, according to Harders and Legrenzi (2008), as a farewell to a Pan-Arab vision. The Agadir Agreement attempted to facilitate a free trade agreement with the EU in the context of greater UE-Mediterranean integration. It was superseded by the Greater Arab

Free Trade Area (GAFTA)–signed in 1998 and projected for 2005–with 18 member states, which, since 1981, has attempted facilitating trade efforts launched by the LAS Economic and Social Council. GAFTA remains a proposal on paper however.

GCC considers the popular uprisings since 2011 a direct security threat and has accepted Saudi Arabia as "regional coordinator", while building an intra-Arab consensus. Gulf states' increasing reliance on their sub-regional organization impacts negatively on the LAS realm of influence. GCC invited the two non-GCC monarchies, Jordan and Morocco, to join the council, making the GCC a more cohesive organization and a viable alternative to LAS. GCC provide its members with: (1) quick decisions on domestic issues; (2) security forces, such as in Bahrain and recently in Yemen. The LAS could only offer preventive diplomatic measures. The LAS has not provided assistance or advice to its member states on handling the protests, while the GCC has pushed for minor political reforms.

Internal struggles for leadership of the GCC have evolved towards dialogue and conciliation more easily than within LAS. Qatar's bid for a reinvigorated role of LAS in Syria caused tensions with Saudi Arabia – the traditional guardian of the GCC. Saudis withdrew their ambassador from Damascus and pushed to end the LAS observation mission in January 2012. However, Riyadh's main role is to keep the council strong, hence the consideration that Qatar could be a minor partner in managing external instability (Colombo 2012). The GCC was actively involved in supporting Arab uprisings outside the GCC area. Their strategy was to provide support for political forces which seemed "friendly" to the monarchies – such as Sunni Islam-rooted movements and parties. GCC members did not support protesters in their own countries and opted for a "stick-and-carrot" policy: promoting economic reforms and investments that improved socioeconomic stability, while suppressing and controlling uprisings both in and outside GCC member states.

4.2.3 Comparative Regionalism

When comparing UNASUR and LAS, common features emerge. Population density and life expectancy are similar. UNASUR has approximately 412 million people living within an area of 17,715,000 km², whereas the Arab League countries have around 362 million in an area of 13,783,000 km²; UNASUR life expectancy is 74 and LAS 71. Both regions have religious majorities: Christians in Latin America and Muslims in the Arab world. The same goes for the predominance of a single language – Spanish in UNASUR and Modern Standard Arabic in LAS– a strong asset for fostering regional integration.

Together, both regions have global importance in many respects. The shared total area accounts for more than the 20% of the earth's land mass and its population (774 million) is larger than Europe's (739 million). But economic differences are significant. UNASUR's GDP amounts to $4.19bn, including large economies like Brazil –almost 55% of the whole block– and tiny economies like Guyana. The Arab

League's GDP is around $2.78bn, also combining unequal economies such as Saudi Arabia and Comoros. In addition, GDP per capita is 25% higher in UNASUR than in LAS ($10,163 and $7670 respectively). Both regions are net exporters of natural resources and raw materials. In the case of Arab countries, oil plays a key role within the vast majority of its economies. Libya, Iraq, Kuwait, Saudi Arabia and the UAE possess almost 40% of the world's proven oil reserves. Oil and gas proven reserves of UNASUR and LAS – together – represent 63% and 30% of the world, respectively. South America is one of the world's main producers of food.

Both regions have embraced a security agenda. Latin America is the most violent region in the world and the only where homicide rates increased between 2000 and 2010. Within LAC, South America shows lower levels of violence than Central America, but considerably higher than the Arab League countries. The average global homicide rate in 2012 was 6.2 per 100,000 inhabitants. In UNASUR it was around 16 whereas in LAS countries it was nearly four times lower (4.6). Nonetheless, it must be stressed that even with lower levels of insecurity, LAS is a less peaceful region when other factors are considered. Current situation in Libya or Syria, with millions of refugees and internally displaced people, or conflicts in Iraq, which has become a battlefield due to the emergence of the Islamic State (ISIS), appear to be much more complicated than any conflict in South America. The Global Peace Index 2014 put many members of the LAS in the list of countries with a very low level of peace.

South America seems to have left its anti-democratic experiences behind and has consolidated government structures elected by the people. After the "Arab Spring", many new governments are facing challenges in consolidating the transition of power in the Arab world. The Syrian conflict and the rise of ISIS have affected the stability of the whole region.

Large sectors of the populations of both regions are young people: an important asset, but also a challenge, as this workforce will require suitable employment. Unemployment in South America has declined in the last 10 years, but the quality and conditions of these jobs are now being contested. In the Arab world, youth unemployment remains high and the lack of opportunities for young people prevalent.

4.3 Interregionalism Between Latin America and the Arab World

UNASUR and LAS group developing countries, which facilitates a common geopolitical approach promoting multipolar world governance, such as the Non-Aligned Movement (NAM) or the G-77. Participation in these forums has facilitated mutual understanding affording coordinated positions in forums such as the UN or the World Trade Organization (WTO). Such contacts paved the way for launching specific interregional forums. The growing network of Arab diplomatic representation in South America – and vice versa – has played an important role in generating a solid interregional dialogue.

4.3.1 The Summit of South American-Arab Countries (ASPA)

In spite of some good bilateral relations between several countries during the last century, interregionalism only began in earnest in the early 2000s. Energy was the driver for this rapprochement. President Hugo Chávez of Venezuela, an OPEC member, travelled to the Middle East in August 2000. His main objective was to discuss oil issues and prepare the next OPEC summit, to be held in September that year in Caracas. Brazilian president, Luis Inacio Lula Da Silva, boosted closer links between the two regions. In December 2003, Lula visited Syria, Lebanon, the UAE, Libya and Egypt with members of his government, private stakeholders and MERCOSUR officials. During his closing speech at the LAS headquarters in Egypt, he advertized his intention to create a permanent interregional dialogue. He encouraged the exploitation of the potential complementarity of both regions and the deepening relationship with the Arab world. To achieve this, he proposed increasing high-level political contacts between leaders of South American and Arab countries with a summit to be held in Brazil. He noted the opportunities for economic cooperation between LAS and MERCOSUR countries, along with other countries in South America and the possibilities of significantly increasing trade, tourism, cultural exchange and investments. Lula was the first foreign head of state to give a speech at the LAS headquarters. At that meeting, Brazil became a LAS observer as Venezuela would also 3 years later. (Mundorama 2003).

Several preliminary meetings took place in order to coordinate the first Summit of South American – Arab Countries (ASPA) held in Brasilia in July 2005.At this event representatives of all countries from both UNASUR and LAS were present, as well as officials from the Arab League, CAN, GCC, and AMU. The meeting had the purpose of strengthening bi-regional relations, increasing cooperation and establishing a partnership to pursue development, justice and international peace.

As a result of this summit, the Brasilia Declaration was approved, containing 102 points. Some relevant political topics were discussed, such as the recognition of the Palestinian state, the support for the negotiations between Argentina and the UK over the Falkland/Malvinas Islands' sovereignty, the respect for the territorial integrity of states and nuclear disarmament. But also economic, social and cultural issues were debated, like the necessity of fostering intra-regional trade, the commitment to sustainable development, the fight against poverty and hunger, technology transfer, the establishment of the South American-Arab Library and the strengthening of South-South cooperation. Jointly with the summit, the first ASPA Businessmen Forum took place, with more than 600 participants from the private sector of both regions. Moreover, some other sectorial meetings were held, following the mandate of the Brasilia Declaration.

The relationship intensified and between the first (2005) and second (2009) ASPA summits, 16 official meetings took place. The strong impact of the first summit encouraged cooperation between the two regions and strengthened interstate relations. In the 2005–2009 period a number of South American countries signed bilateral agreements in different areas: Argentina with Egypt (2005), Algeria (2008) and Tunisia (2008); Brazil with Algeria (2005) and Lebanon (2007); Peru with Algeria (2005) and Morocco (2006); and Venezuela with Yemen (2008). (Organization of American States database).

Some Arab leaders travelled to South America during that period. The president of Algeria −Abdelaziz Bouteflika − visited Brazil, Chile, Peru and Venezuela in 2005, and the King of Jordan (Abdullah II) Argentina, Brazil and Chile. During the second meeting of ministers of economy in Rabat in May 2007, a declaration and an action plan regarding economic cooperation were adopted. The plan established ten fundamental points on which the regions should work together to promote interregional trade.

In March 2009, the second ASPA summit took place in Doha (Qatar). The final declaration had 121 points (preamble and six thematic sections).The Doha Declaration referred to the intensification of links as a result of the first summit and highlighted the issue of Palestine. Additionally, challenges on security in Middle East, sustainable development, nuclear disarmament and the resolution of the Falklands/Malvinas question continued to be key points. The final section defined the ASPA structure (Fig. 4.1).

After the second bi-regional summit, bilateral links became stronger. Agreements were signed between Brazil and Algeria (2010), Uruguay and Qatar (2010), and Venezuela and Libya (2010) and Syria (2010). MERCOSUR concluded other treaties as a block (See Sect. 3.2.1). More Arab leaders visited South America: the Emir of Qatar (Hamad Al-Thani) made a tour of Argentina, Brazil and Venezuela in 2010; the prime minister of Kuwait, Sheikh Nasser Al-Mohammad Al-Ahmad Al-Sabah, visited Argentina, Brazil, Chile and Uruguay the same year. In 2010, Bashar al-Assad (president of Syria) met the presidents of Argentina, Brazil and Venezuela. In 2012, Sheikh Abdullah bin Zayed Al Nahyan of the UAE visited President Ollanta Humala in Lima. In 2014 King Abdullah II of Jordan visited Mexico, and the Lebanese minister of foreign relations toured Latin America in early 2015, including Mexico, Cuba, Brazil and Argentina.

The most relevant visit to South America in that period was that of the president of the Palestinian National Authority, Mahmoud Abbas, in 2009 to Argentina, Brazil, Chile, Paraguay and Venezuela. He requested South American leaders recognize a Palestinian State. Between December 2010 and March 2011, nine UNASUR countries recognized Palestine: Argentina, Bolivia, Brazil, Chile, Ecuador, Guyana, Peru, Suriname and Uruguay. Paraguay and Venezuela had already recognized it (2005 and 2009 respectively). Ten of eleven countries voted in favor of Resolution 67/19 of the UN General Assembly giving Palestine the status of observer within the United Nations General Assembly. After the second ASPA summit additional official meetings were organized, some taking place as sidelines to other multilateral meetings.

Fig. 4.1 ASPA structure (Source: Authors' analysis, based on the Doha Declaration)

The third ASPA summit was scheduled for the first half of 2011.Postponed because of the uprisings, it finally it took place in October 2012, in Lima (Peru). The final declaration, longer than the previous ones, contained 178 points divided into six themes, plus an institutional section. The core topics were the Syrian crisis, agriculture and food security, the development of an action plan committed to education (Kuwait Action Plan), the opening of the Arab-South American Library (BibliASPA) in São Paulo, and progress made in the field of environmental cooperation and health. The third Arab and South American Businessmen Forum accompanied the third summit. Meetings of ministers of economy, culture, environment, health, foreign affairs and energy took place afterwards to continue improving links. The fourth summit of heads of state and government will be held in Riyadh (Saudi Arabia) in 2015.

4.3.2 Interregional Trade and Investment

UNASUR and LAS do not consider each other priority markets. The proportion of interregional trade in the global trade of each region is quite low. In 1997 imports to UNASUR countries from the LAS were only 1.5% of UNASUR's total worldwide imports, whereas exports were 1.9%. It must be taken into account that the main export of the majority of Arab countries is crude oil, and its most important clients are developed and heavily industrialized countries (SELA 2012). These proportions have risen since 2003 and in 2013 reached 2.3% in imports and 3.2% in exports, but are still very low, as the graphic shows (Figs. 4.2 and 4.3).

ASPA propelled an increase in volume and in the proportion of exports and imports between both regions. Exchanges of $5.39bn in 1997, climbed to $34.3bn in 2013. The curve began to rise in 2003, with sustained growth even during the 2008/2009 crisis. The political momentum of the ASPA summit and meetings of ministers of economy facilitated, among other factors, this substantial growth in economic exchange: trade increased fivefold (Fig. 4.4).

Trade balance generates a surplus for UNASUR, which exports more than it imports, a breach that has widened notably since 2005. It is important to note that this exchange is concentrated in few actors. Argentina and Brazil account for more than 70–80% of exports, whereas Brazil accounts for almost 90% of imports during the period (Figs. 4.5a and 4.5b).

Exports from both regions were concentrated in certain products. UNASUR exports mainly raw materials and foodstuffs, whereas for LAS crude oil and its derivatives are the most relevant items. More than 20% of exports from MENA to LAC were crude oil in 2010 (SELA 2012). Main export items from LAC to the LAS are: raw sugar cane; maize; iron ores and agglomerated concentrates; frozen meat; soybeans, including broken soybeans. A high dependence on primary products exports tends to affect these economies, as global markets prices could rapidly change due to external factors.

Both regions have an enormous potential to further develop mutual exchanges. LAS members are foodstuff net importers, whereas South America is a net exporter. On the other hand, the majority of Arab countries are oil exporters and tend to accumulate capital, while UNASUR has an infrastructure deficit, which necessarily

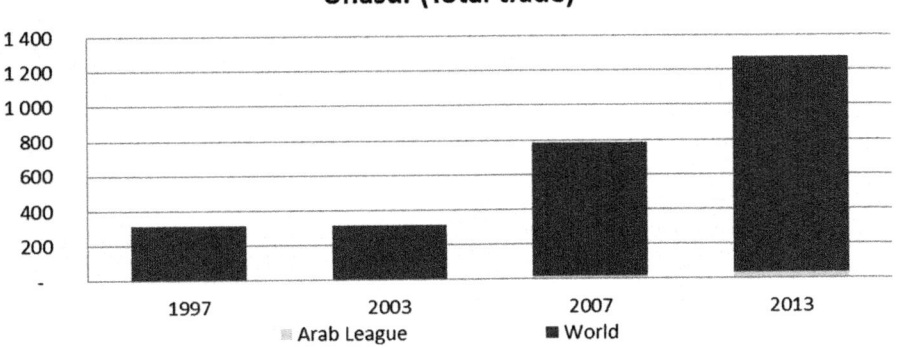

Fig. 4.2 Proportion of UNASUR trade with LAS within UNASUR total trade. Data in billion USD (Source: UNCOMTRADE. Graphics: Authors' own elaboration)

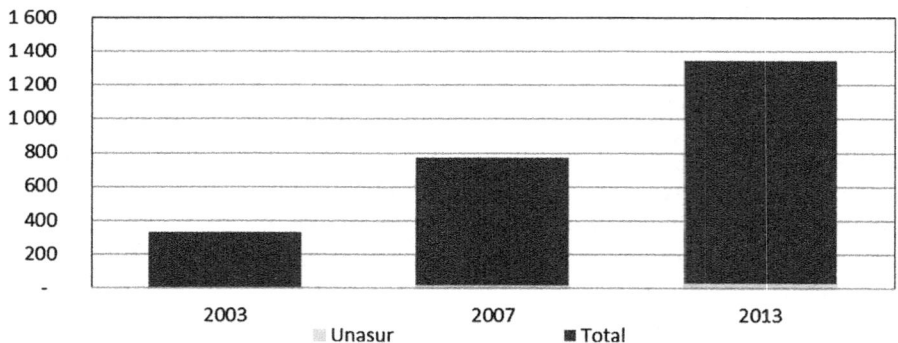

Fig. 4.3 Proportion of LAS trade with UNASUR within LAS total trade. Data in billion USD (Source: UNCOMTRADE. Graphics: Authors' own elaboration)

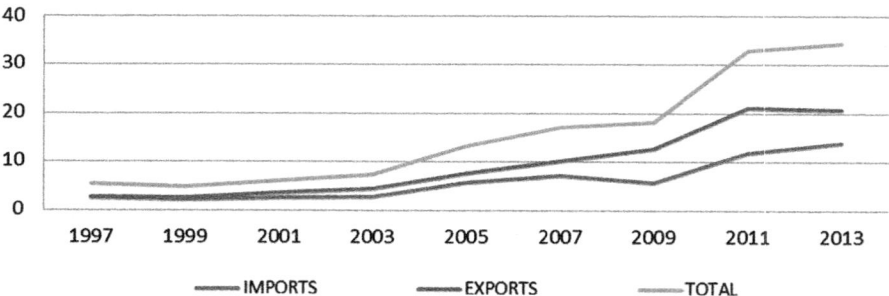

Fig. 4.4 Evolution of trade between UNASUR and LAS. Data in billion USD (Source: UNCOMTRADE. Graphics: Authors' own elaboration)

requires foreign support and investment. So far, the field of investments is still underdeveloped. There are only a few bilateral agreements on investment promotion and some others on double taxation. Arab investors have focused mainly on the services sector, rather than infrastructure. Nevertheless there have been some specific cases of relevant investments (SELA 2012).

On the other hand, South American investments in Arab countries are not outstanding. Chilean oil investments in Egypt, and fertilizer production and port operation in UAE reached around $100 m each. Brazil has opened some branches of Banco Itaú and Banco do Brazil in Dubai, and the mining company Vale invested $790 m in steel production in Oman.

Trade and investments offer opportunities for each region, but require further development, trust and security. The creation of joint chambers of commerce could

Exports by country

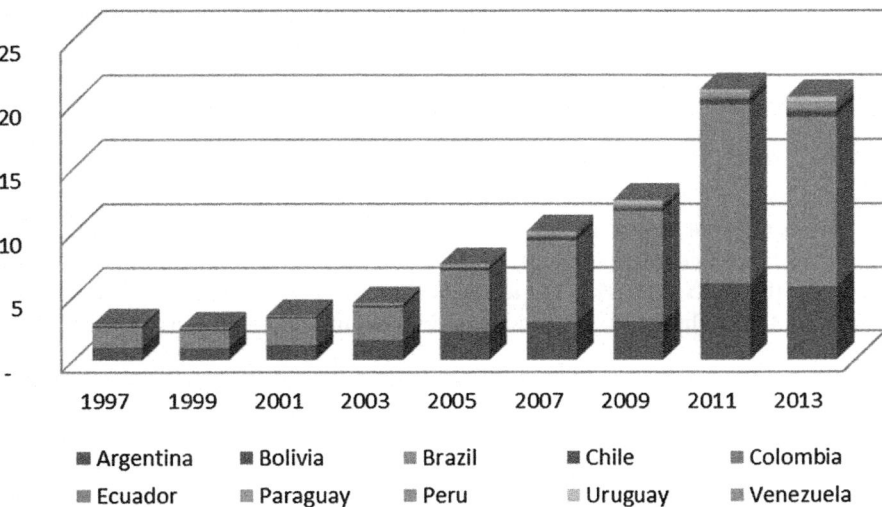

Fig. 4.5a Exports from UNASUR countries to LAS countries (Data in billion USD. Source: UNCOMTRADE. Graphics: Authors' own elaboration)

Imports by country

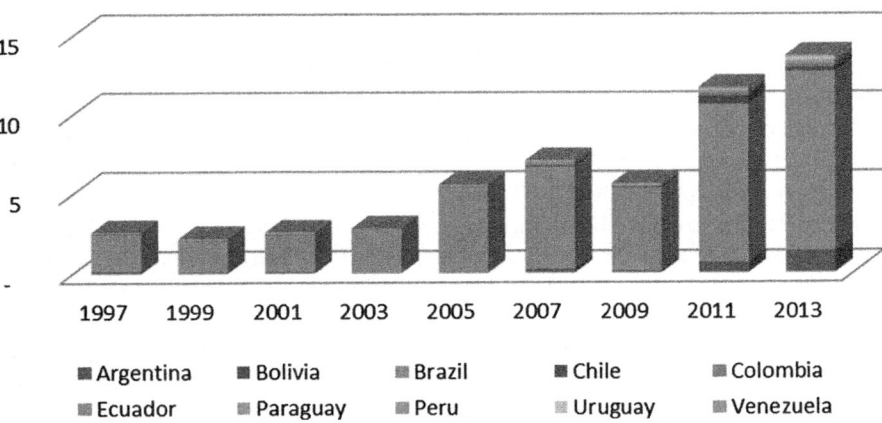

Fig. 4.5b Imports from LAS countries by UNASUR countries (Data in billion USD. Source: UNCOMTRADE. Graphics: Authors' own elaboration)

play a key role in promoting mutual knowledge and fostering interregional exchanges. Today there are more than ten chambers of commerce, mostly based in South America. Furthermore, embassies and consulates, through their commercial departments, are in charge of promoting trade and investments.

4.3.3 Other Public Initiatives

Some sub-regional organizations were invited to be observers at ASPA summits, including CAN and MERCOSUR on the Latin American side and the GCC and AMU on the Arab side. This led to further development of bilateral and interregional relations. The effects of the economic crisis in some of the largest economies of South America may hinder progress in negotiations in the short term. On the Arab side, oil prices, political instability in some North African countries and the conflict in Syria are also obstacles to deepening interregional ties.

4.3.3.1 MERCOSUR and LAS

Core South America partners of ASPA, Brazil and Argentina, are both MERCOSUR members. Therefore several negotiations were opened with some ASPA countries. In July 2004, MERCOSUR and Egypt signed a Framework Agreement aiming to strengthen relations between the Contracting Parties, to promote the expansion of trade and to provide the conditions and mechanisms to negotiate a Free Trade Area in conformity with the rules and disciplines of the World Trade Organization (OAS database). After three rounds of negotiation, in August 2010 a Free Trade Agreement was signed. Only Paraguay, as the least developed country in the block would enjoy better market access to Egypt then rest of members. Nevertheless, the Agreement has not yet entered into force.

In November 2004 MERCOSUR and the Kingdom of Morocco signed a similar Framework Agreement. There was only one negotiation round, held in Rabat in April 2008. Since then no further step towards a Free Trade Agreement has been made. By June 2008, MERCOSUR had signed a Framework Agreement with Jordan similar to the one signed with Egypt in 2004 and started negotiations to reach a Free Trade Agreement. Two more negotiation rounds took place (April and September 2010) and it was foreseen that the agreement would finally be signed at the 15th MERCOSUR summit in Foz do Iguaçu in mid-December 2010, but it did not happen. However, during this summit another two Framework Agreements were signed with Syria and the Palestinian National Authority. In the first case, the outbreak of the Arab Spring and the subsequent Syrian crisis prevented negotiations to start. In the latter, negotiations between MERCOSUR and Palestine resulted in a Free Trade Agreement, signed in December 2011 during the MERCOSUR summit held in Montevideo. Nevertheless, until now, the agreement has not entered into force.

One of the most relevant treaties was the interregional Framework Agreement signed by MERCOSUR and the GCC, the first one between two regional entities. It was signed during the first ASPA summit in Brasilia (2005) and its terms are almost the same as the MERCOSUR-Egypt agreement. The first negotiation round took place in Riyadh in November 2005. A calendar for negotiations towards a free trade agreement between the GCC and MERCOSUR, which should have been concluded by 2006, was established, pending consultations with member states. During the Doha ASPA summit (2009), a joint declaration was signed in which both parties stressed the necessity of starting negotiations regarding the signing of a free trade agreement. All MERCOSUR members have ratified the agreement, but GCC has not yet ratified it.

The last initiative came from Tunisia. At the third ASPA summit, President Moncef Marzouki, remarked on the importance of endeavouring to build an economic system that helps this regional group lay the foundations of a real partnership, achieve development and social justice and boost South-South co-operation. In this context, president Marzouki announced that Tunisia was interested in signing an agreement with MERCOSUR to strengthen economic ties and to ease international trade with the block. Recently, in the joint communiqué issued by the summit of MERCOSUR presidents and heads of state in December 2014, the block expressed its satisfaction with the signing of a Framework Agreement between MERCOSUR and Tunisia, as a way to renew and encourage bilateral relations (Comunicado Conjunto de las Presidentas y los Presidentes de los Estados Partes del MERCOSUR). At the same conference, the signing of a memorandum of understanding between MERCOSUR and Lebanon in order to promote and foster economic and commercial relations between the two parties was welcomed.

4.3.3.2 The GCC and CELAC

Due to the recent creation of CELAC it has not been possible yet to create a specific dialogue with the LAS countries. However they initiated an approach that anticipates a future interregional relationship development. In 2012 and 2013 CELAC Ministerial Troika met with GCC representatives. Moreover, the secretary general of the GCC, (Abdul Latif bin Rashed Al Zayani) was invited to the second CELAC summit held in Havana (2014). Within the Havana final declaration, relations with the GCC were mentioned among the future international activities of CELAC and also the need to develop a roadmap to establish stronger relations was highlighted (point 74). On the other hand, during the 2015 CELAC summit (Belen), LAC leaders agreed to boost relations with extra-regional partners and specifically mentioned the Arab League (point 77), but there is no evidence that they have taken specific actions. (Belen Declaration 2015).

4.4 The Council on Arab World Relations with Latin America and the Caribbean (CARLAC): A Non-governmental Initiative

The LAC-Arab summits held at inter-governmental level has received international attention. Links between regions geographically distant as the Arab world and Latin America can be forged either by top-down inter-governmental relations at a bilateral level, or by private sector migration flows or other forms of circulation.

The Council on Arab World Relations with Latin America and the Caribbean (CARLAC) is a recent non-governmental initiative to strengthen relations between both regions. It aims to consolidate links between LAC and the Middle East and North Africa (MENA), mainly through the participation and inclusion of private actors. In July 2010 a forum on peace in the Middle East was held in the Dominican Republic, sponsored by FUNGLODE. The second meeting took place in March 2011 in Costa Rica and in December of the same year the third conference was held in Cartagena, Colombia. These conferences brought together leaders from both regions, Latin America and MENA, civil society organizations and private stakeholders. The Cartagena meeting was called the "Arab-Latin American Partnership for Development and Peace" and in its final declaration referred to economic and cultural issues and highlighted the necessity to create a council for Arab relations with Latin America, which "will be the driving force in building an intensified and expanded Arab-Latin American partnership". (Cartagena Conference 2011).

The fourth and last Arab – Latin American Forum took place in Abu Dhabi in December 2012. In this occasion CARLAC was officially created, mainly to give continuity to the forum and to elaborate an action plan as a guideline for future meetings. The council would have an executive committee and would work in close collaboration with the Center for Latin American Studies of the University of Jordan, FUNGLODE, other universities, chambers of commerce and civil society organizations. Dr. Leonel Fernandez, ex-president of Dominican Republic and FUNGLODE founder, was elected as CARLAC president. The council would also include ten Latin American and ten Arab leaders. The main aim would be to promote Arab-Latin American cooperation and to further develop bilateral ties. Three main areas would be on the top of the agenda: trade, culture and common vision on global issues. (CARLAC 2014).

In February 2014, the first meeting of CARLAC took place in the Dominican Republic. Its president remarked that the main difference – in comparison with other similar initiatives- is that the council will focus on interregional connections with the participation of non-state actors. In the final declaration, six thematic working groups were created including: food security, investment promotion and finance, tourism and travel, education and culture, energy, infrastructure and development, and innovation and technology. Additionally, it was decided to create four Arab-Latin American relations centers, two in Latin America and two in MENA countries. These centers will be non-governmental institutions and will carry out research and analysis of policies in order to involve companies, governments, civil society, media and the academic world in key issues for both regions (FUNGLODE 2014). This first official meeting of the council brought together forty members, twenty from each region. Within the body, the diversity of profiles were present: from ex-presidents as Leonel Fernandez, Vinicio Cerezo (Guatemala), Ricardo Lagos (Chile) and Andrés Pastrana (Colombia), to congressmen, city majors, ambassadors and presidents of multinational holdings.

4.5 Conclusion: Drivers and Opportunities for Interregional Cooperation

Regionalism in LAC and in the Arab world has followed different paths, therefore it is very difficult to compare its asymmetric realities. However, a multipolar context and the diffusion of power have stimulated regionalism and interregionalism between the two regions, along with the revival of South-South cooperation, in the context of emergence of the South. If, in the past, the non-aligned movement was an engine for cooperation, today the Global South is seeking greater autonomy and emerging powers are using interregionalism as an instrument to be better inserted in this multipolar context. Even when it is recent, interregionalism between LAC and Arab countries can be analyzed under the three prototypes identified by Hänggi (2000): pure interregionalism, transregionalism and hybrid interregionalism.

Regarding the pure regionalism, the weak institutional development of regional organizations in both areas and the intergovernmental structure of decision-making processes, determined the logic of summitry which dominates interregional initiatives as it's explained in the first chapter of this book (Gardini and Malamud). Regionalism in Latin America is more developed, complex and advanced in economic integration than in LAS, but still remains imperfect.

Interregional relations have grown after 2005, when the first ASPA summit took place. This forum started before UNASUR was created – as a transregional relation- but it was later transformed in a region-to-region pure regionalism. Some examples of transregional regionalism resulting in political consensus in international forums can be highlighted, like in the United Nations, where one region supported claims of the other (e.g. Palestine or Falklands/Malvinas issues).

Intra-regional disputes within each region make internal consensus on several issues (e.g.: external relations) a difficult task. In the Arab world the political crisis is a heavy burden. The US invasion of Iraq in 2003, the outbreak of the Arab Spring, the continuing war in Syria and, most recently, the conflict in Yemen are obstacles to regional integration. Furthermore, factors like the emergence of ISIS within a context of a regional crisis or the tremendous drop of the oil price, require enormous efforts from Arab countries trying to contain the situation. In South America, apart from a few inter-state struggles, there is a strong discrepancy on development models between countries like Mexico or Chile (more aligned with liberal theories) and countries like Brazil or Venezuela, which tend to be more protectionists. This difference has delayed the adoption of a common trade agenda in LAC.

Besides multilateral forums, bilateral relations – particularly between countries of South America and LAS- were also boosted. The inter-regional relationship fostered not only a growing trade but also new agreements, meetings and high level visits. Levels of interregional trade have increased steadily, as well as cross-investments, but remain low. Nevertheless, ASPA Summits were also the starting point for negotiations between MERCOSUR and several LAS countries in a Hybrid-regionalist schema and the Framework Agreement signed by Mercosur and the GCC that can be characterized as pure regionalism.

The lack of interconnections and an insufficient infrastructure capacity for exports are important barriers to trade, which require investment in port facilities, the creation of centres and other targeted infrastructure to facilitate this exchange. These limited connections between the two regions were stressed in 2003 by Lula da Silva during his speech in Egypt, saying that also direct flights between Arab and South American countries should be established, which nowadays is a reality. Efforts to negotiate preferential trade agreements have been limited and only a few have come into force. However, there has been significant progress from the previous situation without an interregional legal framework and, when effectively implemented, this can be a push factor to improve the relationship.

Migration flows mainly from the Arab world to the new world were significant during the 19th and 20th centuries, but – as mentioned- the institutional relationship is very recent. Along with the geographical distance, the lack of strong economic and political ties have not favored exchanges and the creation of closer links in the past. These regions are just beginning to know each other better. But language barriers, differing traditions and misperceptions are still present. Student exchanges between schools, universities and research centers, and the creation of interregional studies are extremely important for building knowledge networks.

Not only governments, but civil society involvement is also crucial in order to strengthen links between these regions and to promote convergence of values and intercultural/interreligious understanding. The EU has strategic partnerships with both regions that have been developed through cooperation plans and projects. The possibility of triangular cooperation to spread good practice experiences taking advantage of the new interregional links should be explored.

Mutual knowledge must be promoted in order to create a solid basis for trade and investment. It is important to encourage the creation and development of chambers of commerce to facilitate exchanges and to foster negotiations between stakeholders in the two regions. Private transregional initiatives such as CARLAC are the best complement to public relationships and could enhance the dialogue between the regions and the involvement of other sectors of society such as entrepreneurs, businesses and other members of civil society. The dynamism of these relationships is part of the rise of South-South cooperation, where the interaction of public and private actors is crucial to open the paths for public diplomacy and people to people approaches in a multilevel interregionalism mutually reinforcing.

In conclusion, although there are opportunities and complementarities between these regions, they have not been fully explored. The interregional rapprochement, which began about a decade ago, has promoted a significant increase in mutual trade, investment and diplomatic contacts, and also cultural exchanges have intensified. Not only governments, but civil society involvement is also crucial in order to strengthen links between these regions and to promote convergence of values and intercultural/interreligious understanding.

References

Aggarwal, V., & Fogarty, E. (2005). The limits of interregionalism: EU and North America. *Journal of European Integration, 27*(3).

Baert, F., Scaramagli, T., & Söderbaum, F. (Eds.). (2014). *Intersecting interregionalism regions*. Heidelberg/New York/London: Springer.

Belen Declaration. 2015. *Declaración política de Belén, III Cumbre de Jefas y Jefes de Estado y de Gobierno de la Comunidad de Estados Latinoamericanos y Caribeños (CELAC) 28 y 29 de enero de 2015*, Belén, Costa Rica. http://www.celac2015.go.cr/wp-content/uploads/2015/01/DECLARACION-POLITICA-DE-BELEN-2015-ES-5.pdf. Accessed Apr 2015.

Cartagena Conference. (2011). *Statement by the Cartagena conference on building an Arab-Latin American Partnership for Development and Peace*, December 2, 2011. https://foroarabelatino-americano.wordpress.com/declaracion-ingles. Accessed Apr 2015.

Colombo, S. (2012). *The GCC countries and the Arab spring. Between outreach, patrinage and repression*. Istituto Affari Internazionali. http://www.iai.it/sites/default/files/iaiwp1209.pdf

Council on Arab World Relations with Latin America and the Caribbean (CARLAC). (2014). http://carlac.net. Accessed May 2015.

Decreux, Y., et al. (2012). *The league of Arab States: A regional perspective*. International Trade Forum (pp. 21–24).

Ferabolli, S. (2015). *Arab regionalism: A post-structural perspective*. New York: Routledge.

Fundación Global Democracia y Desarrollo (FUNGLODE). (2014). http://www.funglode.org/?post_type=notice&p=8436. Accessed April 2015.

Gariup, M. (2008). Regionalism and regionalization: The State of the art from a neo-realist perspective. In C. Harders & M. Legrenzi (Eds.), *Beyond regionalism? regional cooperation, regionalism and regionalization in the Middle East*. Burlington: Ashgate Publishing.

Garzón, J. (2015). *Multipolarity and the future of regionalism: Latin America and beyond* (GIGA Working Papers, no. 264). https://giga.hamburg/en/system/files/publications/wp264_garzon.pdf

Hänggi, H. (2000). *Interregionalism: Empirical and theoretical perspectives*. Paper presented at the workshop "Dollars, Democracy and Trade. External Influence on Economic Integration in the Americas". Los Angeles. May 18, 2000.

Harders, C., & Legrenzi, M. (Eds.). (2008). *Beyond regionalism? regional cooperation, regionalism and regionalization in the Middle East*. Burlington: Ashgate Publishing.

Hurrell, A. (1995). Regionalism in the Americas. In L. Fawcett & A. Hurrell (Eds.), *Regionalism in world politics. Regional organization and international order*. New York, Oxford University Press.

Latin American and Caribbean Economic System (SELA). (2012). *Relations between Latin America and the Caribbean and the Middle East: Status and areas of opportunity*. Caracas: Press and Publications Department of the Permanent Secretariat of SELA.

Ministerio de Relaciones Exteriores y Culto. Gobierno de la República Argentina. Comunicado Conjunto de las Presidentas y los Presidentes de los Estados Partes del MERCOSUR. http://www.mrec.gov.ar/userfiles/1._comunicado_ep_final.pdf. Accessed May 2015.

Mundorama, Revista de Divulgação Científica em Relações Internacionais. Discurso do Presidente da República, Luiz Inácio Lula da Silva, no Seminário Empresarial Brasil-Egito Cairo – Egito, 08 de dezembro de 2003 (Presidência da República Secretaria de Imprensa e Divulgação). http://www.mundorama.net/2003/12/08/discurso-do-presidente-da-republica-luiz-inacio-lula-da-silva-no-seminario-empresarial-brasil-egito-cairo-egito-08122003. Accessed May 2015.

Organization of American States (OAS) Agreements database. http://www.sice.oas.org/agreements_e.asp. Accessed May 2015.

Pagani, A., & Martínez Larrechea, E. (2005). *Asimetrías en el MERCOSUR: La bilateralidad argentino-brasileña y el caso uruguayo.* Montevideo: Revista Cuaderno de Negocios Internacionales y Negociación.

Unión de Naciones Suramericanas (UNASUR). (2015). http://www.unasur.org. Accessed May 2015.

Chapter 5
The EU and Africa: Regionalism and Interregionalism Beyond Institutions

Nicoletta Pirozzi and Andréas Litsegård

Abstract This chapter aims at mapping relevant trends of interregionalism between Europe and Africa, by looking at the historical evolution and in light of recent developments. The analysis focuses on institutionalized interregionalism between the European Union (EU) and the African Union (AU), as well as regional organizations in Southern, West and East Africa in the three sectors of trade; security; and environment. It also goes beyond by addressing and comparing formal and informal, state and non-state, patterns of integration at the transnational level. The chapter concludes that it appears that the EU has heavily influenced the development of regionalism in Africa mainly through teaching and support. The relationship between the EU and African regions is fundamentally characterized by the former influencing regional policy of, and providing funds and capacity building to, the latter.

Keywords Atlantic • Interregionalism • Regional organisations • Regionalism • Regions

5.1 Introduction

Europe and Africa are both experiencing deep transformations that affect their integration paths and interregional relationship.

In the last two decades, the European Union (EU) has been characterized by phases of progressive deepening and widening of the integration process and prolonged stalemates. The reforming fatigue that resulted from the adoption and implementation of the Lisbon Treaty, accompanied by the economic and financial crisis erupted in 2008, have questioned the validity and sustainability of the EU model

N. Pirozzi (✉)
Istituto Affari Internazionali (IAI), Rome, Italy
e-mail: n.pirozzi@iai.it

A. Litsegård
School of Global Studies, University of Gothenburg, Gothenburg, Sweden

Center for the Study of Governance Innovation, University of Pretoria, Pretoria, South Africa
e-mail: andreas.litsegard@globalstudies.gu.se

© Springer International Publishing AG 2018
F. Mattheis, A. Litsegård (eds.), *Interregionalism across the Atlantic Space*,
United Nations University Series on Regionalism 15,
DOI 10.1007/978-3-319-62908-7_5

and opened new avenues for alternative – selected and/or differentiated – forms of integration.

Today's Africa is still marked by enduring instability in Libya and Somalia, governance and electoral crises in Central African countries, disease outbreak and epidemics in West Africa and terrorist threats from the Sahel region to the Horn. At the same time, it is characterized by positive developments such as efforts at fostering continental and regional integration through the African Union (AU) and African Regional Intergovernmental Organizations (RIGOs). At the economic level Africa has also experienced some marginal improvements. From the end of the 1990s, economic growth began to recover, rising and staying above population growth. However, the sustainability of this economic development is challenged by factors such as external instability, domestic conflicts, inflexible production systems, and unequal distribution of wealth.

Contemporary regionalism in Africa and Europe cannot be understood by looking only at governmental integration in the framework of continental organizations such as the EU and the AU. Regional and interregional dynamics need to be analyzed through additional levels and forms of interaction. Various types of non-state actors, including social and professional groups, non-governmental organizations (NGOs), community-based and cultural organizations, play an increasingly important role in these processes, both within and outside existing regional and interregional arrangements.

Based on the assumptions outlined above, the chapter aims to map relevant trends of comparative regionalism and interregionalism between Europe and Africa, by looking at the historical evolution and in light of recent developments. The analysis will go beyond formal regionalism and interregionalism by addressing and comparing informal patterns of integration at regional and transnational levels. Except for the (formal and informal) continental regional and interregional processes linked to the EU and the AU, focus is put on other regional actors developed in connection with specific regional areas in Africa and their relationships with the EU. This will be articulated in the three sectors of trade; security; and environment with a view to identifying relevant conclusions on the current status of African-European interregionalism.

For purpose of delimitation, our study focuses on the EU as the most prominent and comprehensive regional organization on the European side. On the African side, we identify the AU as the most inclusive and articulated regional initiative. On a subregional level in Africa, this chapter concentrates on Sub-Saharan Africa, with particular reference to the Southern African Development Community (SADC), the East African Community (EAC) and the Economic Community of West African States (ECOWAS). These are the most innovative and eminent African RIGOs in terms of dealing with trade, environment and security, respectively.

5.2 Comparing Regionalism in Europe and Africa

Equating regionalism and "European integration theory" (Wiener and Diez 2004) is misleading, as the basic conditions of European integration, namely industrial economy and liberal politics, are not "readily transferable to other regional contexts" (Haas 1961: 378). In this chapter, the authors reject the paradigmatic approach that tends to judge the achievements of other integration projects on the basis of the European example. At the same time, the analysis contests the assumption that "Euroexceptionalism" (Acharya 2012: 11), and in particular the uniqueness or sui generis character of the European integration represented by the EU, should be considered as an impeding factor for a comparative study that takes into consideration the EU and other forms of regionalism. Following the approach suggested by Luk Van Langenhove, we adopt "a perspective that, on the one hand, allows us to consider regions of all kinds (wherever they are located) without being 'Eurocentric', but with the possibility of understanding the EU as a special case" (Van Langenhove 2012: 24).

This analysis does not neglect the traditional approaches to regionalism, "which stressed formal structures and intergovernmental interactions" (Acharya 2012: 8), but its scope is enlarged so as to include the basic features of a new regionalism, in which the role of non-state actors and informal processes of interactions represent constitutive elements.

The EU and the AU present many commonalties in terms of institutional architecture and also share some principles and strategic objectives. Nevertheless, if we look at the reality of their achievements in terms of development and implementation of policies in the fields of trade, environment and security, striking differences emerge. It must be recognized that the two organizations evolved at different pace, the AU being a much younger organization than the EU and confronted with different challenges (Paterson 2012: 14–17). While the EU acts in a relatively stable and peaceful context, the AU has to address problems ranging from extreme poverty, endemic war, serious health issues such as HIV/AIDS, malaria and ebola, poor state governance and severe radicalization phenomena.

In the field of trade, the EU stands as the largest market and most integrated region in the world thanks to the realization of the single market and the Economic and Monetary Union (EMU). Both these projects have been recently challenged and put into question: while some member states oppose the completion of the single market in sectors such as financial services, defense and energy, the economic and financial crisis erupted in 2008 has shown the fragility of the EMU and the stability of the Euro. Africa has established the ambitious goals of adopting a continental free trade agreement by 2017 and a continental common market by 2028 (African Union Commission 2015), but these objectives are far from being reached. The low level of intra-African trade accounts for a failure of past attempts to realize market integration in the continent (Paterson 2012). Also, the estimations about informal trade being almost equivalent to the formal sector row against the aspirations of policy-makers to demolish trade barriers (Overseas Development Institute 2013). While many experts question the validity of the market integration model for the African continent, it continues to be regarded by most African leaders as the solution for a progressive integration of Africa in the world economy (Oloruntoba 2013).

The EU is quite advanced in the regulation of environmental issues and has developed an impressive amount of legislation to address climate change, both at domestic level in its member states and through the setting of international standards (European Commission 2013). The AU has shown some activism in this field lately, especially through endorsing the New Partnership for Africa's Development

(NEPAD) Action Plan for the Environment Initiative in 2013 (NEPAD 2003), even if implementation of the initiative lags behind.

In the field of security, the EU remains anchored to the intergovernmental logic and the unanimity rule in the decision-making process, which resulted in a non-linear process of integration and the partial realization of the aspirations of the treaties to develop a truly common security and defense policy (Pirozzi 2015). The AU has set ambitious goals for the resolution of crises and conflicts on the continent through dedicated structures, a continental force to conduct peace support operations, as well as adequate and predictable financial resources. Nevertheless, its ability to cope with security challenges in the region is still hampered by human resource deficiencies, scarce absorption capacity of external funding and persisting imbalances between continental and regional structures (Pirozzi 2009).

The role of alternative processes of integration – such as in the case of transboundary informal trade – and civil society participation – which are more substantial in fields such as environment (UNEP n.d.) and less developed in sectors like security and defense (Miranda et al. 2012) – allow to identify significant margins of improvement for African regionalism. The main challenge lies in the capacity of continental institutions to address governance issues at national level and to build a conducive environment for commitment and participation in the integration project.

In terms of regional integration in Africa, there are many common denominators between the three sub-regions featured in this study. Regional integration is essentially based on economic and trade related premises with the aim of increasing intra-regional trade among the members of the respective organizations. Hence, trade liberalization schemes and monetary convergence have been on the center stage in the creation of various regional governance mechanisms (Matlosa 2006; Matambalya 2012; Hartmann 2013). As will be discussed further below, regional integration arrangements in Africa are deeply influenced by the European model of linear market integration through sequential phases of integrating goods, labor and capital markets, and finally monetary and fiscal integration. This is manifested by a free trade area, followed by a customs union, common market and economic union (McCarthy 2010). It should be mentioned that the enthusiasm for trade integration mainly concerns formal trade. Informal Cross Border Trade (ICBT), where informal traders buy their goods in informal markets and travel with their goods between states (IOM 2010), is generally looked at with suspicion in the three sub-regions and the link between poverty reduction and informal trade is not acknowledged (Godsäter 2016; Nixdorf 2013; Yusuff 2014).

However, with its increasing focus on regional security, West Africa deviates slightly from this picture. ECOWAS and its member states have worked hard to put in place advanced regional security architecture and have been reasonably successful in hindering internal conflicts from spilling over to other countries. The political leaders have slowly developed a regional understanding of peace and security, agreeing that stability in the region can only occur if resources and peacebuilding efforts are pooled (Gandois 2014; Piccolino and Minou 2014). This trend is partly homegrown, stemming from the urge of West African political leaders to collectively solve common peace and security matters, but, nevertheless, must be understood in light of the EU's financial support to ECOWAS' security framework.

The environment is generally of low relevance in regional governance, but the EAC stands out in this regard. The political leaders have gradually come to the conclusion that managing the Victoria Lake resources must be done in a collaborative fashion and have developed a rather sophisticated regional framework in the environmental field (Godsäter 2013). In many regards, this takes place without the supervision of the EU, which has only recently started to show an interest in regional environmental governance.

Lastly, it should be mentioned that regional integration is a slow process in all three regions, of which one manifestation is the low level of intra-regional trade, ranging from 9.5% in Southern Africa (Chigwada and Pamacheche 2012) and 11% in West Africa (Igue 2011) to 19% in East Africa (Matambalya 2012). The member states are, to a large extent, hesitant to give up part of their sovereignty to the regional level, making it very hard to harmonize trade-related policies but also concerning security (TRALAC 2012; Hartmann 2013; Piccolino and Minou 2014; Matambalya 2012), to the great disappointment of the EU. Such state-centrism is linked to a general suspicion towards the role of civil society in regional integration, despite grand declarations stating the opposite. In the trade field Civil Society Organizations (CSOs) are particularly excluded, most notably in SADC. On the whole, regionalism is generally highly top-down, giving little space for popular involvement (Godsäter 2016; Ochwada 2013). However, there are important instances of increasing civil society participation in regional governance, especially in the environmental area (Godsäter 2013). Also, in the security field, even if CSOs generally have a hard time participating in policy-making, ECOWAS deviates from this pattern. Here, NGOs have made a significant contribution to the regional peace and security architecture, especially in terms of implementation (Gandois 2014; Iheduru 2014).

5.3 Interregionalisms Between Europe and Africa

In terms of interregionalism, in its purest form it concerns relations between two clearly identifiable regional organizations within an institutional framework (Baert et al. 2014). However, the nature of interregionalism is much more complex than that, which will be obvious later when the case study is discussed further. In fact, the relations between Europe and Africa seem to cover almost the full spectrum of possible definitions of interregionalism systematized by Francis Baert et al. (ibid: 4–6). In this chapter, we use the following categories to exemplify interregionalism between Europe and Africa in the trade, security and environment sectors: (1) pure interregionalism, which develops between two clearly identifiable regional organizations within an institutional framework; (2) transregionalism, which refers to transnational (non-state) relations, including transnational networks of corporate production or of NGOs; (3) quasi-interregionalism, which is used to describe relations between a regional organization/regional group and a third country in another region (ibid). However, please note that all of the three sectors of focus in this chapter will not be covered in the analysis of all forms of interregionalism below. This is due to the fact that these sectors are not equally relevant for the various interregional relations.

5.3.1 Pure Interregionalism

5.3.1.1 EU-AU Relations

The concept of a Euro-African partnership has evolved over time: the initial approach of a mainly institutional type, based on the donor-recipient logic of the Yaoundé (1963, 1969) and Lomé (1975, 1979, 1984, 1990) Conventions, has gradually evolved into a more balanced partnership to be pursued in the field of development cooperation (Cotonou Convention 2000).

In the last 15 years, the creation of the AU produced an increasing interaction with the EU, which has been modelled on a comprehensive continent-to-continent dialogue. In 2000, the Cairo EU-Africa Summit set in motion a structured political dialogue, which was reinforced by the 2005 EU Strategy for Africa, the first attempt to establish a single framework for continental engagement. These first steps were mainly characterized by unilateral European efforts to design a credible approach to African development and security challenges, without the effective involvement of African actors. To overcome these problems, the new Joint Africa-EU Strategy (JAES) was adopted at the Lisbon Summit in December 2007, guided by the principles of ownership and joint responsibility and aimed at taking the Africa-EU relationship to a more ambitious strategic level, with a strengthened political partnership and enhanced cooperation in all fields (European Union and Africa Union 2007). The two Action Plans, adopted for 2008–2010 and 2011–2013 in order to operationalize the JAES, as well as a Roadmap adopted for 2014–2017, took stock of this evolution and identified priorities for cooperation, the first of which is peace and security. AU-EU relations on peace and security matters take place in different frameworks and at various levels, including Africa-EU Summits held every 3 years (the next one being planned for November 2017 in Abidjan); joint meetings between the EU Political and Security Committee and the AU Peace and Security Council and Africa-EU Defense Ministers meetings; annual Commission-to-Commission meetings between the European Commission and the AU Commission; contacts and meetings between ad hoc delegations from the European Parliament and the Pan-African Parliament (Pirozzi 2009: 19–20). Moreover, a Joint Expert Group on Peace and Security involving AU and EU representatives has been created but it had little impact on the implementation of the partnership due to lack of expertise and resources. An Implementation Team on Peace and Security has also been established by the EU, with a view to gather together all the relevant actors involved in the Africa-EU Partnership, both in the European Commission and in the EEAS (Miranda et al. 2012: 12–13). The role of the EU Delegation in Addis Ababa has also been reinforced in the new system by appointing a double-hatted Head of Delegation/Special Representative for the AU, by enhancing its autonomy in managing and disbursing funds, and by creating a specific section in the Delegation dealing with peace and security issues (Pirozzi 2015). At the operational level, the EU has committed relevant financial and technical resources to help the AU in the process of developing a Continental Early Warning System (CEWS), which consists of a Situation Room located at the AU Commission in Addis Ababa and regional units responsible for data collection and analysis on the basis of early warning indicators, and sustains the development of AU mediation capacities, especially through its support to the Panel of the Wise (PoW), which is composed of highly respected African personalities and designed to both provide advice and undertake action. Moreover, the EU channels its support to AU civilian and military missions mainly through the African Peace Facility, a financial instrument that allocated €1.9 billion to African Peace Support Operations (PSOs) and capacity-building since 2004 (European Commission 2015). In terms of capacity-building, the EU's support is directed mainly towards the operationalization of the African Stand-by Force (ASF), which should be composed by an headquarters in Addis Ababa and stand-by multidisciplinary contingents (civilian, military and police) at regional level to be rapidly deployed at appropriate notice (Pirozzi 2015).

Interregional cooperation on climate change and the environment became a priority of the two organizations at the end of 1990s, in connection with the international debate triggered by the Kyoto Protocol negotiations. Environmental issues became part of the EU's development cooperation approach towards Africa in the Strategy for Africa adopted by the European Commission in 2005. Later, environmental sustainability and climate change were introduced in the JAES among the priorities for Africa-EU partnership, while specific priorities and tools for action were specified by the following Actions Plans. The main actions envisaged are (1) building a common agenda on climate change policies and cooperation, in particular through the integration of regional and national strategies with new instruments, and (2) addressing land degradation and increasing aridity. The Africa-EU partnership in this field led to the definition of key principles such as sustainable development, cooperation, equity and responsibility in the joint documents and declarations, as well as the establishment of a common monitoring framework (ibid: 158–160). However, it has to face a number of political challenges, including the lack of commitment by African governments towards environmental objectives; the still contested division of responsibilities between European and African countries concerning the reduction of CO_2 emissions; and the mutual perceptions of African and the EU as non-credible actors. African leaders frame their EU counterpart as paternalistic, unable to consider the AU as an equal partner, while the EU lamented to the lack of political will on behalf of African policy makers. This mutual suspicion is related to power dynamics between the EU and AU in the environment and climate change field, which are further explored by Lightfoot (2013). He argues that tackling climate change in Africa must be understood in terms of the EU as a normative power, claiming to be a global leader in the strife to combat climate change. The EU has an influence over norms in African states in terms of getting climate change adaptation on the African agenda, through the use of diplomatic and discursive pressure. However, Lightfoot argues that EU states are 'keen on rhetoric but less willing to fund measures to aid adaptation to climate change' (ibid: 251). The EU and African states disagree on the amounts of and rational behind aid and the former is seen as an incoherent actor by the latter. The big brother attitude of the EU, coupled with a discrepancy between policy and action, weaken the relation between the EU and AU, hampering the common combat against climate change in Africa (ibid). Lastly, the institutional limits of the multi-actor and multi-layered approach to the partnership, for example in terms of slow decision-making processes on both sides of the Mediterranean, has negatively affected the partnership, especially the involvement of civil society (Sicurelli 2013: 153). This will be further discussed below.

5.3.1.2   EU-ECOWAS Relations

The cooperation between EU and ECOWAS dates back to the 1970s, the former supporting development and integration in West Africa. However, originally the European Economic Community (EEC) was significantly conditioned by France, resulting in most regional funds going to the Francophone regional cooperation in terms of the Communauté Economique de l'Afrique de l'Ouest (CEAO, West African Economic Community in English). The trend of supporting regional integration among the French-speaking countries continued throughout the 1990s, at the same time as a more all-encompassing regional process evolved in West Africa with the development of ECOWAS, which called the increasing attention of the EU. Hence, later EU funding has marked a break with previous support to regional integration in West Africa, targeting West Africa as a whole. From being neglected, ECOWAS has gradually become the most important regional counterpart to the EU, attracting the majority of donor funds (Piccolino and Minou 2014). Traditionally, the EU has focused on economic integration and support to trade, which attracts the bulk of the so-called European Development Fund (EDF), the main instrument for development cooperation with Africa and elsewhere. However, the EDF has increasingly targeted ECOWAS conflict management activities. In the previous Regional Indicative Programme (RIP) for West Africa, 70% of the money deployed went to deepening regional trade integration, improving competitiveness and European Partnership Agreements (EPAs), with the objective of supporting the establishment of a common market and the creation of the customs union in order to facilitate trade with and within West Africa. At the same time, regional security, stability and peace building had become a strong sector (EU 2008a). In the new Regional Indicative Programme (RIP) 2014–2020, economic integration is reduced to 50% of the total budget, at the advantage of peace, security and regional stability as well as the new area of resilience, food and nutrition security and natural resources (European Union 2015a). With regards to the EPA between the EU and West African states, an agreement was signed in 2014. However, West African states fall under three different trade regimes vis-à-vis the EU, resulting in fragmentation. This can negatively affect regional ECOWAS-led integration in West Africa (Piccolino and

Minou 2014). Similarly, European aid has historically spurred the development of a multitude of overlapping and sometimes competing RIGOs, such as ECOWAS, CEAO and the West African Economic and Monetary Union (not discussed here) (ibid).

In terms of the security aspect, the EU has since 1995 acknowledged ECOWAS as an important regional security organization dealing with conflicts and development in the region. Joint declarations and statements have created an image of partnership between the EU and ECOWAS in the security field (Nivet 2006). Ministerial EU-ECOWAS meetings have been held annually or biannually since 2000. Funding through the EDF has increasingly been channeled to ECOWAS conflict management (Piccolino and Minou 2014). Interestingly here, the EU policy and discursive influence on ECOWAS has mainly taken place in the economic integration area, whose agenda remains deeply shaped by the EU. However, in the security area, it is more uncertain to what extent the EU has been influential on the evolving security agenda of ECOWAS. Some scholars, among them Lucia (2012), believe that the EU is exporting its political values and security norms in its relationship with ECOWAS. Other scholars, such as Piccolino and Minou, want to nuance the EU direct influence arguing that "to the extent that regional integration has contributed to conflict transformation in West Africa, this process has been driven mainly by West Africans themselves" (2014: 24).

5.3.1.3 EU-SADC Relations

As for interregional relations between the EU and SADC, according to one scholar, "[…] the EU's economic hegemony over the region, entrenched through massive financial assistance, has effectively locked SADC into Brussels' sphere of influence" (Qobo 2012: 251). In fact, the EU contributed with 25% of total funding to SADC in 2008 (Buzdugan 2013). In the 10th EDF, through the EU-SADC RIP 2008–2013, 80% was earmarked for assistance to regional economic integration (EU 2008b). The EU seeks to influence the path of regionalism in SADC towards a customs and monetary union, in line with a conventional neo-liberal discourse of trade liberalization and macroeconomic convergence, seeing itself as the model for regional integration (Buzdugan 2013). However, it should be noted that even if the traditional areas of trade integration and business development is still by far the most important areas for the EU, they receive less attention in the new RIP 2014–2020 (slightly above 50% of the total budget). Similar to ECOWAS, peace, security and regional stability, and regional natural resource management have become two (new) priority areas besides economic integration (EU 2015b). It remains to be seen if this represents a trend shift in the development cooperation between EU and SADC. Asymmetrical aid relations between SADC, the EU and other donors have been institutionalized over the years. One manifestation of this is the Joint SADC-International Cooperation Partner Task Force (JTF), which intends to coordinate donors and their counterparts within the Secretariat, in which the EU is responsible for trade and institutional development (Tjönneland 2008). Through the JTF, donors participate in budget programming and joint project planning with SADC and have direct input on policy and strategy (Buzdugan 2013), which has weakened SADC ownership of regional integration. Furthermore, the EU is SADC's largest trading partner. The value of SADC exports to the EU accounts for 30% of total exports and the equivalent value for imported goods from the EU is 29%. Up until now, in trading with EU under the Lomé Conventions, the SADC states enjoyed preferential non-reciprocal access to the EU market. Through the EPA negotiations with SADC members, the EU seems to further "lock in neoliberalism" Southern African regionalism through promoting trade liberalization and open regionalism (Hurt 2012: 507). Furthermore, the EPA negotiations have reinforced already existing trade divisions between Southern African states, in terms of dividing the SADC member states into four separate negotiating blocks, creating their own separate trade paths with Europe (Qobo 2012: 260).

5.3.1.4   EU-EAC Relations

Looking at EU-EAC relations, from the 1980s the EU has evolved as a major funder of regional integration and development in East Africa but the majority of projects were originally implemented by national states and non-state actors. With the 9th EDF, coinciding with the rebirth of the EAC, funding has been transformed from national projects into support for the regional integration efforts as well as the EPA process (European Union 2008b). Up until today, facilitating commercial integration, besides EPAs, has dominated the EU's promotion of regionalism (Theron and Ntasano 2014). In fact, according to two scholars, EAC's market-oriented type of regionalism seems to have adopted EU's linear integration approach without questioning the applicability of the European model in a post-colonial East African context (Bachmann and Sidaway 2010). The former Regional Indicative Program for East and Southern African and the Indian Ocean 2008–2013, in which the EU's support for East African regionalism is situated, highlighted two focal areas: economic integration and political cooperation. Focusing on formal trade, the former received the lion's share of the funding in the last EDF, 85%, compared with 10% for regional political activities and 5% for non-focal areas (EU 2008b).

Of all external trading partners, the EU is the most important one for the EAC (de Zamaróczy 2012). Since 2003, the EAC has been engaged in EPA-negotiations with the EU to replace the previous non-reciprocal trade preferences between the two regions with new trading arrangements that should not only foster interregional free trade but also regional integration and development (Marinov 2013). From 2007, the EAC EPA group has been comprised of the five members of EAC and is the only EPA-grouping in Africa which corresponds with a regional organization. A full EPA was signed in 2014, but the negotiations were greatly delayed partly due to the fact that the EAC demanded binding commitment from the EU on development assistance in order to put in place development safety nets to support the required economic adjustments (Lorenz-Carl 2013). In fact, the EAC "[…] has managed to develop a position towards the EU that lies beyond a simple stereotype of a weak negotiation party from the South" (ibid: 70).

Even though the main priority for the EU's support to East African regionalism is still regional economic co-operation, another focal area in the new RIP 2014–2020 is regional natural resource management. Since 2000, the EU has supported a series of regional projects that deal with environmental degradation and enhanced food production in the Lake Victoria Basin (Delputte and Söderbaum 2012). One specific intervention was the funding of bridging phase activities between Lake Victoria Environmental Management Program I and II (Okurut and Othero 2012). However, by comparison to other donors the EU has not been prominent funder in the environment field in East Africa (ibid). This might change considering that 25% of the new budget for EAC is devoted to resource management, at the expense of economic integration which received "only" 56% (European Union 2015b).

5.3.2 Transregionalism

EU and AU strive to create a multi-actor and multi-layered approach to the partnership. One important component of the JAES is therefore to promote a people-centered partnership (European Union and African Union 2007). In more detail, the two organizations have acknowledged that "the Joint Strategy should be co-owned by European and African non-institutional actors" and they are willing to make it a "permanent platform for information, participation and mobilization of a broad spectrum of civil society actors" (European Union and African Union 2007: 22). This open door to non-state actors spurred the creation of the Africa-EU Intercontinental Civil Society Forum in 2010, a transregional civil society platform made up of a cross-section of African and European CSOs, led by the JAES-recognized Civil Society Steering Group including members from both continents (Africa-EU Intercontinental Civil Society Forum 2010). The forum is an official accompanying event to the EU-Africa Summits. Other notable examples of transnational (non-state) relations are: the Europe Africa Policy Research Network, a network of African and European research institutes aiming to pool and foster policy research capacities, dialogue, information and partnership on issues relating to EU-Africa relations; and the EU-Africa Economic and Social Stakeholders' Network, which brought together representatives of employers, workers, farmers and consumers in the social economy and cooperatives from the two continents at the eve of the latest Africa-EU Summit in 2014 with a view to lay the foundations for regular and structured cooperation. The above-mentioned fora are valuable settings for information-sharing and policy coordination among non-governmental actors alongside and beyond EU-Africa institutional cooperation (Sicurelli 2013: 155). Also, the EU has started to actively support the contribution of African CSOs to continental policy-making in the AU and has recently (December 2016) signed contracts for a total amount of € 20 million for related projects. The initiative is financed under the so-called Pan-African Programme, set up to support sub-regional and continental projects in areas of shared interest of the EU and AU (EU-Africa Partnership 2017). It remains to be seen how this initiative will affect inter-regional cooperation between CSOs from the two continents, for example within the EU-Africa Civil Society Forum, as well as the formal EU-Africa partnership more generally.

One important aspect of the institutional inability of the partnership, mentioned above, is the inability to involve civil society groups, despite the corresponding formal call in various policy documents. Civil society is generally involved in the partnership mainly through a monitoring and consultation role but its inclusion in strategic decision-making and the implementation of financial instruments is still insufficient (Sicurelli 2013: 156). In terms of the Africa-EU Intercontinental Civil Society Forum, from the start there were signs of limited impact of African and European CSOs in the design and implementation of the JAES (Africa-EU Intercontinental Civil Society Forum 2010). Also, the various transregional groups suffered from the ad-hocism of meetings, high turnover of participants and lack of predictable resources, which hampered their effective impact in the creation of a sustainable interregional framework. These problems persisted and the second Africa-EU Civil Society Forum in 2013 stated that, "after reviewing the JAES and the implementation of its two Action Plans [...] the CSOs in both the EU and Africa concluded that the JAES framework, both in design and application, had not enabled them to play effective and predictable roles" (Second Africa EU Civil Society Forum 2013). The roles envisaged were advocacy, watchdog, monitoring and evaluation and participation in political dialogues and the thematic partnerships. Most alarming was the lack of standard operating procedures for CSO participation in the JAES-process as well as difficult access to information and decision-makers (ibid). The Forum therefore called for a structural reform of the framework, making sure that decision-making, implementation, monitoring, and evaluation mechanisms include civil society. Hence, European and African CSOs have so far been rather marginalized in the formal Euro-Afro interregional governance framework, which tends to be state-centric.

5.3.3   Quasi Interregionalism

There are a number of examples of this specific interregional pattern in EU-sub-Saharan African relations, including among others the EU-South Africa relations in the field of trade. Since 1999, these relations have been regulated by a Trade, Development and Cooperation Agreement, which included a free trade area. In 2007, the EU and South Africa entered into a Strategic Partnership, which symbolizes the recognition by the EU of the important role played by South Africa on a regional and international level. Since then, South African and EU's representatives have held regular summits and ministerial meetings (European External Action Service 2015). Another example of quasi-interregionalism is the security co-operation between France and ECOWAS. Since the end of the 1990s, France has actively supported and collaborated with ECOWAS in terms of conflict prevention and peace-building in

West Africa. Some examples are provision of capacity-building support; training peacekeepers; undertaking joint training exercises; seconding military liaison officers; and jointly undertaking peacekeeping operations, such as the civil war in the Ivory Coast from 2002 and onwards (Chafer and Stoddard 2014).

5.4 Conclusion – Assessing EU-Africa Interregionalism: A Partnership Among Equals?

Andrew Hurrell (2007: 132) identifies three ways in which regionalist models come to be diffused around the world: through regional competition, through teaching and support and through conditionality. According to the typological proposal by Malamud and Gardini in Chap. 2, formal region-to-region relations can also be categorized according to the type of involvement of the senior partner – provided there is one, which can be active (through leadership or cooperation) or passive/equal (through emulation and exchange), and the dimension in which the interaction takes place (politico-institutional or socio-economic).

As seen above, pure interregionalism between Europe and Africa has been developed in the full spectrum of possible dimensions, from politico-institutional to socio-economic sectors. Regional competition did not emerge as a defining feature in EU-Africa relations. In its relations with Africa, the EU has traditionally played the role of the senior partner, by exercising leadership in defining goals, monitoring implementation and supporting its partners, and providing technological, financial and economic assistance. The EU has heavily influenced the development of regionalism in Africa through teaching and support. For example, the EU has committed relevant financial and technical resources to help the AU in the process of developing its capacity in the field of peace and security, in particular through the African Peace Facility. Conditionality is also at the heart of the EU-Africa relations, particularly in the fields of trade and development cooperation. The EU has included political conditionality clauses in most of its international agreements since 1995, when the Lomé Convention has defined human rights, democracy and the rule of law as 'essential elements' of cooperation (Del Biondo 2011: 380). This means that, when partner countries do not respect such essential elements, the EU can suspend the agreement, as provided for in Article 96 of the Cotonou Agreement (European Parliament 2008: 3). This article has been invoked by the EU especially in cases of coups d'état or flawed elections (Del Biondo 2011: 381). Moreover, the Cotonou Agreement has extended conditionality, through Article 97, to good governance and corruption. Criticism raised towards conditionality clauses has to do both with their effectiveness (Faust 2013: 1) and the EU's consistency in implementing them (Del Biondo 2011: 390). The 2007 JAES has the declared objective to take the Africa-EU relationship to a more ambitious strategic level by moving away from the traditional donor-recipient relationship based on the conditionality principle and establishing a "partnership among equals" and enhancing cooperation on jointly identified priorities. However, it seems that this principle is still struggling between rhetoric and facts, as the AU remains heavily dependent on the EU in terms of financial support and this inevitably hampers the possibility of African actors to shape the common agenda.

In terms of EU-RIGOs relations, the EU is very dominant in all three regions and fits the teaching and support category above well. The relationship between the EU on one side and SADC, EAC and ECOWAS on the other side is fundamentally characterized by the EU influencing African regional policies and providing funds and capacity building. Being the most important donor for the above RIGOs and having a strong impact on policy-making, the EU exports the European model of linear economic integration. In terms of regional integration in Southern Africa, it is evident that donors, of which the EU is the most prominent, coordinate and lay the policy foundation for many facets of economic integration. Regional security in West Africa, being more internally grown, is a slight exception. It seems as if the many similarities between the EU and ECOWAS regarding the understanding of conflict prevention stem from shared norms among peacebuilding practitioners and are not an export of European ideas to West Africa. Furthermore, in terms of the EU's support to regional integration in all three regions, the commercial, market-oriented approach towards regional integration is explicit in the indicative plans for Eastern and Southern Africa and Western Africa. The bulk of the EDF funds go to this area in comparison with, for example, social issues. Of course, this has a strong discursive impact on the (neo-liberal) view of regional integration on behalf of regional policy-makers. This is further strengthened through the EPA-negotiations which are used to 'lock in' market-oriented and macroeconomic policies within states, particularly in Southern Africa. Nevertheless, in practice, trade liberalization is a slow process in all three regions due to the protection of national interests. It should also be noted that some funds in the field of regional economic integration are allocated to activities related to environmental change in, foremost, East Africa and it seems that the EU will put more emphasis on regional natural resource management in the new EDF. EU's greater emphasis on resource management in development co-operation with EAC, but also ECOWAS and SADC, is linked to its progressive position in the global climate change area (Geddes and Jordan 2012), which has resulted in an increasing will to support climate change adaptation and mitigation in Africa and elsewhere. In terms of ECOWAS, lastly, a decent share of the EDF funds is allocated to regional peace and security even if regional economic integration still dominates the funding portfolio. ECOWAS has become an important partner in security matters for the EU, for example in connection with the Malian crisis and the emerging challenges from the Sahel region deriving from migration and terrorism, which have increasingly drawn upon development resources. The great interest in supporting peace and security in West Africa, also manifested by military operations, should partly be understood by the EU's urge to stop the increasing flow of refugees to Europe. According to two scholars: such 'security-driven responses…[are]…focused on 'keeping people in their place" (Geddes and Jordan 2012: 1032).

Forms of quasi interregionalism, in which regional organizations in Europe or Africa establish institutionalized partnerships with one state in the other continent, represent a distinguishing feature of interregional dynamics between EU and Africa. The cases of EU-South Africa and ECOWAS-France account for differentiated patterns of interregionalism that intersect and overlap with EU-AU-RIGOs relations, making it difficult to rationalize dialogue and initiatives on issues of common concern, both bilaterally and in international fora. This is amplified by the divergences and the competition among governmental and institutional actors both in Europe and Africa. Finally, emerging transregionalism can be considered as a defining feature of EU-Africa relations. Civil society actors from Europe and Africa are increasingly interconnected and involved, even if their relationship is weak and their capacity to influence institutional constituencies is still limited. The impact on established dynamics of pure interregionalism by forms of both transregionalism and quasi interregionalism and in EU's relations with Africa deserves attention for future research.

References

Acharya, A. (2012). Comparative regionalism: A field whose time has come? *The International Spectator, 47*(1), 3–15.

Africa-EU Intercontinental Civil Society Forum. (2010). *Communiqué: First Africa-EU Intercontinental Civil Society Forum*, 10 November, Cairo. http://www.africa-eu-partnership. org/en/newsroom/all-news/first-africa-eu-intercontinental-civil-society-forum-communique. Accessed 3 Mar 2016.

Africa-EU Intercontinental Civil Society Forum. (2013). *Report of the second Africa-EU Civil Society Forum*, Brussels, Belgium, October 23–25, 2013. http://gnrd.net/UserFiles/File/ SECON_AU-EU_CSOs_FORUM_PROCEEDINGS.pdf. Accessed 1 Mar 2016.

Africa-EU Partnership (2017). *European Union supports civil society's voice across Africa.* http:// www.africa-eu-partnership.org/en/newsroom/all-news/european-union-supports-civil-societys-voice-across-africa. Accessed 31 Mar 2017.

African Union Commission. (2015). *Agenda 2063: The Africa we want.* Popular version, September 2015. http://agenda2063.au.int/en/sites/default/files/03_Agenda2063_popular_version_ENG%2021SEP15-3.pdf. Accessed 1 Mar 2016.

Ba, A. Y. (2006). La contribution de l'UnionAfricaine au Maintien de la Paix. *Revue de droit international et de droit comparé, 83*(3), 197–231.

Bachmann, V., & Sidaway, J. M. (2010). African regional integration and European involvement: External agents in the East African Community. *South African Geographical Journal, 92*(1), 1–6.

Baert, F., Scaramagli, T., & Soderbaum, F. (Eds.). (2014). *Intersecting interregionalism. Regions, global governance and the EU.* Springer.

Buzdugan, S. R. (2013). Regionalism from without: External involvement of the EU in regionalism in southern Africa. *Review of International Political Economy, 20*(4), 917–946.

Chafer, T., & Stoddard, E. (2014). The EU, ECOWAS and the multiple dimensions of European-West African relations. In A. B. Akoutou, R. Sohn, M. Vogl, & D. Yeboah (Eds.), *Understanding regional integration in West Africa- a multi-thematic and comparative analysis. WAI-ZEI paper series* (pp. 41–69). Achada Santo António/Bonn: West Africa Institute/Center for European Integration Studies.

Chigwada, T., & Pamacheche, F. (2012). Status and progress of SADC regional trade integration. In M. Tekere (Ed.), *Regional trade integration, economic growth and poverty reduction in Southern Africa* (pp. 77–106). Pretoria: Africa Institute of South Africa.

De Zamaróczy, N. (2012). *Playing Boomerang. East African elites, external actors, and the contestation of East African regionalism.* Paper delivered at the international studies association annual conference, San Diego, 1–5 April 2012.

Del Biondo, K. (2011). EU aid conditionality in ACP countries: Explaining inconsistency in EU sanctions practice. *Journal of Contemporary European Research, 7*(3), 380–395.

Delputte, S., & Söderbaum, F. (2012). European aid coordination in Africa: Is the commission calling the tune? In S. Gänzle, S. Grimm, & D. Makhan (Eds.), *The European Union and global development* (pp. 37–56). New York: Palgrave Macmillan.

European Centre for Development Policy Management. (2014). *Economic partnership agreements: Frequently asked questions, Fiche technique.* http://ecdpm.org/wp-content/uploads/ECDPM-17-10-14-EPA-QA.pdf. Accessed 22 June 2015.

European Commission. (2013). *Environment.* Brussels: EC. http://europa.eu/pol/env/flipbook/en/files/environment.pdf. Accessed 22 June 2015.

European Commission. (2015). *African peace facility.* Brussels: EC. https://ec.europa.eu/europeaid/regions/africa/continental-cooperation/african-peace-facility_en. Accessed 29 Dec 2015.

European External Action Service. (2015). *EU relations with South Africa.* http://eeas.europa.eu/south_africa/index_en.htm. Accessed 29 Dec 2015.

European Parliament. (2008). *The application of human rights conditionality in the EU's bilateral trade agreements and other trade arrangements with third countries.* Strasbourg: European Parliament. http://www.europarl.europa.eu/RegData/etudes/etudes/join/2008/406991/EXPO-INTA_ET(2008)406991_EN.pdf. Accessed 22 June 2015.

European Union. (2008a). *Regional strategy paper and regional indicative programme 2008–2013 for the region of Western Africa.* Brussels: European Commission.

European Union. (2008b). *Regional strategy paper and regional indicative programme 2008–2013 for the region of Eastern and Southern Africa and the Indian Ocean.* Brussels: European Commission.

European Union. (2015a). *Regional indicative programme for Western Africa 2014–2020.* Brussels: European Commission.

European Union. (2015b). *Regional indicative programme Eastern Africa, Southern Africa and the Indian Ocean.* Brussels: European Commission.

European Union and African Union. (2007). *The Africa-EU strategic partnership: A joint Africa-EU strategy and action plan.* Lisbon, 8–9 December 2007, Brussels: European Commission. http://www.africa-eu-partnership.org/sites/default/files/documents/eas2007_joint_strategy_en.pdf. Accessed 22 June 2015.

European Union-The African, Caribbean and Pacific Group of Statea (EU-ACP). (2000). *Cotonou agreement.* Brussels: European Commission. http://www.acp.int/sites/acpsec.waw.be/files/Cotonou2000.pdf. Accessed 22 June 2015.

Faust, J. (2013). *Is the earth flat or is it a cube? European foreign aid, political conditionality and democracy.* German Development Institute Briefing Paper. http://www.die-gdi.de/uploads/media/BriefingPaper_24.2013.pdf. Accessed 22 June 2015.

Francis, D. J. (2006). *Uniting Africa: Building regional peace and security systems.* Aldershot: Ashgate.

Gandois, H. (2014). Economic community of West African States. In L. Levi, G. Finizio, & N. Vallinoto (Eds.), *Democratization of international institutions* (pp. 196–206). London: Routledge.

Geddes, A., & Jordan, A. (2012). Migration as adaptation? Exploring the scope for coordinating environmental and migration policies in the European Union. *Enviroment and Planning C: Government and Policy, 30*, 1029–1044.

Godsäter, A. (2013). Regional environmental governance in the Lake Victoria region: The role of civil society. *African Studies, 72*(1), 64–85.

Godsäter, A. (2016). *Civil society regionalization in Southern Africa: The cases of trade and HIV/AIDS.* Abingdon: Routledge.

Haas, E. B. (1961). International integration: The European and the universal process. *International Organization, 15*(3), 366–392.

Hartmann, C. (2013). *Governance transfer by the economic community of West African States (ECOWAS)* (SFB-Governance Working Paper Series No. 47). Bonn: DFG Collaborative Research.

Hurrell, A. (2007). One world? Many worlds? The place of regions in the study of international society. *International Affairs, 83*(1), 127–146.

Hurt, S. R. (2012). The EU-SADC economic partnership agreement negotiations: 'Locking in' the neoliberal development model in Southern Africa? *Third World Quarterly, 33*(3), 495–510.

Igue, J. (2011). Economic integration in West Africa. In C. Tolentino & M. Vogl (Eds.), *Sustainable regional integration in West Africa* (Discussion Paper C208). Bonn: Center for European Integration Studies.

Iheduru, O. C. (2014). Civil society and regional integration in West Africa: Partners, legitimizers, and counter-hegemonic actors. In L. Fioramonti (Ed.), *Civil society and world regions*. Lanham: Lexington.

IOM. (2010). *Informal cross-border trade sector report*. February 2010. Geneva: IOM. http://iom. org.za/web/images/publications/icbt.pdf. Accessed 25 Oct 2012.

Kimani, N. (2007). *Reinvention of environmental governance in East Africa: Explanatory and normative dimensions*. PhD thesis, Australian National University.

Lightfoot, S. (2013). Climate change and the Africa-EU Strategy: Coherence, leadership and the 'greening' of development. In M. Carbone (Ed.), *The European Union in Africa*. Manchester: Manchester University Press.

Lorenz-carl, U. (2013). When the 'not so weak' Bargain with the 'not so strong': Whose agency matters in the economic partnership negotiations? In U. Lorenz-carl & M. Rempe (Eds.), *Mapping agency. Comparing regionalisms in Africa* (pp. 61–76). Aldershot: Ashgate.

Lucia, E. L. (2012). *A tool for security: How is the EU fostering and shaping ECOWAS security and defense regionalization process?* (GR: EEN Working Paper No. 17). Coventry: University of Warwick.

Makhan, D. (2009). *Linking EU trade and development policies: Lessons from the ACP-EU trade negotiations on economic partnership agreements*. Bonn: German Development Institute. http://www.die-gdi.de/uploads/media/Studies_50.pdf. Accessed 22 June 2015.

Marinov, E. (2013). *Impact of the European Union on regional integration in Africa* (MPRA Paper No. 60313). Sofia: Economic Research Institute at BAS.

Matambalya, F. A. S. T. (2012). The East African community: Can it be a model for Africa's integratioin process? In K. Mengisteab & R. Bereketeab (Eds.), *Regional integration, identity & citizenship in the Greater Horn of Africa* (pp. 195–235). Woodbridge: James Currey.

Matlosa, K. (2006). The role of political parties in regional integration in the SADC region. In A. Bösl, W. Breytenbach, T. Hartzenberg, C. McCarthy, & K. Schade (Eds.), *Monitoring regional integration in southern Africa yearbook* (Vol. 6, pp. 116–139). Stellenbosch: Trade Law Centre for Southern Africa.

McCarthy, C. (2010). Reconsidering regional integration in sub-Saharan Africa. In C. McCarthy, J. B. Cronjé, W. Denner, T. Fundira, W. Mwanza, & E. Bursvik (Eds.), *Supporting regional integration in East and Southern Africa – Review of select issues* (pp. 1–26). Trade Law Centre for Southern Africa: Stellenbosch.

Miranda, V. V., Pirozzi, N., & Schäfer, K. (2012). *Towards a stronger Africa-EU cooperation on peace and security: The role of African regional organizations and civil society* (IAI Working Papers No. 28). http://www.iai.it/sites/default/files/iaiwp1228.pdf. Accessed 23 June 2015.

NEPAD. (2003). *Action Plan for the environment initiative*. Addis-Abeba: NEPAD. http://www. nepad.org/system/files/Environment%20Action%20Plan.pdf. Accessed 23 June 2015.

Nivet, B. (2006). *Security by proxy? The EU and (sub-)regionalorganisations: The case of ECOWAS* (Occasional Paper No. 6). Paris: European Union Institute for Security Studies.

Nixdorf, L. (2013). Regional integration and informal cross-border trade in the East African community. In U. Lorenz-Carl & M. Rempe (Eds.), *Mapping agency. Comparing regionalisms in Africa* (pp. 133–147). Aldershot: Ashgate.

Ochwada, H. (2013). The history and politics of regionalism and integration in East Africa. In K. Omeje & T. R. Hepner (Eds.), *Conflict and peacebuilding in the African Great Lakes region* (pp. 47–64). Bloomington: Indiana University Press.

Okurut, T. O., & Othero, D. M. (2012). A holistic approach to natural resource management: A case of Lake Victoria Basin. In V. I. Grover & G. Kraatzberg (Eds.), *Great Lakes: Lessons in participatory governance* (pp. 349–363). Boca Raton: CRC Press.

Oloruntoba, S. (2013). *The political economy of regional integration and development in Africa: Rethinking the theoretical models.* Paper presented at the African economic conference. Johannesburg, 28–30 October 2013. http://www.afdb.org/en/aec-2013/papers/paper/the-political-economy-of-regional-integration-and-development-in-africa-rethinking-the-theoretical-models-1038/. Accessed 2 Mar 2016.

Overseas Development Institute. (2013). *The history, impact and political economy of barriers to food trade in sub-Saharan Africa: An analytical review.* ODI Report, December 2013. London: ODI. http://www.odi.org/sites/odi.org.uk/files/odi-assets/publications-opinion-files/8803.pdf. Accessed 2 Mar 2016.

Paterson, M. (2012). *The African Union at ten: Problems, progress, and prospects.* International colloquium report. Berlin, 30–31 August 2012. Cape Town/Berlin: Centre for Conflict Resolution/Friedrich Ebert Stiftung. https://www.fes.de/afrika/content/downloads/AU_Report_FINAL.pdf. Accessed 2 Mar 2016.

Piccolino, G, & Minou S. (2014). *The EU and regional integration in West Africa: What effects on conflict resolution and transformation?* (Working Paper Series No. 5). Pretoria: Centre for the Study of Governance Innovation.

Pirozzi, N. (2009). *EU support to African security architecture: Funding and training components* (Occasional Papers No.76). Paris: EU Institute for Security Studies. http://www.iss.europa.eu/uploads/media/op76.pdf. Accessed 23 June 2015.

Pirozzi, N. (2015). *EU crisis management after Lisbon: A new model to address security challenges in the 21st century?* Cambridge: Intersentia.

Qobo, M. (2012). The European Union. In C. Saunders, C. Dzinesa, A. Gwinyayi, & D. Nagar (Eds.), *Region-building in Southern Africa* (pp. 251–263). London: Zed Books.

Rudloff, B., & Weinhardt, C. (2011). *Economic partnership agreements between the EU and the African, Caribbean and Pacific Group of States.* SWP Comments 3. Berlin: German Institute for International and Security Affairs. http://www.swp-berlin.org/fileadmin/contents/products/comments/2011C03_rff_wht_ks.pdf. Accessed 23 June 2015.

Sicurelli, D. (2013). Africa-EU partnership on climate change and the environment. In J. Mangala (Ed.), *Africa and the European Union. A strategic partnership* (pp. 149–169). New York: Palgrave Macmillian.

Silvestre, C. (2009). *EU-AU relations: What role for civil society?* Brussles: Open Society Institute. http://www.opensocietyfoundations.org/sites/default/files/silvestre_20090409.pdf. Accessed 23 June 2015.

Söderbaum, F. (2001). Turbulent regionalization in West Africa. In M. Schultz, J. Michael, J. Öjendal, & F. Söderbaum (Eds.), *Regionalisation in a globalizing world* (pp. 61–81). London: Zed Books.

Söderbaum, F. (2004). *The political economy of regionalism. The case of Southern Africa.* New York: Palgrave Macmillan.

Theron, S., Ntasano, E. C. (2014). *The EU, regional co-operation and conflict in the Great Lakes Region* (Working Paper Series, No. 7). Pretoria: Centre for the Study of Governance Innovation.

Tjønneland, E. (2008). *From aid effectiveness to poverty reduction: Is foreign donor support to SADC improving?* (Vol. 4). Gaborone: Lightbooks.

TRALAC. (2012). *The regional indicative strategic development plan: SADC's trade-led integration agenda. How is SADC doing? Trade Law Centre* (TRALAC Trade Brief No. S12TBO2). http://www.tralac.org/files/2012/04/S12TB022012-SADC-RISDP-SADC-agenda-20120418. pdf. Accessed 23 June 2015.

UNEP. (n.d.). *Increased role of civil society, Africa environment outlook 2.* Nairobi: UNEP. http:// www.unep.org/dewa/Africa/publications/AEO-2/content/019.htm. Accessed 23 June 2015.

Van Langenhove, L. (2012). Why we need to 'unpack' regions to compare them more effectively. *The International Spectator, 47*(1), 16–29.

Wiener, A., & Diez, T. (Eds.). (2004). *European integration theory.* Oxford: Oxford University Press.

Yusuff, O. S. (2014). Gender dimensions of informal cross border trade in West-African Sub-Regiona (ECOWAS) borders. *International Letters of Social and Humanistic Sciences, 18,* 19–33.

Chapter 6
Assessing Interregional Relations Between North America and Sub-Saharan Africa

John Kotsopoulos and Madeleine Goerg

Abstract This paper explores the extent of interregional cooperation between North America and Africa in the area of development. As an initial contribution to the study of interregional relations between North America and Africa the analysis focuses on governmental and intergovernmental organisations. Through the prism of quasi-interregionalism, the authors explore relations between the United States and African regional organisations and similarly Canada and African regional organisations. The chapter also considers the motivations of Canada and the U.S. in seeking relationships at the interregional level in Africa. Using primary documents and interviews, the paper demonstrates that while overarching strategies for interregionalism may be still absent, focus on regional entities and institutions in Africa is gaining ground and coordination between the U.S. and Canada can be seen in areas of mutual interest on the continent.

Keywords Atlantic • Interregionalism • Regional organisations • Regionalism • Regions

6.1 Introduction

Since the end of the Cold War, the burgeoning growth of relationships between regional organisations around the globe has broadened the focus of once Eurocentric interregional studies (Söderbaum 2012). Organisations such as the Association of South East Asian Nations (ASEAN) have developed a wide range of international relationships, with other regional organisations and third countries too. Latin America is similarly going through a "new era" of regional integration (Mouline

J. Kotsopoulos (✉)
Center for the Study of Governance Innovation, University of Pretoria, Pretoria, South Africa
e-mail: john.kotsopoulos@governanceinnovation.org

M. Goerg
German Marshall Fund of the United States, Brussels, Belgium
e-mail: madeleine.goerg@gmail.com

© Springer International Publishing AG 2018   95
F. Mattheis, A. Litsegård (eds.), *Interregionalism across the Atlantic Space*,
United Nations University Series on Regionalism 15,
DOI 10.1007/978-3-319-62908-7_6

2013). Africa also boasts a large number of regional organisations with many enjoying formal ties with other regional bodies within the continent and beyond.

The purpose of this chapter is to explore the extent of interregional cooperation between North America and Africa. Such a proposition might strike the observer as counter-intuitive, given the paucity of North American regional organisations with any relations beyond the continent. Indeed, it has been asserted that "the North American continent did not experience a formal process of regionalisation in the twentieth century" (Ayres and Macdonald 2015: 182). Functional regional organisations did exist of course, centred on security such as the North American Aerospace Defence Command (NORAD) or area-specific trade agreements like the Canada-US Auto Pact (1965). The economic and political asymmetry between the United States, Canada, and Mexico precluded more ambitious regional initiatives until the end of the century, with the establishment of the North American Free Trade Agreement (NAFTA). Still, NAFTA represents a free trade area rather than a regional institution and as such does not have the agency to interact with other regional groupings. Instead, strategic economic and political issues have taken on a bilateral focus in North America (Söderbaum 2014). For instance, recent focus has concerned the Transatlantic Trade and Investment Partnership (TTIP) negotiations between the EU and the U.S. as well as a free trade agreement (FTA) with Canada and the EU.

In notable contrast to North America, African regionalism is extensive – to the point where some have considered the number of overlapping institutions and jurisdictions as a "spaghetti bowl" (Draper et al. 2007: 7). Some 14 regional economic communities (RECs) exist, despite decades-old legislation from the former Organisation for African Unity (OAU) to limit them to five. While efforts have been made to account for an African brand of regionalism (Bach 1999), and particularly the topical issue of regional economic integration, comparatively less analysis exists concerning African interregional relations beyond the continent.

Yet focusing exclusively on region to region relations omits a range of other relationships. An obvious example is the African Union (AU), which is engaged in comprehensive interregional relations with the EU but also maintains partnership agreements of varying depth with a host of third countries, including China, India and Korea, to name a few. Furthermore, in August 2014 the United States hosted the first US-Africa Leaders Summit (White House 2014), an indication of not only Africa's renewed prominence on the international scene, but also of a willingness to engage it at a continental rather than bilateral level.

It is therefore evident that any narrow analytical approach risks missing what exists of North American-African interregionalism altogether. Exploring the ties between sides of the Atlantic with dramatically different levels of integration will require a more varied definition of interregionalism. The starting point is the work of Hänggi (Hänggi 2006) and his attempt to create a typology of interregionalism and the extension of that typology by Malamud and Gardini (see Chap. 2 in this volume). Hänggi outlines three core categories of external relations of a regional organisation, with Malamud and Gardini complimenting his list with a further two:

- relations with regional organisations in other regions;
- involvement in transregional relations;

- relations with third states in other regions (Hänggi 2006);
- overlapping interregionalism;
- interregionalism by stealth (Malamud and Gardini, this volume).

Of all five categories, Hänggi's third denoting relationships between regional organisations and third countries – otherwise known as hybrid or quasi interregionalism – is the most appropriate here. This type of interregionalism is by no means a universally accepted category (Ruland 2006), yet it reflects a useful conceptual tool through which to analyse relations between regional organisations and third countries (Baert et al. 2014).

Given the aforementioned lack of North American regional organisations engaged in trans-continental relationships, the chapter will look at the separate cases of the United States and Canada and their respective *development* cooperation with African regional organisations. Development in this context is considered an umbrella for all activities which relate directly or indirectly to development, including the ever increasing prominence of trade as a tool for development[1] as well as security as an enabler of development. The focus on development is also crucial because it takes into account the historical prominence that development aid played in framing North American relations with Africa. While civil society and non-governmental organisations are increasingly present in the development arena, few studies have provided in depth analyses of the implications of this changing landscape. The same can be said about the role of private sector actors in development cooperation. Given the sparse literature on interregional relations between North America and Africa, and the preeminent role governmental and inter-governmental organisations continue to play in this space, this chapter will focus on official development cooperation.[2]

This chapter will also consider the motivations of actors such as Canada and the U.S. in seeking relationships at the interregional level in Africa (rather than bilateral), and the implications of such relationships on all parties involved. Building on Aggarwal and Fogarty (2006) and their explanation of the limits of EU-North American interregionalism, this study will therefore account for the difference in interregionalism taken as a *process* and interregionalism as a *policy strategy*. The latter reveals functional motivations, such as if programming is more efficient at the multilateral rather than the bilateral level. Likewise interregionalism as strategy reveals regional organisations' limitations, such as human resource capacities, and

---

[1] The US-African Leaders summit in August 2014 had as its theme "Investing in the Next Generation" – a reflection of the prominence of trade and investment in current relations with Africa.

[2] It is acknowledged that other forms of interregionalism, namely transnational linkages between civil society organisations, may also provide potentially fruitful avenues of inquiry; civil society linkages often touch on a wide variety of areas, including development organisations, activist networks, religious institutions, diaspora associations, and the list goes on. A study of interregionalism in civil society (Söderbaum 2012) as it applies to North America and Africa provides an interesting topic for future investigation.

thus why countries such as the U.S. and Canada might in some instances prefer to channel programming bilaterally or even through third party institutions.

Interregionalism as process accounts for the effects of interregional relations on the parties involved. The act of engagement can bestow legitimacy and status on an organisation. For instance, western countries electing to support the AU but previously showing far less interest in its progenitor the OAU is indicative of faith in the legitimacy of the former and circumspection with respect to the latter. Moreover interregional relations oblige parties to articulate interests, further contributing to their own identity and agency, or "actorness" (Baert et al. 2014).

Finally, the chapter touches on any cooperative links between Canada and the U.S. in Africa, in order to discern whether North American cooperation is prioritised, even if it occurs outside the framework of any formal North American regional organisation. Cooperation could provide evidence of growing integration on both sides of the Atlantic basin. Several semi-structured interviews were conducted in late 2014 and early 2015 with officials from the U.S. and Canada (Department of Foreign Affairs, Trade and Development) to better address the question of North American cooperation. Other sources used include official U.S. Government and Government of Canada documents and secondary resources. It should also be noted that Mexico has not been considered in this study due to its far less prominent role in Africa.[3]

6.2 Moving Towards the Regionalisation of U.S. – Africa Relations?

6.2.1 Providing Context for U.S. Engagement with Africa

While relations with Africa remain relatively low on the list of foreign policy priorities for the U.S., they have become increasingly important over the past decade. In terms of policy goals, engagement with the continent has shown continuity over the Clinton, Bush, and Obama administrations. Released in June 2012, the four pillars of the *U.S. Strategy Toward Sub-Saharan Africa* include strengthening democratic institutions and spurring economic growth, trade and investment, advancing peace and security, and promoting opportunity and development, which frame American engagement with African actors. Across these policy areas, the horizontal objectives consist of engaging the youth, empowering marginalised groups and women, addressing the needs of fragile and post-conflict states, and working with the UN and other multilateral actors (White House 2012).

Under former Secretary of State Hilary Clinton the role of development policy was elevated and put on a par with foreign and security policy as part of a 'whole of government' approach. Development policy is now more clearly identified by the

---

[3] Mexico has, for example, only five embassies on the continent (Mballa 2009).

U.S. as a foreign policy tool, with an emphasis on "American know-how, American dollars, American values" (Wolff 2010: 1). The State Department and USAID serve to centralise most of the efforts toward the African continent as U.S. engagement remains dominated by development cooperation.

Over the past decade, decisions which might have pointed toward an emerging continental approach toward Africa have tended to retain strong bilateral components. In 2006, the U.S. opened its diplomatic mission to the AU, which is housed in the U.S. Embassy to Ethiopia. Four years later, the Annual U.S.-AU High-Level Dialogue was launched and has taken place five times since (in 2010, 2011, 2012, 2014, and 2015). The partnership between the AU and the U.S. was further formalised in 2010 with an assistance agreement (U.S. Department of State 2011). The Mission to the AU, however, lacks the necessary resources to propose and implement continent-wide strategies and programming. The mission has ten staff members and largely relies on the resources of the U.S. Embassy to Ethiopia (Williams 2015). Likewise, the U.S.-Africa Leaders Summit, held in August 2014, the Young African Leaders Initiative Network, and the African Growth and Opportunity Act (AGOA) negotiations follow bilateral patterns, with a limited role for the AU or other regional organisations.

The largely bilateral nature of U.S. engagement with the African continent is not specific to the region but rather reflects a broader American approach whereby 83% of its global Official Development Aid (ODA) disbursed in 2012 was allocated on a bilateral basis (OECD 2014). Of the $8,3 billion disbursed in 2013, around $300 million were allocated for regional programming (OECD 2014, OECD 2015). While the numbers remain relatively low, a closer look at American development policy and USAID's programming point to some budding regional, if not continental, approaches and a growing recognition of the role of regional organisations on the continent. While cooperation with RECs is not a stated strategic goal in the *U.S. Strategy Toward Sub-Saharan Africa*, it is presented as a horizontal approach under the "Spur Economic Growth, Trade, and Investment" and "Advance Peace and Security" pillars (White House 2012: 3, 5). In both policy areas, regional integration is a key tool to achieving the stated goals.

According to U.S. officials, the past 10 years have witnessed a shift in thinking about regional integration. Long seen as the purview of the EU, the U.S. is now increasingly involved in building capacity for regional organisations. Indeed, in recent years USAID has given a more prominent role to regional organisations in its strategic planning. This change reflects both a belief that regional integration will further economic development and stability in Africa and an attempt to better integrate USAID and the State Department while more effectively harnessing American resources, expertise, and cooperating with allies (Department of State 2010). The Department of State's *First Quadrennial Diplomacy and Development Review* published in 2010 recognises the fact that despite its "organisation around regional bureaus, the structures within those bureaus prioritize bilateral relationships, with strong country desks and deep links to bilateral embassies in the field" (Department of State 2010: 52) and urges regional bureaus to assert themselves to address increasingly regional and transnational policy challenges. Regional bureaus are expected to "develop more effective regional strategies on core policy objectives, situate bilateral relationships in a regional context, and strengthen our engagement with regional institutions" (Department of State 2010: 52).

On the African continent, regional programming is broken down into five bureaus: the Central African Regional (USAID/CA); the Sahel Regional; Southern African Regional (USAID/SA); the East African Regional (USAID/EA); and the West African Regional (USAID/WA), each with their own focus areas.

The Central Africa Regional focuses on the Congo Basin through USAID's Central Africa Regional Program for the Environment (CARPE), which covers the Democratic Republic of Congo (DRC), Republic of Congo, Central African Republic (CAR), Cameroon, Gabon and Equatorial Guinea (USAID Central Africa Regional 2015a). The Sahel Regional was created to address the chronic vulnerability of the region. The Sahel Joint Planning Cell (JPC) attempts to bridge the gap between humanitarian and development activities by pooling resources and expertise (USAID Sahel Regional 2015b).

The Southern Africa Regional covers Botswana, Lesotho, Namibia, and South Africa. Programming focuses on five policy areas including agriculture and food security, democracy, human rights and governance, economic growth and trade, environment, and global health (USAID Southern Africa Regional 2015d). Not surprisingly, given the size of its economy, cooperation with South Africa plays a significant role in the Southern Africa Regional's activities.

The East Africa Regional bureau's programming covers five policy areas, agriculture and food security, economic growth and trade, environment, global health, and crises and conflict, and spans the Great Lakes region of Burundi, Rwanda, Tanzania, and Uganda, and the Horn of Africa region that includes Djibouti, Ethiopia, Kenya, and Somalia. Activities in the region are further complemented by the Assistance Agreement for Comprehensive Regional Development with the East African Community (EAC), which aims at increasing regional economic integration and development (USAID East Africa Regional 2015c, U.S. Mission to the African Union 2014).

USAID's West Africa Regional mission primarily aims at building capacity for the Economic Community of West African States (ECOWAS). Relative to the other four regional missions, the West Africa Regional has among the most extensive regional programming, covering seven policy areas including agriculture and food security, clean and efficient energy, economic growth and trade, environment, global health, promoting peaceful political transitions, and working in crises and conflict. Formal cooperation agreements between the ECOWAS Commission and USAID have further consolidated the relationship between the two organisations (USAID West Africa Regional 2015e, ECOWAS Commission 2007, 2012, 2014).

A short overview of USAID's five regional missions points to the varying depth and breadth of U.S.-Africa regional cooperation in Africa. While the East and West Africa Regional missions include formal cooperation frameworks with RECs, the countries included in the other regional missions are more a function of the policy areas covered than membership to a specific regional organisation.

6.2.2   Varying Degrees of Regional Approaches: A Closer Look at key Policy Areas

Agriculture, food security, and trade account for more regionalised policies when compared to energy, security, and health. USAID activities in agriculture and food security count among the closest partnerships the U.S. forms with regional organisations, RECs particularly. The RECs consist of the eight regional organisations recognised by the African Union and include ECOWAS, Common Market for Eastern and Southern Africa (COMESA), EAC, and the Southern African Development Community (SADC), with whom USAID regional missions partner. Most activities in this policy area fall under the Feed the Future (FtF) program, which is the U.S. Government's global hunger and food security initiative. FtF is a global program, which combines bilateral and regional activities in Asia, Africa, and Central America. The bulk of the programming, however, is done in Africa, which hosts 11 national and three regional programs while FtF has three national and one regional program in both Asia and Central America (Feed the Future 2015).

On the African continent, FtF programming supports the Comprehensive Africa Agriculture Development Programme (CAADP), a continent-wide policy framework and instrument of the African Union's New Partnership for Africa's Development (NEPAD). In West, East, and Southern Africa, USAID supports the respective RECs as they set out regional policies and priorities. Partnering with regional institutions is a "top priority for the U.S. Government" (U.S. Government Document 2011a: 5). The decision to elevate agriculture and food security programming to the regional level is based on recognition that challenges in this policy area are inherently regional. In addition, regional activities compliment bilateral programs in the various regions. Regional cooperation is most visible in West Africa, with both ECOWAS and the West African Economic and Monetary Union (WAEMU), and in East Africa with support to COMESA and the EAC.[4] While the activities in West and East Africa are more closely linked to regional strategies, USAID/SA is also increasingly working with SADC. Although regional programming is done primarily in partnership with the respective RECs, USAID also engages with other policy-relevant regional actors (U.S. Government Document 2011b, USAID East Africa 2015c).

Promoting economic growth through global and intra-regional trade is also high on the U.S. Government's Africa agenda. Given the place of agriculture in African economies, trade and agriculture programs are closely linked in USAID's three main regions, West, Southern, and East Africa. Indeed, USAID's trade work furthers and integrates FtF objectives. Regional trade hubs aim at increasing Africa's international competitiveness, bolstering intra-regional trade, and ensuring food security for African countries. U.S. trade with African countries falls under the African Growth and Opportunity Act (AGOA), a unilateral preferential access

---

[4] With the exception of Tanzania, the EAC member states are also members of COMESA. Burundi, Kenya, Rwanda, and Uganda claim membership to both the EAC and COMESA.

program negotiated on a bilateral basis with eligible African states and approved annually by the U.S. Congress. The West, East, and Southern Africa trade hubs provide support for African governments and business seeking access to the U.S. market under the AGOA provisions. The U.S. also has trade and investment framework agreements (TIFAs) with eight African countries and three regional groupings (COMESA, EAC, WAEMU) and a Trade, Investment, and Development Cooperative Agreement with SACU (Office of the USTR 2015). These agreements, however, are less ambitious than free trade agreements. Although the Obama administration has taken steps to coordinate American policies toward Africa with its *whole of government* approach, a 2013 report published by the Wilson Center and Manchester Trade Limited Inc. argues that "more still needs to be done in concert with Congress to produce a truly sustainable U.S. footprint in Africa" (McDonald et al. 2013: ii).

A closer look at energy, security, and health, shows the unequal regionalisation of U.S. Africa policy. Although Power Africa comes closest to a continental project with a continental "pot of money", the initiative will focus initially on six African countries in West and East Africa (Ethiopia, Ghana, Kenya, Liberia, Nigeria, and Tanzania). Furthermore, USAID's West Africa Regional is the only regional mission for whom power and clean energy are a defined area of work (USAID West Africa 2015e).

U.S. support to peace and stability in Africa spans a number of agencies, including USAID, the Department of Defence, and the Department of State. The U.S. Mission to the AU also plays a role in this policy area. Despite initial scepticism on the part of African governments (Barkely 2009), the U.S. Africa Command (AFRICOM) has come to play a central role in U.S.-Africa security cooperation. Since its inception in 2007, AFRICOM has expanded its programs to help build capacity for the African Peace and Security Architecture of the African Union. Paul Williams, however, argues that the increased support for peace and security operations in Africa has taken place without an overarching peacekeeping strategy and remains largely bilateral rather than through direct support to the AU (Williams 2015).

Health, which falls under USAID's Global Health initiative, is perhaps the least regionalised policy area. USAID health programming in Africa focuses on HIV/AIDS, nutrition, tuberculosis, maternal and child health, family planning and reproductive health with some support to regional organisations like the East, Central & Southern Africa Health Community (ECSA) and the West African Health Organisation (WAHO).

6.2.3   Assessing the 'Regionalisation' of the U.S.' Africa Policy

The past decade has seen a shift in USAID's approaches to development cooperation with growing recognition of the importance of regional organisations. Although these steps remain tentative, together, the five regional missions cover the full range of USAID's policy areas. The *First Quadrennial Diplomacy and Development*

Review lays out approaches for regional engagement in Asia, which could possibly be extended to Africa (Department of State 2010). The document also foresees the creation of regional hubs, presumably building on existing regional USAID bureaus. Indeed, with the exception of South Asia, Africa is the only region for which regional integration is a priority for the American government. However, USAID programming continues to follow thematic logics by policy area rather than regional lines. Presidential initiatives, such as Power Africa, focus on specific policy areas and key pilot countries, and many USAID programs are developed based on the analyses of on-the-ground needs and are subject to the approval of the United States' Congress on an annual basis. This more granular and nimble approach hinders, to a degree, the development of longer-term regional strategies.

Over the past 10 years, USAID started delivering more capacity building programs focused on regional organisations and regional integration. These activities are, among others, discussed with EU policy makers in the framework of USAID-EuropeAid policy dialogues in an attempt to coordinate efforts. According to a USAID representative, however, these particular discussions do not rank very high on the U.S. and the EU's respective agendas. While regional strategies and cooperation with regional organisations have been developed for programming on agriculture, food security, and trade; in the areas of energy, security, and health, work with regional organisations continues to be on a more ad hoc basis.

According to Bach, "[r]egionalism refers to ideas or ideologies, programs, policies and goals that seek to transform an identified social space into a regional project. Since regionalism postulates the implementation of a program and the definition of a strategy, it is often associated with institution building or the conclusion of formal agreements" (Bach 2013: 92). In the case of East and West Africa, USAID activities support and work with existing regional projects, namely the EAC and ECOWAS. USAID, however, does not systematically work with or build capacity for RECs, as recognised by the AU. Programming, at times, favours more policy-relevant groupings. In Central Africa, for instance, the regional mission which focuses on land management works with the Congo Basin countries rather than partnering with the ECCAS. Since few USAID initiatives, other than Power Africa, are specific to the African continent, USAID seems to first identify issues and policy areas and then find the appropriate partners, which would be in line with the project-based approach of the organisation and is consistent with a interregionalism as a policy strategy, rather than process.

As discussed in the previous sections, the degree to which USAID develops and implements regional strategies and partners with RECs or other regional bodies varies greatly between regions and policy areas. Doidge argues that "if actorness refers to the ability of an organisation to purposively act in the international system, then *ipso facto* the strength of its actorness will dictate the types of activities it is able to undertake successfully" (Doidge 2007: 234). In this context, the actorness, or lack thereof, of the various RECs likely plays into partnership and cooperation possibilities with USAID. Programming by the West Africa Regional is embedded in regional strategies undertaken by ECOWAS in a way that might not be possible in other, less regionally integrated, parts of the continent. Indeed, regionalism in Africa still focuses on ambitious agendas, which would require real transfers of sovereignty to the regional body and strong institutions. For Bach, this translates into a "sharp disconnect between highly ambitious federalist ambitions and poor transcription of stated ambitions on the ground" (Bach 2013: 102). USAID's challenge in strengthening the regional bureaus could also be a function of this disconnect. Furthermore, in policy areas such as peace and security, the ability to develop regional approaches through cooperation with regional organisations, like the AU, may depend on the degree to which competencies are delegated to regional or continental bodies. While African states might participate in AU missions and use the training provided by the U.S. to do so, security and defence matters tend to remain the prerogative of sovereign states.

According to U.S. officials, the regional missions were created in part to make up for the decrease in the number of bilateral missions between the mid-1980s and mid-1990s (Interview 2014/2015). Indeed, budget considerations and attempts at rationalising the use of resources and expertise have, in part, underpinned the move toward more regional approaches. This could be interpreted as an interregional strategy. However, the budget allocation process for USAID remains a challenge for the implementation of its regional approach. While the *First Quadrennial Diplomacy and Development Review* demands that regional bureau spend "significant time and resources" (Department of State 2010: 52) to develop cooperation frameworks and strategies with regional organisations, access to funds is limited. Indeed, funding, which is allocated in the annual budget and approved by the United States' Congress, remains largely bilateral. While regional missions have some autonomous funds, the amounts pale in comparison with allocations for bilateral aid. The slow development of regional or continental approaches toward Africa is in part linked to institutional constraints on American actors dealing with the continent.

Doidge's argument that "where qualitative differences are at their greatest, internally focused aspects of interregionalism are likely to be performed, while at the same time externally focused aspects will remain unachievable" (Doidge 2007: 242) helps frame the interregional relations between the U.S. and Africa. Interregionalism between the two is predominantly internally focused, with an emphasis on capacity building, rather than externally focused with an ability to influence global debates (Doidge 2007), which might be expected of two regions more on a par with one another. Gardini and Malamud make the distinction between senior and junior regions in certain region-to-region arrangements. This contrast can be extended to hybrid or state-to-region interactions. Using the typology proposed by Gardini and Malamud, American engagement with Africa's regions falls under active state-to-region relations, with a combination of a *leadership role* in the politico-institutional realm and a *cooperation role* in the socio-economic arena. The former is expressed through U.S. support to African processes of cooperation, coordination and integration, and the latter through the provision of technical, financial, and economic assistance.

6.3 Canadian Engagement with Africa

6.3.1 Providing Context for Canada's Relations with Africa

The following section will explore Canada's evolving approach to Africa and changing relations with African regional organisations. The analysis will examine trends, including any Canadian tendencies towards formal cooperation with the United States in Africa as well as any notions of a nascent Atlantic area of cooperation. The idea of interregionalism as strategy or process will also be considered, with most of the evidence pointing towards the former in Canada's Africa programming.

Canada's historic relationship with Africa has centred on development assistance and humanitarian aid, with trade comparatively less significant (Black 2004). This aid-first agenda has only recently begun to change through gradually increasing trade links and some conflict and security support programming. Canadian involvement in Africa had (and continues to be) channelled through a mix of bilateral and multilateral relationships, though the focus accorded to these relationships is shifting. For decades, roughly 15 embassies were maintained in Africa, finely balanced between Francophone and Anglophone countries as a reflection of the linguistic composition and political sensibilities in Canada. Multilateral relations were mostly channelled through the Commonwealth, UN and eventually la Francophonie. Conspicuously absent were relations with African regional entities such as the OAU, though this has changed in recent years.

Canada's approach to Africa has provided a canvas to project its (self-) image as a moral, "middle power", not only through the provision of aid but also the support of African independence movements in the 1960s and explicit backing from the 1970s of the struggle against white-minority regimes in Southern Africa (Elder 2013). This approach has had its champions – Nelson Mandela, for instance, made a special point of including Canada in the first group of countries he visited after his release from prison – but has also garnered criticism. Some pundits have deemed Canada's approach as one tied to an image of Africa as an entity in need of charity, an "impoverished continent" (Akuffo 2013: 125), allowing Canada to serve as a "helper state" (Ibid). "…Canadian policy towards Africa is about *us* – about our own moral self-affirmation and sense of collective identity and purpose – as it is about the African counties and people Canadians have engaged" (Black 2004: 138). This self-interested approach has been abetted by the fickleness regarding Canada's Africa policy, which has moved up and down Canada's foreign policy agenda over the years (S. Brown 2013a).

However, an increasing embracement of the development-trade nexus as a sustainable path to growth and alternative to an open-ended aid regime, coupled with a new and less apologetically instrumental approach to foreign policy launched by the administration of former Prime Minister Stephen Harper, has had some perceptible effects on just who Canada is interacting with on the continent. Specifically, the growing trade agenda has given new impetus for cooperation with Africa's RECs. The case for hybrid interregionalism in Canada's relations with Africa starts there.

The organisation of the government of Canada's foreign policy, aid and trade instruments has changed over time, reflecting a changing philosophy about the place of international development in Canada's foreign relations (Culpeper 2013). From 1968 to 2013, Canada's aid funding was channelled through the Canadian International Development Agency (CIDA), underlining at the time the importance given to development aid as a process in its own right. Some critics, however, considered the agency's de-coupling from Department of Foreign Affairs and International Trade as an antiquated approach to the developing world and a perpetuation of the image of Africa as entity in need of charity. In 2013 CIDA was folded in to the newly christened Department of Foreign Affairs, Trade and Development (DFATD). How much this amalgamation may lead to improved integration of foreign policy and development goals, as well as broadening the scope of aid funding, remains unknown at this early stage. There is, however, some reserved excitement by some within DFATD about a clearer strategic – that is, political -- dimension to aid funding (DFATD interview 2015).

Linked to institutional change has been a gradual shift in philosophy about the purpose of aid, its distribution and the accountability surrounding it. This is likely a reflection of a larger "post-Washington Consensus", with a neo-liberal and trade oriented philosophy challenging the outcomes of traditional aid distribution. Greater interest in accountability has resulted in Canada's Official Development Assistance Accountability Act (ODAAA) and quasi-corporate funding mechanisms like the Millennium Challenge Corporation (MCC) in the US. The 2005 Paris Declaration and the 2008 Accra Agenda for Action have also provided the principles for aid effectiveness, which guide Canadian policy (DFATD interview 2014).

6.3.2 Assessing Regional Approaches to Africa

Canada is one of the most prominent donors of ODA in the world (6th ranked in the world in 2011).More specifically, in terms of net ODA, Canada allocated US$4.91 billion in 2013, making it the 9th largest DAC donor (by comparison, the USA is the largest donor with US$31.5 billion in 2013) (OECD 2015). The largest chunk of this aid (~40%) went to Sub-Saharan Africa, with four of the five largest recipients also stemming from the region (Department of Foreign Affairs 2012–13). Grants normally made up the highest percentage of aid with technical cooperation usually second. The distribution of funding is divided between bilateral and multilateral ODA. In 2012 roughly 29% of a total of CAD4.8 billion in funding went to multilateral sources (Department of Foreign Affairs 2012–13) – an explicit reminder that Canada's contribution to multilateral entities like regional organisations was of substantial importance.

Canadian programming is divided between bilateral and multilateral initiatives with more funding apportioned to the bilateral side at a ratio of approximately 3 to 1.[5]

---

[5] Government of Canada ODA development assistance funding was around $5 billion in 2012–13 with 4 billion allocated for bilateral projects and $1.4 billion for multilateral. (DFATD 2012–13, pp: 13–14).

A tension exists between the two with Canada's historical "good multilateral citizen" approach (Black 2004) juxtaposed with an increasing wish to prioritise bilateral projects driven by Canadian organisations (DFATD interview 2015). Analysis of Canada's 2013 ODA funding demonstrates that at the bilateral level development assistance and humanitarian assistance are both targeted, with Tanzania and South Sudan being the largest recipients in each category respectively (Department of Foreign Affairs 2012–13).

Canada's largest funding commitment to a multilateral organisation is for the Global Fund to Fight AIDS, TB and Malaria. For food security, funds have been channelled through UN's World Food Programme (WPF), making Canada the organisation's third largest donor. Last but not least, the G8/G7 has played a crucial role as a conduit for some of Canada's initiatives and the promotion of its development interests. The "Muskoka Initiative", launched at the G8 Summit in Canada in 2010, successfully committed its members to mobilise new funding of up to US$5 billion in pursuit of Millennium Development Goal (MDG) targets especially related to MNCH (*Muskoka Declaration: Recovery and New Beginnings* 2010). In 2012 Canada also used the G8 New Alliance for Food and Nutrition Security initiative to pledge C$219 million, with Ghana and Ethiopia the chief bilateral recipients.

One area of Canadian ODA programming where substantial funds do go towards regional entities is under the category of International Financial Institution (IFI) support. In fact, about half of assistance to multilateral organisations is destined for IFIs, with more than half of that designated for World Bank initiatives (Department of Foreign Affairs 2012–13). Beyond the World Bank, the leading recipients of Canadian funding are the Asian Development Bank ($171 million) and the AfDB ($147 million) – which shall be explored in more detail below.

Finally, there is of course non-ODA spending which also directly or indirectly links to Canada's development agenda and its multilateral relations in Africa. This is especially true when the scope of what is deemed aid is broadened to include the security-development nexus or the trade-development nexus.

In promoting peace and security, Canada's support touches mostly multilateral efforts, including contributions to several UN Trust Funds designated to support UN or African led initiatives most recently in Mali, Somalia and the Central African Republic (DFATD 2014b). There is also Canadian support for the ECOWAS and its African-led International Support Mission to Mali (AFISMA), though funding is indirect and through the UN. A more direct relationship is evident with the AU, where Canada was an early contributor to training and communication for the 2013 "Mission internationale de soutien à la Centrafrique sous conduite africaine" (MISCA) in the Central African Republic (Ibid). Prior to that CIDA aid money was used to support the African Standby Force (ASF) and the African Peace and Security Architecture (APSA).

Canada's most prominent relationships with regional bodies in Africa are with the AfDB and the AU. The former has become an important conduit for Canadian funding aimed at larger regional initiatives such as the NEPAD Infrastructure Preparation Facility with C$25 million committed over two phases of the project (Department of Foreign Affairs Trade and Development 2013).

Canada is in fact one of the largest non-regional stakeholders in the Bank and is one of the Bank board's 20 members. It supported the Bank's 2010 General Capital increase with a commitment of C$331 million, representing 4.9% of the burden share (AfDB). The bulk of that commitment is "callable", which is a type of guarantee of liquidity that allows the Bank to borrow on the international market at low interest rates (DFATD interview 2015). The AfDB represents Canada's chief multilateral gateway to Africa along with the AU.

Returning to the AU, in 2015 there is only one direct funding agreement between it and Canada focussing on support for pillar 5 ("institutions, capacity building an communication") of the AU Commission's Strategic Plan for 2014–17 (African Union Commission, 2013). However, Canada does also support the AU's Comprehensive Africa Agriculture Development Programme as a member of the Development Partners Task Team, contributing expertise in the establishment of an accountability framework and strengthening regional donor coordination (G8 Deauville Summit 2011). It should be added here that one interviewed Canadian diplomat based in Addis Ababa felt there was plenty of scope for future cooperation with the AU but it was not necessarily the most suited conduit for funding for a given area since its capacity was still in the progress of expanding (DFATD interview 2014).

6.3.3 Trends in Canadian Regional Policy in Africa

The above effort to identify Canada's main partners in Africa and specifically its interactions with regional organisations leaves a mixed picture. The historic role of Canada in Africa has changed, reflecting not only institutional changes within Canada but also a changing consensus about engagement with Africa, manifested not only in the Millennium Development Goals, but also in the Africa-driven agenda of the AU, NEPAD and AfDB, among others. Shifting understandings of development, which have broadened to include areas such as trade, security, good governance, democracy and the rule of law, have also affected programming.

What is not discernible from the figures, documents or interviews is any form of specific or exclusive cooperation between the U.S. and Canada in Africa either with respect to bilateral partners or regional organisations on the continent. Interviewees noted that good cooperation with the U.S. existed in diplomatic fora, but as part of a larger set of "like minded" nations. For instance, at the AfDB, the eight non-regional chairs maintain close relations, in particular the UK, France, U.S. and Canada (DFATD interview 2015). This might point to coordination between Atlantic partners, though at this stage it is not explicitly deemed as Atlantic cooperation. The proximity of worldviews and familiarity between Atlantic and Western countries likely facilitates interaction. At the AU, Canada cooperated with the U.S. within the joint partners group, including in the sub-committee forum comprised of mostly western donors seeking to exchange views on approaches to engaging the AU

(DFATD interview 2014). Cooperation was also evident on Joint Programming Arrangements.

As for an Atlantic space, again it is nearly impossible to state that a pattern of interaction based on geographic proximity was evident. Taking Canada's preeminent bilateral 2012–13 ODA funding recipients in Africa in order: Tanzania, Cote d'Ivoire and Ethiopia (2012–13 ODA funding), no such pattern can be surmised. The lack of a special Canada-U.S. approach to African issues further underlines just how tenuous hybrid interregional relations are between Africa and North America, let alone within the Atlantic Basin exclusively.

It is evident that Canada has a "natural" interest in multilateralism as a means of conducting foreign and development policy stretching back decades. This of course makes hybrid interregionalism a distinct possibility, though as the ODA data clearly indicates, bilateral relations still remain predominant while most of the multilateral ties are with UN-related bodies rather than African. Yet multilateralism has also been of strategic interest since donor coordination is best done this way. Moreover regional organisations are identified by DFATD as often easier partners to work with since by their very nature they are set up to facilitate external funding.

There also remains the question of capacity for both Africa and Canada. For instance, the AU continues to grow both in size and ambition, but it is still a relatively young organisation. There are areas where funding is better targeted at the country level than the regional (DFATD interview 2015). Canada has also rationalised its own capacity in the area of development, cutting 15% of CIDA staff dealing with bilateral issues during the merger with the Department of Foreign Affairs in 2013. What's more, the Africa branch at DFATD has been amalgamated into one larger entity with less than a dozen trade commissioners stationed in sub-Saharan Africa (as opposed, for example, to twenty trade commissioners at the Canadian High Commission to the UK alone) (DFATD interview 2015).

6.4 Conclusions

The results of our survey of North American and African interregional relations are mixed, at best. Having established a generous framework of hybrid or quasi inter-regionalism – which to many regionalism scholars is a contested concept in itself – we have been able to show a pattern of growing relationships between the U.S. and some African regional organisations, particularly the AU. These relationships, however, are not necessarily the expression of a grand strategy for American engagement with African regional organisations. They also start from a low base and are unlikely to become the focus of U.S. foreign policy for the administration of President Donald Trump. Much the same applies for Canada, where an overarching strategy for interregionalism is absent, yet focus on regional entities in Africa or institutions such as the UN with interests on the continent is apparent.

In terms, however, of enhanced or formal North American cooperation in Africa, the results, at least in the field of development, are muted. As expected, there is little or no North American regionalism with a focus on Africa in development or even related areas such as trade, security, or governance. This does not mean that the U.S. and Canada fail to coordinate in areas of mutual interest on the continent. In fact both are usually together as part of a wider group of "like minded nations" in international fora and, as shown, at the AU joint partners group or the AfDB regional chairs grouping. Still, this ad hoc style does not represent anything more systematic for the moment.

Similarly, with respect to the existence of an Atlantic area, the results are inconclusive at best. None of the interviewed officials from the U.S. or Canada indicated a policy preference or trend for cooperation with Atlantic facing countries or regional organisations. No such pattern of interaction was discernible.

Still, rapidly changing circumstances are creating new opportunities for cooperation. For one, there has been an inexorable growth in African regionalism, not only at the continental level in the AU, but also at the level of RECs, with a demonstrated interest in continued regional integration. While the nation-state remains immutable in Africa, regionalism has never been stronger. This is particularly true about regional "actorness", with regional organisations increasingly perceived as attractive partners. The case of NEPAD is a telling one, with huge amounts of funding mobilised on a relatively quick time scale in the early twenty-first century as a response to the ambitions of a new generation of African leadership. The "Africa Rising" narrative, while contested in many circles, has also emboldened African actors, both bilateral and multilateral to take control of their own destiny (Akuffo 2012). This is evinced in the burgeoning growth of South-South relations and the perceived diminution of the importance of the Global North. Intra- and interregionalism *as process* is evident not just through relationships between regional organisations on the continent but also in terms of the legitimacy and prestige interaction with actors such as the U.S. bestows on organisations like the AU and NEPAD.

In terms of interregionalism *as strategy*, this study has revealed the utilitarian attractiveness of hybrid or quasi interregional relations in Africa for both the U.S. and Canada. Though bilateral programming remains predominant, there is an increasing realisation that Africa has developed some strong and transparent homegrown institutions that in some instances provide a superior conduit for external funding. Again, the importance and attractiveness of the AU as a (positive) work in progress is underlined here.

Looking forward, it might be possible to see strategies akin to the EU's 'complex interregionalism.' Hardacre and Smith define 'complex interregionalism' as the result of the EU's policy of differentiation between levels of relations (2014). Indeed bilateral relations do not necessary stand in opposition to inter-regionalism but rather can coexist. The U.S. and Canada will likely continue to pursue both bilateral and regional avenues of cooperation depending of the strategic goals for engagement and the policy area.

References

African Development Bank. (2015). Canada. http://www.afdb.org/en/topics-and-sectors/topics/partnerships/non-regional-member-countries/canada/. Accessed 04 Apr 2015.

African Union Commission. (2013). African Union Strategic Plan 2014–17. Addis Ababa.

Aggarwal, V., & Fogarty, E. (2006). The limits of Interregionalism: The EU and North America. In F. Söderbaum & L. Van Langenhove (Eds.), The EU as a global player (pp. 79–98). Abingdon: Routledge.

Akuffo, E. (2012). A New Love for Africa?. OpenCanada.org. Accessed 10 Oct 2014.

Akuffo, E. (2013). Canada's engagement with African regional peace and security architecture: Constructivist analysis and implications for policy. In R. Medhora & S. Yiagadeesen (Eds.), Canada-Africa relations (pp. 115–130). Waterloo: The Centre for International Governance Innovation.

Ayres, J., & Macdonald, M. (2015). Is North America Unravelling? Transformations of regionalism in North America. In S. Dosenrode (Ed.), Limits to regional integration (pp. 179–198). Farnham: Ashgate.

Bach, D. (Ed.). (1999). Regionalisation in Africa: Integration and disintegration. Bloomington: Indiana University Press.

Bach, D. (2013). Thick institutionalism vs lean integration – New regionalism in Africa. In C. Moore (Ed.), Regional integration and social cohesion; perspectives from the developing world (pp. 93–106). Brussels: P.I.E. Lang.

Baert, F., Scaramagli, T., & Söderbaum, F. (Eds.). (2014). Intersecting interregionalism. Dordrecht: Springer.

Barkely, R. L. (2009). AFRICOM: Security, development and humanitarian functions. New York: Nova Science Publishers, Inc.

Black, D. (2004). Canada and Africa: Activist aspirations in straitened circumstances. In I. Taylor & P. Williams (Eds.), Africa in international relations (pp. 136–154). Abingdon: Routledge.

Brown, C. (2013a). Canadian nation building in Africa: Building whose nation? In R. Medhora & S. Yiagadeesen (Eds.), Canada-Africa relations (pp. 79–89). Waterloo: The Centre for International Governance Innovation.

Brown, D. E. (2013b). AFRICOM at 5 Years: The Maturation of a New U.S. Combatant Command, Strategic Studies Institute and U.S. Army War College Press.

Brown, S. (2013c). Canadian aid to Africa. In R. Medhora & S. Yiagadeesen (Eds.), Canada-Africa relations (pp. 181–194). Waterloo: The Centre for International Governance Innovation.

Culpeper, R. (2013, April 8). CIDA merger links aid to trade and diplomacy. Toronto Star.

Department of Foreign Affairs, Trade and Development. (2012–13). Statistical Report on International Assistance.

Department of Foreign Affairs, Trade and Development. (2013). Harper Government Supports Regional Economic Development in Africa.

Department of Foreign Affairs, Trade and Development. (2014a). Pan Africa Regional Program. http://www.international.gc.ca/development-developpement/countries-pays/panafrica-pan-africain.aspx?lang=eng. Accessed 4 Apr 2015.

Department of Foreign Affairs, Trade and Development. (2014b). Promoting Democracy, Governance, Human Rights and Rule of Law. http://www.international.gc.ca/ss-africa-afrique-ss/pdghrrl-pdgdhpd.aspx?lang=eng. Accessed 4 Apr 2015.

Department of Foreign Affairs, Trade and Development. (2014c). Promoting Peace and Security. http://www.international.gc.ca/ss-africa-afrique-ss/peace_security-paix_securite.aspx?lang=eng. Accessed 5 Apr 2015.

Doidge, M. (2007). Joined at the hip: Regionalism and Interregionalism. Journal of European Integration, 29(2), 229–248.

Draper, P., Halleson D., & Alves, P. (2007). SACU, Regional integration and the overlap issue in Southern Africa: From Spaghetti to Cannelloni?. South African Institute of International Affairs.

ECOWAS Commission. (1999, 10 August). *ECOWAS, USAID Sign Agreement on West African Gas Project* – N°: 45/1999. Press Release. http://news.ecowas.int/presseshow.php?nb=45&lang=en&annee=1999. Accessed 24 Sept 2014.

ECOWAS Commission. (2000, 13 December). *USAID Boosts ECOWAS Power Pool Project* – N°: 108/2000. Press Release. http://news.ecowas.int/presseshow.php?nb=108&lang=en&annee=2000. Accessed 24 Sept 2014.

ECOWAS Commission. (2007, 14 September). *ECOWAS and USAID Sign Three Agreement Amendments for $24.65 Million Dollars to Support Regional Initiatives* – N°: 88/2007. Press Release. http://news.ecowas.int/presseshow.php?nb=88&lang=en&annee=2007. Accessed 24 Sept 2014.

ECOWAS Commission. (2012, 7 September). *ECOWAS, USAID to Strengthen Cooperation* – N°: 241/2012. Press Release. http://news.ecowas.int/presseshow.php?nb=241&lang=en&annee=2012. Accessed 24 Sept 2014.

ECOWAS Commission. (2014, 17 September). *ECOWAS, USAID Strengthen Cooperation for Regional Development and Stability* – N°: 162/2014. Press Release. http://news.ecowas.int/presseshow.php?nb=162&lang=en&annee=2014. Accessed 24 Sept 2014.

Elder, D. C. (2013). Canada's diplomacy in Africa. In R. Medhora & S. Yiagadeesen (Eds.), *Canada-Africa relations* (pp. 23–41). Waterloo: The Centre for International Governance Innovation.

G8 Summit Deauville. (2011). *Deauville accountability report G8 commitments on health and food security: State of delivery and results*.

G8 Summit Muskoka. (2010). Muskoka declaration: Recovery and new beginnings.

Hänggi, H. (2006). Interregionalism as a multifaceted phenomenon. In H. Hänggi, R. Roloff, & J. Ruland (Eds.), *Interregionalism and international relations* (pp. 31–62). London: Routledge.

Hardacre, A., & Smith, M. (2014). The European Union and the contradictions of complex interregionalism. In F. Baert, T. Scaramagli, & F. Söderbaum (Eds.), *Intersecting interregionalism* (pp. 91–106). Dordrecht: Springer Netherlands.

Interview with Canadian DFATD official, by telephone, 09/10/2014.

Interview with Canadian DFATD official, by telephone, 14/01/2015.

Interviews with U.S. officials 2014 and 2015.

Mballa, L.-V. (2009). A discreet look at Africa from Mexico. *Voices of Mexico, 84*, 79–81.

McDonald, S., Lande, S., & Matanda D. (2013). Beyond AGOA – An updated case for a Trans-Atlantic Trade & Investment Partnership between Africa and the United States. *Wilson Center & Manchester Trade*.

Mouline, S. (2013). 21st century regionalism: Where is Latin America Headed? *Council on Hemispheric Affairs*.

OECD. (2014). *Development co-operation report 2014: Mobilising Resources for Sustainable Development – United States*. OECD Publishing.

OECD. (2015). *StatExtracts. Aid (ODA) disbursements to countries and regions* [DAC2a].

Office of the United States Trade Representative. Africa. https://ustr.gov/countries-regions/africa. Accessed June 15 2015.

Reichle, S. (2010). Statement by Senior Deputy Assistant Administrator Susan G. Reichle, Bureau for Democracy, Conflict, and Humanitarian Assistance. In *U.S. Congress, Subcommittee on National Security and Foreign Affairs; Committee on Oversight and Government Reform, July 28, 2010*. http://www.usaid.gov/news-information/congressional-testimony/statement-senior-deputy-assistant-administrator-susan-g. Accessed 12 June 2015.

Rüland, J. (2006). Interregionalism: An unfinished agenda. In H. Hänggi, R. Roloff, & J. Rüland (Eds.), *Interregionalism and international relations* (pp. 295–313). London: Routledge.

Söderbaum, F. (2012). Theories of regionalism. In M. Beeson & R. Stubbs (Eds.), *The Routledge handbook of Asian regionalism* (pp. 11–21). Abingdon: Routledge.

Söderbaum, F. (2014). Introduction: Intersecting interregionalism. In F. Baert, T. Scaramagli, & F. Söderbaum (Eds.), *Intersecting interregionalism* (pp. 1–12). Dordrecht: Springer Netherlands.

The White House. (2012). *U.S. strategy toward Sub-Saharan Africa*.

The White House. (2014). *U.S.-Africa leaders Summit*. https://www.whitehouse.gov/us-africa-leaders-summit. Accessed 1 Mar 2016.

U.S. Agency for International Development. (2015a). *Central Africa Regional*. http://www.usaid.gov/central-africa-regional. Accessed 2 Feb 2015.

U.S. Agency for International Development. (2015b). *Sahel Regional*. http://www.usaid.gov/sahel-regional. Accessed 2 Feb 2015.

U.S. Agency for International Development. (2015c). *East Africa Regional*. http://www.usaid.gov/east-africa-regional. Accessed 2 Feb 2015.

U.S. Agency for International Development. (2015d). *Southern Africa Regional*. http://www.usaid.gov/southern-africa-regional. Accessed 2 Feb 2015.

U.S. Agency for International Development. (2015e). *West Africa Regional*. http://www.usaid.gov/west-africa-regional. Accessed 2 Feb 2015.

U.S. Department of State. (2010). *Leading through civilian power – The first quadrennial diplomacy and development review*.

U.S. Department of State. (2011). *The United States and the African Union – Fact sheet*. http://www.state.gov/r/pa/prs/ps/2011/04/161212.htm. Accessed 30 June 2014.

U.S. Government. (2015). *Feed the future – The U.S. Government's Global Hunger and Food Security Initiative*. http://www.feedthefuture.gov. Accessed 2 Feb 2015.

U.S. Government Document. (2011a). *Feed the future – EAST AFRICA FY 2011–2015 multi-year strategy*.

U.S. Government Document. (2011b). *Feed the future – West Africa FY 2011–2015 multi-year strategy*.

U.S. Mission to the African Union. US and EAC Promoting Regional Integration and Development. http://www.usau.usmission.gov/regional-integrity.html. Accessed 24 Sept 2014.

USAID. *Trade Africa.*. http://www.usaid.gov/tradeafrica. Accessed 2 Feb 2015.

Williams, P. D. (2015). Enhancing U.S. support for peace operations in Africa. *Council on Foreign Relations, Council Special Report No. 73*.

Wolff, P. (2010). US development policy: A strong player back on the map. *Deutsches Institut für Entwicklungspolitik*.

Chapter 7
EU-Latin American Relations as a Template for Interregionalism

Anna Ayuso and Gian Luca Gardini

Abstract The interregionalism between Latin America and the Caribbean and the European Union evolved for over 20 years. The complexities and overlapping of Latin American regionalisms are reflected in several interregional formal links between the two shores of the Atlantic characterized by a density and multiplicity of mechanisms and forums, involving a diversity of actors – from states to NGOs, from regional organizations to business and institutional bodies. This constitutes a multi-layered network of agreements, summits and other cooperation mechanisms that is the result of the interplay between the development of the regionalist phenomenon and the dynamics of globalization. This is one reason why the EU-LAC interregion-alism can be considered a sort of template in practice for the conceptualizations of, and theorizing about interregionalism, as it illustrates all the three prototypes identi-fied by Hanggi: mechanisms of pure interregionalism, transregionalism and hybrid interregionalism. In this chapter we discuss; first, the historical evolution of the EU-LAC interregional relations. Second, we concentrate on the four existing cases of interregionalism with LAC sub-regional organizations. Third, we analyze the region-to-region summits between the EU and the 33 LAC countries. Finally, we draw conclusions about the dynamics of EU-LAC.

Keywords Atlantic • Interregionalism • Regional organisations • Regionalism • Regions

A. Ayuso (✉)
Barcelona Centre for International Affairs (CIDOB), Barcelona, Spain
e-mail: aayuso@cidob.org

G.L. Gardini
Friedrich-Alexander-University of Erlangen-Nürnberg, Erlangen, Germany
e-mail: gian.luca.gardini@fau.de

© Springer International Publishing AG 2018
F. Mattheis, A. Litsegård (eds.), *Interregionalism across the Atlantic Space*,
United Nations University Series on Regionalism 15,
DOI 10.1007/978-3-319-62908-7_7

7.1   Introduction

Formal and institutionalized interregional relations between the European Union (EU) and its predecessor the European Economic Communities (EEC) on the one hand, and Latin American and Caribbean countries (LAC) on the other, are well established and have been in place for over 20 years. Broader political and cultural links between the two regions have a history of centuries. The formal links between regional organizations on the two shores of the Atlantic are characterized by a density and multiplicity of mechanisms and forums, involving a diversity of actors – from states to NGOs, from regional organizations to business and institutional bodies – that constitute a multilayered network of agreements, summits and other cooperation mechanisms. This is essentially the result of the interplay between the development of the regionalist phenomenon and the dynamics of globalization.

There is indeed a debate on whether interregionalism is a by-product of the proliferation of regionalisms or a response to increasing interdependence and globalization. In fact the question is ill posed, at least in the case of the EU-LAC interregionalism, as this is clearly the result of both forces. This is a first reason why the EU-LAC interregionalism can be considered a textbook case of interregionalism. On the one hand, the mushrooming of regional cooperation and attempts at integration in Latin America, coupled with the successes and strength of the EU partly explain the complexity of this case of interregionalism. On the other hand, the desire of the EU to present itself internationally as a global actor, has led Brussels to promote its own institutional and political model in other regions of the world and later on to relate with these areas through instutionalized region-to-region mechanisms, or – better said – on a regional organization to regional organization basis.

About the proliferation of regionalisms and their impact on the interregionalist phenomenon, it is relevant to note the multiplicity of Latin American regional organizations. This is in stark contrast with what happens in Europe, where the European Union is the only game in town. Or at least other organizations and forums, such as the European Free Trade Association or the Council of Europe, are currently compatible with or subservient to the EU and its goals. In Latin America, a plethora of competing organizations and schemes purport to pursue Latin American unity and integration but in fact they result in diversity and fragmentation if not in outright divergence (Gardini 2010). This specific aspect of Latin American regionalism has of course had an impact on the features of the EU-LAC interregionalism, and is itself as much the result of history as it is of politics.

The variety of LAC regionalisms is explained not only by the different national interests and development strategies that characterize Latin America today. Most of all, Latin American regional organizations were established in three different historical phases and are the product of the values and ideals prevailing in each of those periods. Each phase added new organizations to the existing ones, often without dissolving or adapting the more obsolete or less effective of them. In the 1960s and 1970s the so called "closed regionalism" model brought into existence the Latin American Free Trade Association (LAFTA), the Central American Common Market (CACM), the Andean Community (CAN) and the Caribbean Community

(CARICOM). In the 1990s, the wave of so called "open regionalism" led to the creation of the North American Free Trade Area (NAFTA), the Common Market of the South (MERCOSUR) and the reform of the Andean Community. As this model was increasingly questioned in the new millennium, a new set of organizations was created between 2004 and 2012, such as the Bolivarian Alliance for the Americas (ALBA), the Union of South American Nations (UNASUR), the Community of Latin American and Caribbean States (CELAC) and the Pacific Alliance (PA).

Given the impossibility of finding one single regional interlocutor in Latin America, the European Union has almost necessarily had to establish several mechanisms of dialogue and cooperation with some of these organizations. Since the EU started institutionalized region-to-region relations with Latin America between the late 1980s and the 1990s, it established relations with those Latin American and Caribbean organizations that it deemed most representative of the continent at that time. For this reason, the EU took the initiative and created interregional mechanisms with all the thirty-three Latin American and Caribbean countries (EU-LAC summits, now EU-CELAC) and also with the most significant sub-regional organizations. So we now also have an EU-MERCOSUR, an EU-Central America, an EU-Andean Community, and an EU-CARICOM summit or interregional arrangement. At present there are no interregional mechanisms between the EU and the Latin American sub-regional organizations created in the twenty-first century. The shortcoming of the present system, as well this fast-changing regional equilibria within Latin America, call for a revision of the EU-LAC interergionalism.

A second reason why the EU-LAC interregionalism can be considered a sort of template in practice for the conceptualizations of, and theorizing about interregionalism is that it meets or illustrates all the relevant theoretical points (see Malamud and Gardini in this book). First, EU-LAC interregionalism presents all three prototypes identified by Hanggi (2000). That is to say that there are forms/mechanisms of pure interregionalism, transregionalism and hybrid interregionalism, as we will discuss in the following sections. Second, EU-LAC interregionalism is largely characterized by summits, which constitute the pinnacle of the bi-regional relation and set the pace and political agenda for most of the other complementary mechanisms. Third, EU-LAC interregionalism shows all the identified patterns of interregional behavior: on the political level, the major partner (the EU) displays leadership while the junior partner (LAC) largely responds with emulation. On the socio-economic plane, the major partner has traditionally provided cooperation. More recently, and with the maturity of the interregional relationship, the fast-changing global context, and the evolution of regional circumstances in both Latin America and Europe, the bi-regional dealings have taken the form of a more balanced exchange, characterized increasingly by trade rather than aid.

The chapter unfolds as follows. In Sect. 7.2, we discuss the historical evolution of the EU-LAC interregional relations. In Sect. 7.3, we concentrate on the four existing cases of interregionalism where the EU deals with LAC sub-regional organizations. In Sect. 7.4, we analyze the region-to-region mechanism, basically in the form of summitry, between the EU and the 33 LAC countries, emphasizing the innovations and challenges of the newly created EU-CELAC format. Finally, we draw conclusions about the dynamics of EU-LAC interregional relations.

7.2   The Evolution of the Bi-regional Relations

Relations between Europe and LAC have a long and deep-seated history. Latin America was colonized primarily by Spain and Portugal, and events that took place in Europe, such as the Napoleonic wars, were at the root of Latin American independence in the early nineteenth century. Up until the end of the First World War the wealth of many LAC countries, for example Argentina, was dependent upon commercial ties with European powers, particularly Great Britain (Brown 2008). Following the Second World War and with the onset of the Cold War, European former colonial powers lost their status as world powers and relations with Latin American were put on the back burner.

The establishment of the European Economic Community in 1957 did little to reverse this trend, and LAC increasingly became a side-line in EU international affairs. However, when Spain and Portugal joined the EU in 1986, interregional relations took on a new verve, with European political and economic presence reaching new heights. LAC did not become a priority area for the EU; quite the contrary in fact. Nonetheless, in its quest for a global player status the EU has adopted a rather active and dynamic position regarding LAC (Gardini 2012).

The process of democratic transition in the region experienced during the 1980s and 1990s fuelled the re-launch of the LAC integration projects and led to a process of sub-regionalization of the relationship of the European Community institutions with LAC. This started with the creation of the San José dialogue between the European Community (EC) and Central America in 1984 in support to the Regional Peace Process and was intensified from 1987 with the dialogue between the EC and the Rio Group that was institutionalized in 1990. In the 1980s the first agreements between the EEC and LAC regional organizations were formalized, first with the Andean Group in 1983 and then with the CACM in 1985. These are first examples of traditional or pure interregionalism, that is formal regional organization to formal regional organization.

With the second regionalist wave and the "open regionalism" initiatives in LAC the EU support for regional integration processes became one of the pillars of the bi-regional relationship. This included a preference for bargaining collectively with existing bodies and the development of sub-regional cooperation strategies with those blocks. The strategic partnership launched in 1999 by the Heads of State and Government of LAC and the EU aimed at consolidating a space for political cooperation and inter-regional cooperation complemented by the gradual establishment of a Euro-Latin American free trade area. Europe tried to distance itself from a purely commercial approach and promote a regulatory role incorporating three dimensions: political, through multilevel dialogues; economic, including trade and investment; and development cooperation, incorporating social policies. The political dialogue institutionalised in the EU-LAC Summits and the EU-Rio Group Summits are examples of transregionalism, bringing together a formal regional organization (the EU) and a quite loose group of states from one region (LAC countries acting individually).

The strategic partnership between EU and LAC was developed not only as a top-down process lead by governmental agencies but integrates multiple consultation mechanisms and frameworks that incorporate relations between social partners and parliamentarians and a large number of actors forming a multilevel relationship. The existence of such dense social network is a specific quality pattern of the EU dialogue with LAC. Another particularity of EU-LAC cooperation is the horizontality through the so-called decentralized cooperation programs that put into direct contact institutions and actors of both regions.

At the beginning of the twenty-first century a new generation of Latin American regionalism emerged with more flexible features. Stressing social policies instead of trade-related issues, this wave was labelled as "post-liberal regionalism" (Sanahuja 2013). At the political level, the creation of CELAC in 2011 introduced a new framework for dialogues. It aims to harmonize the dialogues at different levels, including bilateral strategic partnerships with Mexico and Brazil and possibly the incorporation of new significant regional groupings in Latin America such as UNASUR and the Pacific Alliance. Starting with the 2013 Santiago de Chile Summit, the biannual EU-LAC Summits were replaced by EU-CELAC Summits. The international and regional scenarios of the twenty-first century are quite different from those that generated the current EU-LAC model of relation. At the commercial level, the entry into force of the free trade agreements between the EU and CARICOM, Central America, Colombia and Peru, as well as the renegotiation of existing agreements with Mexico and Chile and the new agreement with Ecuador frame a new map of agreements. These achievements contrast with the lack of progress in the negotiations with MERCOSUR. This picture should also be analyzed in the context of the negotiations for a Trans-Atlantic Partnership between the EU, Canada and the US (the TTIP) and the lack of momentum in the WTO negotiations. The future of the Atlantic space and its governance also depend on these developments.

In terms of development cooperation, the twenty-first century accelerated changes that have altered the relationship between the developing world and the traditional powers. The incorporation of heterogeneous actors, new instruments and forms of cooperation, new standards of quality and greater accountability in relation to the results of political action have all brought in significant innovation. Changes have also concerned the agenda after the end of the cycle of the Millennium Development Goals (MDGs). Participatory processes of regional, national and thematic scope of the post-2015 agenda have affected the meaning of mutual responsibility and the role of the traditional Official Development Assistance. New approaches to cooperation seem to distinguish emerging powers and middle-income countries, as well as various forms of South-South and triangular cooperation that have been proliferating in LAC with Brazilian leadership (Ayllon et al. 2014).The EU-CELAC relationship can no longer be conceived as a strictly North-South link as in the past. This is not only because of the emergence of Latin American powers, but also because many of the new EU member states have similar per capita income levels to those of some LAC countries, and cannot be considered traditional donors (Ayuso and Villar 2014a, b).

7.3   Interregionalism Between the EU and LAC Sub-regions

Interregional EU-LAC relations build on very diverse experiences of and approaches to regional cooperation. Like other approaches to the governance of interdependence, interregionalism encompasses political interactions, formal institutional relations, material transactions and cultural exchanges among the parties (Garzón 2015). Given the trends towards fragmented or modular regionalism in LAC (Gardini 2015), group-to-group institutional dialogue – in Hänggi's words, 'pure interregionalism' (Hänggi 2000) – comprise EU-LAC relations as well as relations between the EU and sub-regional cooperation schemes. This section studies the variety of EU-LAC institutionalised interregional relations focusing on: EU-SICA, EU-CAN, EU-CARICOM, and EU-MERCOSUR. The format of relation that the EU offers to these LAC sub-regions is based on three pillars: political dialogue, economic exchanges, and development aid. For all four cases, the bi-annual political summit represents the pinnacle of the relationship. While these case studies embody the Hänggi prototype of pure interregionalism, the practice of EU-LAC interregionalism involves LAC region-wide organizations such as CELAC, LAC sub-regional organizations, and individual LAC countries. This way EU-LAC interregionalism in practice comprises all of Hanggi's prototypes: pure interregionalism, transregionalism and hybrid interregionalism.

7.3.1   EU and Central America

The relations between the EU and Central America are probably the more advanced of the EU support to LAC regional integration. The 1984 San Jose process pioneered the EU political dialogue with the region. The San José dialogue is now incorporated – as one of three pillars – in the new Partnership Agreement signed in 2010. This Partnership agreement is evidence of the EU commitment to Central American integration. It includes mechanisms to address asymmetries both between the two regions and within Central America, but its effectiveness has yet to be assessed in practice. Cooperation on trade issues to promote liberalization has been added to an increased contribution to regional programs, including new funding for a Support Regional Integration Fund.

The cooperation pillar in the Central America Strategy 2007–2013 continued the traditional institutional support linked to trade issues (creation of the customs union, adoption of international standards, legislative harmonization, investments promotion, intellectual property protection and harmonization of fiscal policies), but also included democracy, human rights and security, and measures to mitigate the impact of the free movement of goods, capital and persons.In fact, in the new Latin American regional program 2014–2020, Central America is the only integration process maintaining its specific regional program.

The first pillar of the regional programme is primarily intended to deepen economic integration through the harmonization and implementation of regulatory policies, standards and statistics, support for intra and extra regional trade, promotion of SMEs, improving infrastructure and promoting regional productive value chains. However, the most important trading partner for Central America is the United States. The second pillar includes prevention against violence with special attention to vulnerable groups; reintegration and social rehabilitation, strengthening law enforcement and operational regional cooperation and promoting a culture of peace among citizens. The third pillar focuses on adaptation to climate change and regional risk management and disaster reduction in Central America, a region particularly affected by such threats.

7.3.2 EU and Andean Community

The Andean Pact, created in 1969, was the integration process in LAC with most similarities with the EEC. Its institutional and legal structures were developed in parallel (De Lombaerde et al. 2008) but differed as the CAN institutional structure remained intergovernmental, and internal and communitarian laws were kept separate. The failure of the import substitution policies, the effects of the debt crisis in LAC in the 1980s and the political instability in the member states contributed to stall the project for a decade. Following the new dynamics of open regionalism in the 1990s, the Trujillo Protocol (1996) was a new starting point for the Andean Community of Nations (CAN) towards the establishment of a free trade zone but also to improve integration in international markets.

Negotiations for an EU-CAN association agreement were launched in 2007, just after the signature of the Free Trade Agreement (FTA) between Colombia and Peru with the US. These two negotiations of FTA with the EU and the US entailed the withdrawal of Venezuela over economic policy divergences from the CAN in 2006 and its application for membership to MERCOSUR. The initial scheme for the EU-CAN negotiating process as "bloc to bloc" was maintained with the four remaining CAN members for the development cooperation and political dialogue pillars. But trade negotiations failed, as Bolivia left the talks and Ecuador followed suit. Thus, two bilateral trade agreements with Colombia and Peru were signed in 2010 in a transregional scheme. This was an achievement for the extension of the EU map of trade agreements but it also can be seen as a failure in the EU inter-regionalist strategy with the CAN. However, a trade agreement was eventually achieved in 2014 with Ecuador.

Currently the CAN integration process is threatened. After Venezuela, Bolivia also signed an adhesion agreement with MERCOSUR, but without leaving the CAN. Ecuador is now negotiating its accession to MERCOSUR, whereas Colombia and Peru are part of the newly created Pacific Alliance. The creation of the Pacific Alliance highlighted political differences among the four members of the CAN. The competition between the open model of liberalization of the Pacific Alliance and the protectionist model of MERCOSUR weakened the CAN integration process. Even if EU-CAN trade relations have grown in recent years with a positive balance of payments for the Andean countries, the main trading partner of CAN remains the United States. Except Bolivia, whose main markets are Brazil and Argentina, the EU is gradually being displaced from the second place by China. The dynamism of the Pacific Alliance and the interest of the two fastest growing countries of the CAN, Colombia and Peru, in the Asian market have devalued the relationship with the EU, which seems to be doomed to languish. The legal framework for EU-CAN cooperation and political dialogue still depends on the Agreement adopted in 2003, which is pending for the ratification by some European countries. Changes in the EU development policy resulted in the ineligibility of Colombia, Peru and Ecuador for bilateral cooperation under the 2014–2020 EU Cooperation Program. Only Bolivia remains an eligible country for bilateral cooperation but paradoxically it is the only CAN country that has no FTA with the EU.

This loss of importance in the EU-CAN relations may be partially offset by European involvement in the Peace Process in Colombia and by the growing priority of the security issues related to drug trafficking and transnational crimes for the EU. A specialized Drugs High Level Dialogue CAN-EU exists since 1995 to exchange best practices and enhance further cooperation, co-existing with the Coordination and Cooperation on Drugs Mechanism between the EU and LAC. This will continue to be an axis for stronger co-operation but the security cooperation bodies created in UNASUR will probably acquire a more prominent role at the expense of CAN.

7.3.3   EU and CARICOM

Overlapping cooperation schemes exist in the Caribbean reflecting the political diversity of this space (Sutton 2012) composed of 12 island sovereign states and different dependent territories including Overseas Countries or Territories (OCT) linked to European countries (France, United Kingdom and Netherlands) and islands dependent from border countries (Belize, Colombia, Honduras, Mexico, Nicaragua, Panama, US and Venezuela). The small size of these territories and the diverse colonial past caused a fractioned regionalism. Currently the main organizations are the Organization of Eastern Caribbean States (OECS) created in 1981 and the CARICOM created in 1973 and reformed in 2001 to create a future single market.

The CARICOM 15 member countries have a total population of just 16.5 million, representing a very small proportion of LAC. The small size makes these countries sensitive to external fluctuations. Trade with the rest of LAC is low and a negative trade balance of payments is a shared trend. The role of the US in the Caribbean economies is crucial and the EU has a much less relevant position. Only in three cases (Belize, Guyana and Suriname) the EU represents over 10% of the total trade and only with the first one does it supersede the US. Furthermore, the EU faces competition of other Latin American countries, such as Mexico and Brazil, for investment opportunities and trade.

Despite weak economic links, historical and cultural relations between the EU members and the Caribbean are strong. Sixteen Caribbean countries are part of the African, Caribbean and Pacific (ACP) group. This group was created in 1975 by the European Economic Community to establish a strategic partnership through cooperation programs and priority access to European markets. After the British adhesion to the EEC, this agreement added the Caribbean countries to the "Regime of Association" started previously with the African countries. Currently, bi-regional relations are largely framed under the 2000 Cotonou Agreement. Political dialogue is held at different formal and informal levels and geographic and/or sectorial levels. It includes High-level summits, ministerial meetings, parliamentary meetings and civil society encounters. The EU political dialogue is channeled through CARIFORUM, a political consultation Group established in 1992 that incorporates Cuba, not belonging to the Cotonou Agreement.

The Economic Partnership Agreement (EPA) between the EU and CARIFORUM was signed in 2008. It removes all tariffs and quotas from Caribbean exports to the EU. Caribbean countries offer a gradual opening of markets over a period of 25 years, but they are allowed to exclude sensitive products and industries. Improved rules of origin intend to have positive effects on the development of industries to export products to Europe. The implementation of the EPA has been difficult and with important delays in a context of the EU crisis and the economic downturn in most Caribbean states (Byron 2014). EU-Caribbean cooperation priorities however have to be coordinated now with the most recent overarching EU-CELAC Action Plan. Constituting 42% of CELAC membership in terms of numbers of countries, the Caribbean sub-region has a real chance to enhance its role and bargaining power within LAC and in its relations with the EU.

7.3.4 EU and MERCOSUR

The MERCOSUR area has the strongest and deepest historical and cultural bonds with Europe. It is thus unsurprising that this area also has the strongest political and economic ties with the EU. The EU has always assisted MERCOSUR as part of its support strategy for regional integration schemes elsewhere in the world, and by 1992, within a year of its creation, the EU had made an agreement to supply the newly formed South American bloc with technical assistance. Although a possible EU–MERCOSUR association agreement is in the pipeline, relations between the two blocs at the moment are amply regulated by the 1995 Framework Agreement for Inter-regional Cooperation, which covers three fields: political dialogue, cooperation and commercial issues.

Political dialogue took shape in 1996 and includes meetings between heads of state and government, ministers and diplomats. These meetings usually take place in tandem with the EU–LAC summits (now CELAC) to save time and economic resources. The key themes on the current agenda are the conclusion of the EU–MERCOSUR association agreement, better coordination of positions in multilateral fora, and intensification of cooperation in innovation and technology. Sub-regional cooperation, which is a complement to EU cooperation with individual member states in MERCOSUR, concentrates on assistance to help complete the common market of MERCOSUR and reinforce regional institutions and civil society. In particular, EU funds were used to support the MERCOSUR secretariat and the conflict resolution instrument, as well as measures for harmonization in the customs, statistical, veterinary and macroeconomic sectors. The EU is MERCOSUR's main trade partner: it accounts for nearly 20% of the bloc's commercial relations; the EU is also a major exporter of commercial services to MERCOSUR, as well as the biggest foreign investor in the region (DG Trade 2015).

Given their political and economic links, it seemed logical for the EU and MERCOSUR to strengthen their exchanges by concluding an association agreement and creating a free trade area. Talks that had begun in 1999 ground to a halt in 2004. The EU decided to re-launch the negotiations in 2010. There were multiple and complex reasons for this lack of progress between 2004 and 2010. As well as the changing international situation, particularly the shifting trends and equilibriums in trade surpluses, it is important to note that the bilateral association agreement was closely linked with multilateral negotiations on similar topics within the World Trade Organization. The multilateral draft under discussion at the WTO was more favourable to MERCOSUR countries than the EU bilateral proposal. For this reason, the parties prioritized multilateral discussions, at least until 2006, when the collapse of the Doha Round provided a possible incentive to re-engage in bilateral dialogue. However, other difficulties persisted.

The European Commission's own estimates confirm that a potential liberalization, whether partial or complete, would have relatively more positive effects for the EU than for MERCOSUR. This can be explained by the fact that over 60% of products that MERCOSUR countries export to the EU are already free from import duty. This is true for both industrial and agricultural products. On the other hand, the EU's most important export sectors (automotive, transport components, mechanical and electrical products) are subject to relatively high customs duties when entering MERCOSUR. Considering that the EU also has an undeniable comparative advantage in services and investments, the inclusion of these sectors in the free trade agreement linked to the association agreement would be another advantage for Europe. More importantly, the EU Common Agricultural Policy, through which European farmers are subsidised, is perceived as an obstacle to negotiations by MERCOSUR members. Yet, for both economic and social/environmental reasons, both fair and justified it has to be said, the EU does not seem inclined to make significant concessions in this domain.

The re-launch of negotiations in 2010 was due to a number of reasons but a conclusion is not within reach yet. First, the rise of China forces the EU to look for new markets to compete globally and to defend more effectively its market quota abroad. China also offers MERCOSUR countries an alternative trade partner to the US and the EU, thus increasing their leverage with the latter. Secondly, the stalemate of multilateral negotiations at the WTO seems endless, which increases the convenience of the bi-regional option to both parties. Thirdly, the global crisis that shook the EU hard requires strategies to reactivate growth and employment, and fostering trade relations with MERCOSUR may be part of such a strategy. Fourthly, Brazil's rise ought to produce tangible results in terms of commercial expansion. The Lula and Dilma administrations were unable to produce any significant preferential trade agreement but it is in the area of trade that big powers and would-be ones will increasingly compete globally. With the changed mood in Brazil under Temer uncertainty prevails.

7.4 From EU-LAC Summits to the EU-CELAC Format

Historically there have been two official mechanisms for interregional political dialogue between Europe and Latin America: EU–LAC summits and EU–Rio Group summits. The first are biennial bilateral meetings between heads of state and government to identify the basic drivers and priorities for the bi-regional relationship. The first summit took place in Rio de Janeiro in 1999. The 2010 Madrid Summit may well have marked the end of an era and a cooperation model. With the creation of CELAC in 2011, and the first EU-CELAC Summit, celebrated in Santiago de Chile in January 2013, Latin America and the Caribbean now attempt to speak with one voice in international venues. This is meant to increase the global weight of Latin America and to make it heavier than that of sub-regional groupings (Appelgren 2013). The second mechanism, the EU–Rio Group summits of ministers, used to take place every 2 years, alternating with the EU–LAC summits. Now both mechanisms are incorporated in the new EU-CELAC system.

The first element that has to be kept in mind is that CELAC is a political project (Bonilla 2013). This means that CELAC is not meant to produce direct economic benefit but to pursue political objectives and coordination. Interestingly, CELAC has been perceived as a promising step both by Latin Americans and international partners. Europeans have stressed in fact how CELAC provides a framework to work with everyone in Latin America, and therefore to overcome regional complexities and sub-regional fragmentation (Schafer 2013). CELAC indeed provides an umbrella framework for all the EU-Latin American and Caribbean regional and sub-regional dialogues, with the latter now taking place at the fringes of the main political event thus saving time, human and financial resources.

The EU-CELAC interregional mechanism also responds to a fast changing international scenario (Sanahuja 2013). EU-LAC institutionalized bi-regional relations started in the 1980s, in a context of Cold War, conflict in Central America, and democratic transition. Today, distribution of power and wealth are significantly different. The North Atlantic area is losing importance while the Asia-Pacific is rising. New partners are available for both Europe and Latin America and the EU itself seems to be less important to Latin America. In this sense, the new format of EU-CELAC Summit may offer an opportunity to rethink EU-LAC interregionalism.

Yet, CELAC embodies all the contradictions of Latin American and Caribbean regionalisms and attempts at unity (Ayuso 2015). CELAC can be seen as a response to a changing context but also as a counter-hegemonic project in opposition to the US and the US-led Organization of American States. While diversity of members is taken as a given, the ability to reach significant consensus on issues with practical impact remains to be seen. Some members favour institutionalization and others prefer a loose and flexible structure. While CELAC boosted an Action Plan to develop economic relations with China, only a few members have actively opened their economies towards Asia while for instance MERCOSUR countries have so far resisted.

The first two EU-CELAC Summits confirmed the problems that all summitry exercise have, in particular the ability to deliver concrete measures (Maihold 2010, Whitehead and Barahona de Brito 2005). In 2013, the Santiago Summit produced a final Declaration in 48 points, while the 2015 Brussels Declaration comprised 77 points. These are hardly lists of priorities. Besides limited practical results, summitry often poses problems to leaders, diplomatic services and domestic constituencies in terms of time, energy, money, opportunity cost and a swollen, diluted agenda. Yet, the EU-CELAC mechanism is an effort to address the challenges facing the two regions. It reflects the need for structured dialogue at the highest political level, and it is certainly perfectible. Most of all, the format of the summit, including several sectoral collateral summits, seems to reflect a genuine societal demand that goes beyond government agendas.

Both the 2013 and the 2015 EU-CELAC Summits brought together societal actors and state bodies other than the executives. In spite of the costs associated and other criticisms, this is a laudable step to reduce the democratic deficit and involve an ampler sample of the institutional spectrum from the two regions. On the fringes of the main political summit, a business summit and an academic summit fostered dialogue between significant stakeholders from civil society. The parliamentary summit and the Courts of Justice summit involved the other key branches of the state in the process. Demand for these parallel events stemmed from those involved and their desire to shape the bi-regional relation. The tangible effects on the main political event may be limited. In 2015, several leaders, especially from Latin America, objected to start the opening plenary with the recommendations from civil society meetings. While this shows the complex interaction among stakeholders of the bi-regional relation, these difficulties do not diminish the potential value of this pluralistic and inclusive format.

7.5   Conclusions

Four tentative conclusions can be made about the dynamics of EU-LAC interregional relations.

Firstly, interregional dynamics with the European Union reflect the complexities and fragmentation of LAC regionalism. The EU had to establish several sub-regional mechanisms of political dialogue and economic relations due to the variety of sub-regional integration schemes in Latin America and the Caribbean. Historically the interregional dynamics have been propelled by the EU and have essentially reflected its priority and vision, including incentives and concrete policy in favour of the deepening of regional integration. This is consistent with the theoretical argument that, at the political level, the major partner (the EU) exercises a leadership role while the junior partner (LAC) is more of an emulator. Interestingly, and following European priorities and needs, civil society has been more directly involved in EU-LAC interregional mechanisms than in LAC regionalism. This also contributes to explain the great variety of actors involved in EU-LAC interregionalism. With the creation of CELAC and the maturity of the bi-regional relationship, Latin America and the Caribbean are bound to play a more proactive role, especially in terms of agenda setting, in interregional relations with Europe. This also is consistent with the theoretical expectations that in socioeconomic matters the junior partner will assume more responsibility with time.

Secondly, in theoretical terms, EU-LAC interregionalism fits Hänggi's model in all its dimensions: pure interregionalism, transregionalism and hybrid interregionalism. This can be observed at the three levels of relations that the EU offers to LAC countries: political dialogue, trade, and cooperation. At the level of political dialogue, EU relations with MERCOSUR, SICA and CARICOM are examples of pure interregionalism; EU-LAC Summits before CELAC and EU-Rio Group Summits are examples of trasregionalism, where LAC countries acted individually within a regional loose framework vis-à-vis a regional organization, the EU; the EU strategic partnerships with Mexico and Brazil provide examples of hybrid interregionalism. At the trade level, bi-regional agreements with SICA and CARIFORUM and negotiations with MERCOSUR are examples of regional organization to regional organization relations, which is pure interregionalism; FTA agreements with CAN members Colombia, Peru and Ecuador are examples of transregionalism; bilateral agreements EU-Chile and EU-Mexico are hybrid cases. At the level of development cooperation, the EU-Central America regional plan is a form of pure interregionalism while EU bilateral country programs with less developed countries are cases of hybrid regionalism; the transregional form is more problematic at this level and paves the way to a broader discussion about CELAC.

Thirdly, the case of CELAC falls between pure interregionalism, transregionalism and possibly new forms of interregionalism. On the one hand, CELAC is an attempt to give Latin America a unitary voice in its relations with global partners, not only the EU but also China and others in the near future. In this sense, the EU-CELAC Summit may be seen as a case of regional organization to regional organization relations, or pure interregionalism. On the other hand however, practice reveals that CELAC has no juridical personality and no real institutional structure, such as a secretariat, and the body speaking on behalf of the members with a single voice, the pro-tempore-presidency, has no power to commit the member states or the organization as such. In this sense, EU-CELAC relations can be understood as a case of transregionalism, where a regional organization, the EU, deals with a group of states acting individually, although with some degree of coordination. Or, alternatively, EU-CELAC summits can be seen as a new form of interregionalism that reflects the evolution and peculiarities of LAC regional processes. This perspective helps remove an EU-centric vision of regionalism and interregionalism, and opens a space to new varieties emerging as results of developments and concepts in regions other than Europe.

Fourthly, the summitry dimension is an inescapable element of EU-LAC interregionalism. Theoretically, the processes of regionalization and globalization, limiting the control of nation states on their own policy choices encourage states to engage in interregional cooperation. Also, rhetorical commitments produce actual effects (Schimmelfennig 2003). So, political support for interregionalism, as expressed in final declarations and political statements, reinforces and propels the interregional mechanisms. Perhaps more convincingly, the multi-bilateralism approach (Hill and Smith 2011; Le Gloannec 2004) suggests that interregional summits actually provide convenient venues to take forward bilateral affairs and agendas. In addition to theoretical explanations, there are very practical and pragmatic reasons for the resilience and flourishing of interregional summits. Firstly, they provide a forum for discussion and political direction in interregional relations. Secondly, with the increase and diversification of regional organizations and aggregations, interregionalism is a logical step to connect new regional actors, powers and agendas. Thirdly, in spite of constant complains about exclusion, civil society demand for and participation in interregional summits legitimizes their existence and continuation.

For all these four reasons, EU-LAC interregionalism is a perfect template in the practice of international affairs of all the theoretical arguments developed by International Relations as a discipline. The tension between regional and global forces and developments, the applicability of Hänggi's prototypes, the importance of summits, as well as the predictable behavior of the major and junior partner in political and socioeconomic domains are all reflected in EU-LAC interregional relations. This is perhaps one of the few cases in which theory and practice almost fully meet in the political and social sciences.

Overall, the rhetoric of shared values and principles underpinning EU-LAC interregional relations, and more broadly cross-Atlantic relations, collides with a reality full of nuances, in which both regions seek to enhance their place in the world. The relative decline of the EU and the rise of LAC, and the periphery overall, in the international system, may have a significant impact on the future of the Atlantic. On the one hand, their dynamic will foster a new balance of power, including agenda setting power and the ability to spread values, across the four shores of the Atlantic. On the other hand, these shifts will affect mechanisms of interregional relations across the Atlantic. With specific reference to EU-LAC interregionalism, "over the years, the two sides have progressively built up a broad-based relationship of equals" (EEAS 2014). This statement suggests that the goal of an equal partnership has been an incremental process. The goal now seems to be within reach.

References

Appelgren, C. E. (2013). CELAC, Desafío y riqueza de la diversidad. In M. S. Ortiz (Ed.), *La Diplomacia de las Cumbres: Retos y Oportunidades de los nuevos Regionalismos* (pp. 41–48). San José: FLACSO.

Ayllón, B., Ojeda, T., & Surasky, J. (Eds.). (2014). *Cooperación Sur-sur. Regionalismos e Integración en América Latina*. Madrid: Los libros de la Catarata and Instituto Universitario de Desarrollo y Cooperación- UCM.

Ayuso, A. (2015). Los dilemas existenciales de la CELAC, Opinión CIDOB, n°. 301, http://www.cidob.org/publicaciones/serie_de_publicacion/opinion/america_latina/los_dilemas_existenciales_de_la_celac, Accessed 5 Feb 2016.

Ayuso, A., & Villar, S. (2014a). Integration processes in Latin America *CGR Gulf Papers*, Gulf Research Centre-Geneva-/October, pp. 22 http://www.grc.net/index.php?frm_module=contents&frm_action=detail_book&frm_type_id=&pub_type=11&publ_id=16&sec=Contents&frm_title=Research%20Papers&book_id=85009&op_lang=en&sec_type=h&publ_type=54, Accesed 22 February 2016.

Ayuso, A., & Villar, S. (2014b). Latin America, the Caribbean and Central and Eastern Europe: potential for the economic exchange. EU-LAC Foundation, March, pp. 69 https://eulacfoundation.org/en/documents/latin-america-caribbean-and-central-and-eastern-europe-potential-economic-exchange, Accessed 22 Feb 2016.

Bonilla, A. (2013). Genética y naturaleza de la CELAC. In M. S. Ortiz (Ed.), *La Diplomacia de las Cumbres: Retos y Oportunidades de los nuevos Regionalismos* (pp. 101–106). San José: FLACSO.

Brown, M. (Ed.) (2008). *Informal empire in Latin America: Culture, commerce, and capital*. Wiley-Blackwell.

Byron, J. (2014). A Caribbean perspective on regionalism: What role for CELAC? *Revista Cubana de Economía Internacional*, n° 3.

De Lombaerde, P., et al. (Eds.). (2008). *Del regionalismo latinoamericano a la integración interregional*. Madrid: Siglo XXI y Fundación Carolina.

DG Trade. (2015). MERCOSUR. Online: http://ec.europa.eu/trade/policy/countries-and-regions/regions/MERCOSUR/ Accessed 15 Mar 2015.

European External Action Service. (2014). *Multiannual indicative regional programme for Latin America*. Brussels: European Union. Online: http://eeas.europa.eu/la/docs/mip_alr_vf_07_08_14_en.pdf, Accessed 16 Mar 2015.

Gardini, G. L. (2010). Proyectos de integración regional sudamericana: hacia una teoría de convergencia regional. *Relaciones Internacionales, 15*, 11–31.

Gardini, G. L. (2012). *Latin America in the 21st century*. London: Zed Books.

Gardini, G. L. (2015). Towards modular regionalism: The proliferation of Latin American cooperation. *Revista Brasileira de Politica Internacional, 58*(1), 210–229.

Garzon, J.F. (2015). Mulipolarity and the future of regionalism: Latin America and Beyond GIGA *Working Papers* n° 264, January, pp. 33 https://giga.hamburg/en/system/files/publications/wp264_garzon.pdf, Accessed 12 June 2016.

Hänggi, H. (2000). Interregionalism: Empirical and theoretical perspectives, paper prepared for the workshop "Dollars, Democracy and Trade. External Influence on Economic Integration in the Americas". Los Angeles. May 18 http://www.cap.lmu.de/transatlantic/download/Haenggi, Accessed 24 Feb 2016.

Hill, C., & Smith, M. (2011). *International relations and the European Union*. Oxford/New York: Oxford University Press.

Le Gloannec, A. (2004). The unilateralist temptation Germany's foreign policy after the Cold War. *Internationale Politik und Gesellschaft, 1*, 27–39.

Maihold, G. (2010). La productividad del proceso de cumbres euro-latinoamericanas. Una evaluación a diez años de Rio. In C. Gerardo (Ed.), *Las Negociaciones entre América Latina y el Caribe con la Unión Europea* (pp. 21–60). Montevideo: Ediciones Trilce.

Sanahuja, J. A. (2013). Towards a new framework of relations between the European Union and Latin America and the Caribbean, EU-LAC Bi-regional relations paper, Hamburg: Foundation EU-LAC. https://eulacfoundation.org/en/documents/towards-new-framework-relations-between-european-union-and-latin-america-and-caribbean. Accessed 25 Jan 2015.

Schäfer, R. (2013). EU-CELAC: Five strengths. In M. S. Ortiz (Ed.), *La Diplomacia de las Cumbres: Retos y Oportunidades de los nuevos Regionalismos* (pp. 87–90). San José: FLACSO.

Schimmelfennig, F. (2003). *The EU, NATO and the integration of Europe. Rules and Rhetoric.* Cambridge: Cambridge University Press.

Sutton, P. (2012). The European Union and the Caribbean Region: Situating the Caribbean Overseas Countries and Territories. *European Review of Latin American and Caribbean Studies, 93*, 79–94.

Whitehead, L., & Barahona de Brito, A. (2005). Las cumbres mundiales y sus versiones latino-americanas: ¿Haciendo una montaña de un grano de arena? *América Latina Hoy, 40*, 15–27.

Chapter 8
The North Atlantic: A Case of Bicontinental Regionalism

Riccardo Alcaro and Patrick Reilly

Abstract Form and content of interregional relations reflect the dynamics generated by the specific regionalism existing in the regions considered. Nowhere is interregionalism's subordination to regionalism clearer than in the North Atlantic. The experiences with regionalism of Europe and North America differ considerably, as the former has experimented radically in regional integration while the latter has made only modest steps. Consequently, interregionalism provides for a poor analytical grid to understand North Atlantic relations. The latter are better grasped instead if a regionalism-informed conceptual framework is applied, as after all the North Atlantic displays features that fit a regionalism prism. After outlining a conceptual framework to understand regions, the chapter briefly compares Europe's and North America's regionalism before delving into the analysis of the North Atlantic as a sui generis bicontinental region.

Keywords Atlantic • Interregionalism • Regional organisations • Regionalism • Regions

8.1   Introduction

Interregionalism is, by definition, an attempt to conceptualise the relationship between two regions. Regions are an elusive entity, however. In empirical terms, they may designate a geographical area, an economic zone, an administrative unit, or even an area characterised by relative ethnic or religious homogeneity. In conceptual terms, the concept of region can alternatively indicate an area defined by the overlapping actions of states, treat multiple states as a more or less a single entity, or identify

R. Alcaro (✉)
Istituto Affari Internazionali (IAI), Rome, Italy
e-mail: r.alcaro@iai.it

P. Reilly
German Marshall Fund, Washington, DC, USA
e-mail: reillykp@gmail.com

© Springer International Publishing AG 2018   131
F. Mattheis, A. Litsegård (eds.), *Interregionalism across the Atlantic Space*,
United Nations University Series on Regionalism 15,
DOI 10.1007/978-3-319-62908-7_8

a level of governance between the state and the international system.[1] The empirical and conceptual diversity of regions involves that intra-regional interaction – what International Relations studies generally refer to as 'regionalism' – varies greatly. This fluidity has important consequences for anyone investigating interregional relations, as the form and content of interregionalism inevitably reflects the unique dynamics generated by the specific regionalism existing in the regions considered.

Nowhere is interregionalism's dependence on and subordination to regionalism more evident than in the North Atlantic. Europe and North America are an exceptional case of region-to-region interaction, because transoceanic relations unfold mostly in a bicontinental space, alternatively called the (North) Atlantic community or, more often, the 'West'. This chapter consequently analyses North American-European relations in regionalist, rather than interregionalist, terms. In the first section, we present a comprehensive analytical framework to understand and potentially compare regions, showing how distinct Europe and North America's experiences with regionalism are and how such differences are only minimally reflected in the transatlantic relationship. Although interregional dynamics are not entirely absent, underlying the transatlantic relationship is a complex web of interactions that can only be appreciated in analysing it through a regionalist frame. The second section applies the conceptual framework to investigate transatlantic regionalism.

8.2 An Analytical Framework to Understand and Compare Regions

8.2.1 Five Parameters to Assess Regionalism

Regions can be conceptualised, understood and eventually compared in various manners. Drawing heavily from the most recent literature on regionalism, we single out five broad parameters.

The first concerns the *functions performed by regionalism*. Regions complement or supplement states in the exercise of three fundamental state functions: delimit and regulate a common market; provide public goods; exert sovereign authority over individuals and vis-à-vis other states (Van Langenhove 2012: 20–21).

The *drivers of regionalisation* constitute the second parameter. States, elites, interest groups and others engage in regionalism for a variety of reasons, ranging from strategic considerations regarding security and power, to calculations about their material well-being, to the ambition to lend a political dimension to what they perceive as a community of nations that share an historical legacy, values and norms. Motivations of a different nature can, of course, co-exist and actually mutually reinforce each other.

The third parameter is the *degree of 'regionness'*. We borrow the term 'regionness' from Björn Hettne (2014: 56) to indicate the degree to which regions have acquired internal cohesion, including in terms of regional identity (ibidem: 56–57).

---

[1] The concept of region, as it defines a separate level of governance, is applicable to subnational governance too (Van Langenhove 2012: 18).

Regions move up and down the 'regionness' scale depending on how states have addressed the security dilemma, that is, whether their relations are more competitive or more cooperative[2]; how homogeneous their economic systems are, implying a lesser or greater mobility of goods, capital, labour and people; and whether the governance regimes under which they operate are convergent (ibidem: 61–62).

The fourth parameter describes the *capacity of regions to shape the international system*. Certain regions have "actorness", that is, the capacity to act in a purposive and organised fashion. Other regions stop short of having a distinct actorness but still structure the international system – they have "impersonal" actorness, so to speak. Following Hurrell (2007: 136–141), we distinguish four ways in which regionalism structures the international system. First is the capacity of a region to embody a cultural specificity that reverberates into the world. Regions can provide for a larger horizon in which the cultural specificity of a nation state is less exposed to degradation because it is part of a bigger, culturally plural entity. Secondly, regions structure international relations as organisational mechanisms between the national level and the multilateral one. A degree of institutionalisation of regional relations is implied here, albeit not necessarily a strong actorness. Thirdly, regions structure international relations when they act as powers or 'poles' (Hurrell 2007: 139). As such, regions are cohesive blocs that influence the global power structure. Fourthly and lastly, regionalism organises interstate relations according to behavioural patterns not reducible to state-based multilateral interactions (Hettne 2014: 57; Baert et al. 2014b: 181). In region-based multilateralism the emphasis is on collective management of transnational challenges, which implies a relaxation, although by no means the relinquishment, of state-determined behavioural patterns. Regional multilateralism relies on structured dialogue, consensus-based decision-making and repeated practices of interaction.

The last parameter concerns the *disintegrating potential of regions*. The experiments in regionalism undertaken by Europe and North America are not immune to the risk of regression. These moves away from regionalist logic are the flip-side of the regionalisation drivers – when the latter wane or disappear, so regional structures inevitably weaken. But there are also disaggregating factors not directly related to the causes of regionalism, for instance an over-reliance on elites (Fioramonti 2012: 158, 2014: 225 and ff.).

8.2.2   Europe and North America Compared

In terms of *functions*, Europe and North America stand quite apart. In Europe, regional institutions provide for a highly integrated economic space, they allot resources for the promotion of public goods, and they exert – within

---

[2] The literature on the security dilemma is vast. Our analysis uses Alexander Wendt's understanding of it as a social construction resulting from the intersubjective understanding of states rather than an objective state of reality that reflects the supposedly anarchic nature of international relations (Wendt 1992: 397; see also Wendt 1999).

limits – authority over states and citizens while relating to external actors as a sovereign or semi-sovereign entity. The European Union (EU) and the regimes inherent to it, such as the Schengen agreement for the free movement of people, perform almost all of the functions outlined above. The exception is the European Court on Human Rights (ECtHR), which has exerted supranational jurisdiction over the states party to the European Convention on Human Rights (ECHR) since 1959. By contrast, in North America there is little common economic space, only a limited and carefully delineated bilateral provision of public goods, and no regional legal authority.

European regionalism has multiple *drivers* (Pollack 2012), some emanating from security (Rosato 2011) and economic interests (Moravcsik 1993 and 1998), and others from ideational factors such as a common identity and the universal rejection of war as an instrument to solve intra-European disputes (Christiansen et al. 2001; Wiener and Diez 2009). The drivers of North American regionalism, mostly centred on the North American Free Trade Agreement (NAFTA), are economic-only (Graham 1997: 126). However, it is worth noting that advocates of deeper North American integration insist that it is warranted by broader political interests and ideational proximity (Pastor 2003: 11).

Considering the degree of *regionness*, a striking degree of convergence in political regimes characterises North America and Europe. A commonality of political values shapes a regional environment in which intra-regional borders have lost any meaning in terms of national defence. Regional economies have also drawn closer, though to varying degrees. In Europe, the regional dimension is as important as and at times even more important than the national one. This is due to the EU's partly supranational decision-making, a high level of economic integration, and the fact that security is primarily an extra-regional matter. Europe can thus be described as a *regional polity*, the highest form of regional integration (Hettne 2014: 57). North America lacks most of the institutional structures, both formal and informal, created by Europe, but is nonetheless a space regulated by rules and generally cooperative practices. As such, it is what Hettne would term an advanced form of *regional society* (ibidem), two steps down the regional polity.

Both Europe and North America occupy an important place in the international system because of their geographical, demographic and economic size. They have a considerable 'presence', a pre-condition for having a powerful *capacity to structure international relations* (ibidem: 59). European integration is premised on the idea that pluralism – of religion, language and historical tradition – is not an impediment to the establishment of viable regional frameworks, and that a supranational identity layer can co-exist with a national one. In this respect, a *European* identity articulates the international system's cultural diversity more than an Italian, German or French one do. The contours of such an identity outline a broad political-cultural agenda based on a preference for dialogue and multilateral cooperation, a strong emphasis on environmental protection and sustainable development, and cosmopolitanism (Habermas and Derrida 2003). North America has not developed a comparable sense of its own self as the bearer of a region-wide cultural specificity. To a varying degree, societies in the US, Canada and Mexico embrace the same idea of pluralism in defining their own culture, most notably in the US, whose original myth is built around the idea of a 'cultural melting pot' (Kazal 1995: 438). While there is no distinctly *North American* cultural identity per se, some of the characteristics of each individual country's identity, such as the belief in individual rights and a market-based rather than centrally directed economy, are shared regionally.

Regions also shape international relations as governance mechanisms placed in-between the national and multilateral levels. The main way in which the EU performs this function is between the EU's relationship with the United Nations (UN). EU-UN cooperation has mostly taken the form of delegation, whereby the EU has conducted military or civilian missions abroad under a UN Security Council (UNSC) mandate or in support of local UN efforts (Tull 2012: 135–139; Novosseloff 2012: 150–161). In North America, the situation is more complicated. Mid-level governance from the region is mostly confined to the economic sphere. NAFTA follows World Trade Organisation (WTO) provisions, while the now abandoned Trans-Pacific Partnership (TPP) between the US, Mexico, Canada and a number of other Pacific countries also aimed to strengthen these norms in places where they are currently lacking. Through this drawing of regional norms embodied in NAFTA, North America, as a region, still shapes international trade relations.

Regions also define the international power structure. Europe as a region influences the global system, though not in the one respect of which power is generally assumed to consist, military power (Nuttall 2000; Merlingen and Ostrauskaite 2006; Howorth 2014; Menon 2014). Yet in non-military areas, the EU has emerged as one of the 'poles' around which international relations revolve (Hill and Smith 2005). The EU speaks for the largest trade bloc in the world. Occupying such a prominent position in world trade allows it to compel countries desiring access to the common market to abide by EU-set standards and rules, so much so that the Union has been defined a 'regulatory power' (Robberecht 2013). Furthermore, thanks to its considerable negotiating power, the EU has often tipped the scales in concluding multilateral agreements and more than once proved decisive for their entry into force – notable examples include the Rome Statute establishing the International Criminal Court (ICC), the anti-personnel land mine treaty and the Kyoto Protocol on greenhouse gas emissions limits. In contrast with Europe, regionalism in North America can in no way be conceived in 'polar' terms. The reason is simple: the lack of any incentive for the US to set up regional institutions to which 'polar' functions could be transferred. This is not to say that the US has no interest whatsoever in exerting its power through regionally defined alliances and partnerships. But North America is not the locus wherein this takes place. Instead that locus has traditionally been the 'Atlantic community', or the West, which does behave as a 'pole' insofar as it is a bloc resting on US hegemony, as we discuss below.

Another way in which regionalism shapes international relations is the ability to present viable alternatives to state-based relations. At first sight, Europe stands out again as a testament to the transformative potential of regionalism (Hettne 2014: 62). However, there is scant empirical evidence that European integration has changed the dynamic of multilateral cooperation around the world. Post-modern

Europe has remained an isolated case in a world in which states continue to be dominant. Lacking any form of supranational authority, the logic according to which regional integration would naturally proceed through functional spillovers from one policy area into another has not taken place in North America. But the liberal logic of absolute gains has played out powerfully, to the extent that North America's landscape is one in which rules can constrain power in regional interactions where key national interests are at stake.

Finally, North America and Europe differ in terms of *internal vulnerability*. Europe's integration has made EU countries largely dependent on one another. The lack of a supranational authority in key areas such as foreign affairs, defence, and currently most importantly immigration and fiscal policy creates ample room for conflict. Such conflicts have been a constant in the EU's history, but in the context of the Eurozone and migration crises and the British referendum that has put the United Kingdom (UK) on the way out of the EU, a rollback of European regionalism is definitely conceivable. While Brexit will bring about diminished membership, the unsolved difficulties in the eurozone governance system may still lead to a break-up of the common currency, and the divisions over migration to the permanent suspension of the passport-free Schengen system. With anti-EU forces rising even in founding countries such as France, the Netherlands and Italy, the prospect of a dissolution of the EU, unthinkable just a few years ago, is now a possibility. Conventional wisdom had it that the relatively low degree of regional integration achieved by North America shielded it from possible reversal. The underlying reasoning was that no party to NAFTA has any incentive to roll back regionalised trade patterns, as breaking infrastructure links and supply chains, as well as limiting market access, would entail high costs and no immediate benefit. Yet, the election as US president of Donald Trump, who during the campaign regularly referred to NAFTA as a bad deal for the US, points to a shakier consensus base for North American regionalism than previously assumed. It remains to be seen whether this will bring about the regression of North American regionalism to a simpler, more competitive form of interaction. But the relative success of Trump's anti-regionalist discourse is a further warning against considering regionalism as a purely functional project rather than a political one. Like all political undertakings, it depends extensively on consensus, an element of analysis that (with the exception of Europe) the literature on regionalism tends too often to neglect or take for granted.

In conclusion, the comparison of Europe and North America's experiences with regionalism tells a story of differences rather than similarities. As the focus of the analysis shifts to European-North American relations, the question arises about the extent to which the two regions' different forms of regionalism inform interregional relations.

8.3   The West: More Region than Interregional Space

Interregionalism is a contested concept. Baert et al. (2014a: 4–6) distinguish 'pure' interregionalism involving regional organisations from more spurious forms of region-to-region contacts. None of these, however, fits the North Atlantic case. North Atlantic relations unfold in two dimensions: state-to-region, e.g. EU-Canada and EU-Mexico relations, both of which have recently been upgraded thanks to formal free trade agreements[3]; and bicontinental regionalisation in the framework of the North Atlantic Treaty Organisation (NATO) and EU-US relations, particularly in the now remote eventuality that the Transatlantic Trade and Investment Partnership (TTIP) is negotiated and ratified. State-to-region relations are a form of spurious interregionalism, which Baert, Scaramagli and Söderbaum call 'quasi-interregionalism' and some experts exclude from the interregionalism taxonomy altogether (Doidge 2014: 37). In this respect, the gap between Europe and North America's regional experiences shapes transcontinental relations indirectly: because regionalism has made strides in Europe but has only made marginal progress in North America, regional organisation to regional organisation relations are basically absent.

Even the state-to-region dimension – namely EU-US, EU-Canada and EU-Mexico – is an incomplete frame for transatlantic ties. Underlying relations between European countries and Canada and the US is a deeper and more complex web of interactions unfolding in a shared political, cultural and institutional setting. Transatlantic or North Atlantic relations – terms generally used as a substitute for 'US-European' relations (although Canada is often included too) – are in fact usually referred to as if they were a complex but single entity, the 'West'. While other historically Anglophone countries outside the North Atlantic, such as Australia and New Zealand, are often included in the 'West' and are part of the mostly Western Organisation for Economic Cooperation and Development (OECD) and the Western European and Other Group (WEOG) in the UN, they do not drive the West to any degree like the North Atlantic does. Thus, however imprecise terminologically the term 'West' is, we believe it is legitimate to use it to describe the nature of US-European relations.

Measured against the parameters of the conceptual framework outlined in the previous section, not only do transatlantic relations exhibit traits typical of regions, but also act as a relatively cohesive region. The conclusion is that the West is more a region than an interregional space.

---

[3] The EU and Mexico signed a trade agreement in 1997 that was later upgraded into a free trade area for goods and services. The EU-Canada Comprehensive Economic and Trade Agreement (CETA), a more ambitious document, is more recent (2014).

8.3.1 Functions of Western Regionalism

No Western structure exists to provide a common economic space, public goods or jurisdiction over citizens and states. Nevertheless, Western regionalism does perform certain state functions.

The EU and US economies, while not formally integrated, have achieved a considerable degree of mutual interpenetration (Hamilton and Quinlan 2016). Exchanges between transatlantic economic policymakers, operators and regulators take place on a regular basis, sometimes through institutionalised settings such as the EU-US Transatlantic Economic Council (TEC). The regular nature of these interactions has gone far enough to trigger socialisation processes. These established practices not only sustain transatlantic economic interdependence, but also contribute to cementing a sense, however loose, of community or at least strong partnership (McNamara 2008). The launch of the TTIP negotiation in 2013 originated from a desire to fill a perceived gap in the transatlantic economic dimension, especially in regulatory cooperation. With the wave of anti-trade forces mounting, TTIP is unlikely to be concluded in the near term. Yet, the economic ties it was meant to reinforce are are infinitely more difficult to break than a trade negotiation, and they will continue to generate a demand – functional, if not political – for greater regulation.

While there is no Western mechanism to transfer money to states, transatlantic regionalism does provide for a public good due to its protection of borders and populations via NATO. The Atlantic Alliance performs this state function asymmetrically – for the US, NATO is less a defence asset than it is an instrument of power projection. But other member states have sub-contracted significant parts of their defence to it, including a few that have done so entirely. This trait marks the West as a very peculiar form of regionalism, one organised hierarchically rather than horizontally.

8.3.2 Drivers of Western Regionalisation

Western regionalisation seems to fall neatly in a monocausal explanation. The bipolar structure of global power during the Cold War triggered aggregation around the two main superpowers, most notably in Europe, where opposite Eastern and Western blocs were created and codified in the Warsaw Pact and NATO. Considerations of national security, as well as strategies of counterbalancing and bandwagoning (Waltz 1979: 126), determined the choices of the US and (West) European governments.

However, while the monocausal explanation sheds light on the initial driver of Western regionalisation, it does not explain its sustainability. NATO's obstinacy to outlive the Soviet threat has posed a theoretical challenge to realists, though they argue that the Alliance's endurance is a residual element of the past that will fade away eventually unless a new common threat, such as a resurgent and hostile Russia, re-emerges (Mearsheimer 1990; Waltz 1993, 2000; Kagan 2003). Liberal institutionalists counter that common transatlantic institutions – both formal like NATO and informal such as the many contact groups comprising the US and a restricted number of EU countries – are established instruments to manage both intra-West relations and external challenges. They provide systemic incentives that keep the transatlantic relationship from dwindling (Keohane 1993; McCalla 1996; Haftendorn et al. 1999). Social constructivists contend that transatlantic relations reflect an evolving "configuration of interests, interdependencies, institutions and identity" (Risse 2012: 3). A multi-causal explanation of the West's sustainability – if not of its inception as an institutionalised region in the NATO framework – appears to capture reality more than a monocausal, security-only one.

8.3.3 The West as a Regional Community

For realists, there is no West beyond a threat-determined temporary coalition of sovereign states pursuing self-help. Yet, the West fares well when measured on the regionness scale (Hettne 2014: 56–57). The security dilemma has been overcome and political regimes have achieved a remarkable degree of convergence, with the US, Canada, and EU countries all espousing pluralist democratic systems. Macroeconomic homogenisation is limited, and yet since the 1990s supply-side economics and free trade discourse and practices have largely dominated the economic agenda in both Europe and North America. The West is thus characterised by well-established frameworks of relations, most notably NATO and the various EU-US cooperation forums, and premised on commonality or compatibility of interests but also values and normative practices, whereby violence as an instrument to solve intra-regional disputes is unthinkable.

For non-realist theorists the complexity of transatlantic relations is such that it has warranted the use of a wider panoply of categories to define and understand them. These categories are now part and parcel of the regionalism dictionary. In the 1950s Karl Deutsch pointed out the peculiarity of the West as an imaginary "pluralistic security community" detached from geography and based on "dependable expectations of peaceful change" (Deutsch et al. 1957: 9). Adler and Barnett have argued that security communities are characterised by the sharing of identities, values and meanings; directness and many-sidedness of intra-regional relations; and diffused reciprocity among regional states, both because of interest-based considerations and out of a sense of mutual obligation (Adler and Barnett 1998). Thomas Risse also argues that, while the concept of security community was originally applied to elites, there is no theoretical impediment to extend it to the "attitudes and activities of ordinary citizens", whereby societal links are posited as a supporting pillar of the security community (Risse 2012: 3). The combined effect of Risse's four 'Is' – interests, institutions, interdependence and identity – puts the West into the higher end of regional scale (Hettne 2014: 56–57). As a *regional community*, the West is one step behind the EU's 'regional polity' but ahead of North America's 'regional society'.

8.3.4 Shaping International Relations: The West and the 'Outer' World

Thanks to the combined effect of its economic, political and cultural influence, the West makes for a powerful agent of change in international relations.

The West contributes to articulating the cultural diversity of the international system, standing for political pluralism, rule of law, individual rights and the separation between religion and state. At the same time, Western culture is not only one among others. Because of their universalism, Western values and norms (at least the core highlighted above) make up the pillar of international law as well as the normative framework of global governance mechanisms.

The irresistible universalistic zest of Western norms contrasts with the preservation of cultural diversity. Alternative cultural discourses have had to adapt to this 'imperial' aspect of Western norms, sometimes succumbing (as in the Balkans), sometimes finding forms of more or less working syncretism (as in India), but often clashing with it (as in Russia or even more so in China). Besides, while norms may be universal in essence, they will always retain a strong element of cultural specificity as long as one region pretends to be the standard-bearer of such norms. Western norms are often perceived by non-Western countries as a rhetorical cloak in which the West opportunistically wraps its interests, particularly when it comes to peace and security (Tocci 2014). At times, however, the opposition is genuine: Western values, particularly individual rights contrasting with deep-seated social and religious habits (gay rights, for instance), are rejected on their own merit. Yet, even when challenged, the extent of the West's cultural impact is undeniable. Western culture remains the world's irremovable terms of reference.

The outreach of Western culture is largely a function of the fact that the West is not only a cultural region but also a geopolitical 'pole'. The West contributes to structuring the global balance of power more than any other region. It does so in part according to traditional patterns of regionalism, that is, structured, formalised or well-established cooperation among regional states. Thus, we see Western power emanating and expanding from NATO and the broader partnerships between the US (and Canada) and the EU. In part, however, the nature of Western power is such that the West is less a 'pole' itself than it is a system of alliances and partnership *around* a pole, the US (Alcaro 2016: 203–8).

On the surface NATO is a standard organisation in which all members enjoy equal status. However, the imbalance of power between the US and its allies involves decisions that are not taken on the basis of consensus but hierarchy. In intergovernmental regional organisations, all member states' interests must be accommodated, whereby the result is often, though not always, a lowest common denominator-based policy. By contrast, in hierarchical structures the decision-making procedure, *de facto* if not *de jure*, is such that the leader's decisions prevail because, by providing social order and security, the leader obtains loyalty and support from the followers (Lake 2006).

NATO's internal dynamics are not always as straightforward. The subtleties of US leadership entail a relationship between leader and followers that necessitates the former to convince, cajole and woo the latter. In such a structure, ample room for disagreements remains. Nevertheless, divergences can hardly stop the leader from pursuing its objectives, even if they might at times be so severe to imperil the well-functioning of NATO. Most of the times, dissenting followers eventually reach an accommodation so that both parties can pursue the benefits of their asymmetrical but mutually satisfying relationship.

Notwithstanding the remote possibility of TTIP to ever materialise, the case is illustrative, because it would reflect 'interdependence' rather than one-way dependency. The aim of TTIP is to create a transatlantic market based on a largely harmonised or compatible regulatory regime that would provide the US and the EU with the ability to set 'the rules of the game' in global regulations and trade. The sheer magnitude of the transatlantic market would eventually compel other countries to abide by its rules and standards in order to get access to it (Hamilton 2014). Ratification of TTIP, as unlikely as it appears now, would, in other words, reinforce the status of the West as a 'pole'.

In the security field, NATO has battled with the difficulty of reconnecting with the global security framework of the UN since the Alliance started to intervene outside its traditional Euro-Atlantic remit. After the rift over Kosovo, where NATO intervened lacking formal authorisation by the UN, the Alliance has operated with a UN mandate in Afghanistan, Libya and off the coasts of Somalia. NATO has also stated its intention to act as a 'hub' for other security-focused regional organisations and insisted that its growing focus on the 'global commons' (space, air, sea and cyberspace) is in the interest of all. In this regard, NATO does provide a middle level of security governance between the multilateral and national level, although only a limited and contested one.

The role of Western regionalism in bringing change to established behavioural patterns in international relations is difficult to assess. It was a US-led coalition that set up the UN and Bretton Woods systems and gave legitimacy and authority to institutions of international law, multilateralism and free trade. Western regionalism has nonetheless remained state-based and is organised more hierarchically than intergovernmentally. This explains the selective commitment to multilateralism often displayed by Western countries, especially the US, and highlights the inherent tension that characterises Western regional structures. The capacity of Western regionalism to be a harbinger of change in international relations depends on where the balance tilts.

8.3.5   Disintegration Risks in the West

Western regionalisation processes have not lost steam yet. NATO has expanded its membership and EU-US ties have grown thicker even if TTIP, which is a long way from becoming a reality, is not taken into account. Cooperation on issues such as checking Russia's revanchist instincts or Iran's nuclear ambitions attests to the lingering existence of such a thing as a 'Western security interest'. The TTIP negotiation at least points to a desire to codify and increase interdependence within a transatlantic institutional economic framework.

The picture, however, is by no means all rosy. For the West, the risk is not so much that of disintegration as of looser ties. This may result, first, from a diminished capacity to act jointly – a problem that already besets NATO, given Europe's reluctance to spend on defence. Also relevant is the likely inability to overcome domestic resistance to TTIP, which would prevent greater cooperation on regulation and trade. A massive imbalance in priorities, particularly if US-China relations take on an antagonistic tone (which could pit US strategic goals against Europe's commercial interests), or an isolationist turn, if large domestic constituencies traditionally supportive of the Western alliance dwindle and fade out, should also be factored in. A looser relationship would not amount to the end of the West as a region, at least not immediately and not irreversibly. Yet it would attest to the fact that regionalism is not a one-way street and that not even a relationship that continues to provide benefits for both leader and followers, rests on a massive economic foundation, and unfolds in a common normative framework, is immune to roll-backs.

8.4   Conclusions

Regionalism has proceeded at a quite different pace in Europe and North America. The gap between Europe's high degree of regionalisation and North America's modest advances has impinged on transoceanic relations, whereby conventional categories of interregionalism do not fit the picture. State-to-region interactions – EU-US, EU-Canada, EU-Mexico – play a more prominent role, but more important still is the fact that US-European (and to a lesser extent Canadian-European) relations unfold within a single, bicontinental regional setting. For this reason, it is more appropriate to analyse North Atlantic relations through the lenses of a regionalist framework. The specificity of the North Atlantic region can be measured by the functions performed by regions, the drivers of regionalisation, the cohesiveness of regions, their capacity to structure the 'outer' world, and their vulnerability.

A brief analysis of Europe and North America's respective regionalisation processes shows that, while North America is mainly a geographic and commercial region and Europe stands apart because of its structural reliance on common rules, the 'West' or North Atlantic is a region in which strategic interests mingle with normative convergence. This adds an important element of porosity to the term region.

In terms of functions, the West fares worse than not only Europe but North America too. The West lacks any legal regional authority and has no regulated economic common space. Yet Western regionalism stands out in at least one respect, in that a regional organisation, NATO, provides for the territorial defence of most if its twenty-nine member states.

Western regionalism, similarly to European regionalism, has multiple drivers, although in the West material factors – US power and security interests in particular – have such a pre-eminent position that some scholars consider other drivers, such as norms, values and a shared identity, accessory. In fact, security may have played a prominent role in generating a transatlantic desire to integrate, but other factors, material (economic) and especially ideational help explain the West's sustainability.

The West has after all achieved a relatively high degree of 'regionness', actually higher than North America has. Security policymakers in Europe, the US or Canada look at the North Atlantic as an asset, not a source of concern. The US and European economies are deeply interpenetrated. Decision-making remains a sovereign matter but the leader-followers relationship between the US and its allies in Europe often result in the grouping act as one. All this earns the West the status of a 'regional community'.

As much as and arguably more than European regionalism, Western regionalism contributes to shaping international relations, although the process is anything but linear and certainly not uncontested. The West's relationship with the 'outer' world is characterised by an internal tension, in that the West is both a container of a cultural specificity and the bearer of a normative core that is conceived of as transcending any cultural specificity. Western cultural outreach is a function of its power, which largely resides with the US. Hence, the manner in which the West mostly affects the international constellation of power is binary: either it generates convergence with US strategic preferences or antagonism. This does not mean that Western international action is entirely power-determined and consequently arbitrary. On the contrary, the West is a strong promoter of liberal forms of state interaction.

Finally, the West shows elements of internal vulnerability, just as Europe and lately North America have. North America's regionalism has only made limited progress and has remained firmly in the hands of national governments, which in theory should shelter it from disintegration risks. However, the recent rise in popular opposition to trade deals in the US, and especially to NAFTA, could spawn a regionalist retrenchment. Europe's regionalism is even more at risk of reversal. The EU's intergovernmental-supranational hybrid form of decision-making, coupled with the imbalance between the degree of integration and governance mechanisms (painfully on display in the eurozone), has made the whole edifice of European regionalism more vulnerable to internal and external shocks. Assessing the vulnerability of Western regionalism is more difficult. NATO has an increasing problem of imbalance in military capabilities, while TTIP is a project in the making with little chance of being concluded. At the same time, the fundamental bargain underlying the US-European relationship, the provision of security by the leader (the US) in exchange of loyalty from the followers (European countries plus Canada), continues to provide benefits for both parties. The West looks more volatile on the surface than it does when its foundations are considered.

The specific features of North Atlantic interactions have very little that can be conceptualised as interregional (Baert et al. 2014a, b: 181). At best, they might be regarded as falling into the category of quasi-interregionalism, namely state-to-region relations, although the concept does not enjoy widespread scholarly support. The relative importance and marginal agency of state-to-region relations contributes to drawing an incomplete picture of transoceanic relations. Transatlantic relations exhibit traits that cannot be understood in interregional or quasi-interregional terms. Collective defence via NATO; convergence of political regimes; deep economic interpenetration; common normative background and shared interests; and capacity to act as a single entity or pole: these are the typical traits of a region and, consequently, regionalism studies have a strong claim to examine North Atlantic relations in their own right (Table 8.1).

Table 8.1 Comparing regionalism in Europe, North America and the North Atlantic/West

Parameter	Europe	North America	North Atlantic/West
Functions of regionalism	Common economic space provided by EU single market	Partial common economic space provided by NAFTA	Potential common economic space if TTIP is ratified
	Resource allocation by EU institutions		Provision of security and defence by NATO
	(Partial) sovereignty over EU member states by EU institutions over communitarised areas and by ECtHR over ECHR member states		
Regionalisation drivers	Multicausal explanation for both inception and sustainability of regionalisation process:	Monocausal explanation of inception and sustainability of regionalisation process:	Monocausal explanation of inception of regionalisation process:
	Commonality of interests, both geopolitical and economic	Commonality of economic interests	Commonality of threat
	Common identities and shared values		Multicausal explanation of sustainability of regionalisation process:
	Common institutions		Converging interests (economic and strategic)
	Spillover effects of integration process		Economic interdependence
			Common institutions
			Shared values and identity

(continued)

Table 8.1 (continued)

Parameter	Europe	North America	North Atlantic/West
Degree of regionness	Regional polity:	Regional society:	Regional community:
	Security dilemma overcome	Security dilemma irrelevant, though not overcome	Security dilemma overcome
	Macroeconomic homogeneity	Partial macroeconomic homogeneity	Increasing macroeconomic homogeneity
	Common political regimes	Increasing convergence of political regimes	Common political regimes
Capacity to structure international relations	*Cultural specificity:*	*Cultural specificity:*	*Cultural specificity:*
	Support for dialogue and multilateralism, political pluralism, environmentalism and sustainable development, cosmopolitanism	Cultural pluralism	Promotion of democracy, human rights, secularism, rule of law
	Mid-level governance:	*Mid-level governance:*	*'Pole' in global constellation of power:*
	Top-down or delegation (UN-EU cooperation)	Bottom-up (NAFTA in keeping with WTO provisos)	Security, with US in the lead
	Bottom up or policing (e.g. ECHR as implementation of UDHR)	*No 'pole' role*	Economic and regulatory, particularly if TTIP is ratified
	'Pole' in global constellation of power:	*Promoter of state-based multilateralism*	*Promoter of state-based multilateralism*
	Trade, regulations, norms		
	Promoter of regionalism-based multilateralism		
Disintegration risks	Scenarios of partial disintegration	Improbable yet not implausible scenario of disintegration via US withdrawal from NAFTA	Medium-to-low risk of disintegration, though the relationship may become looser
	Diminished membership: Brexit (actual); Grexit (potential)		
	Greater disarticulation of EU governance system and/or roll-back of competencies to national level		

References

Adler, E., & Barnett, M. (1998). Security communities in theoretical perspective. In E. Adler & M. Barnett (Eds.), *Security communities* (pp. 3–28). Cambridge: Cambridge University Press.

Alcaro, R. (2016). The paradoxes of the liberal order: Transatlantic relations and security governance. In R. Alcaro, J. Peterson, & N. Tocci (Eds.), *The West and the global power shift* (pp. 197–219). London: Palgrave Macmillan.

Baert, F., Scaramagli, T., & Söderbaum, F. (2014a). Introduction. In F. Baert, T. Scaramagli, & F. Söderbaum (Eds.), *Intersecting interregionalism. Regions, global governance and the EU* (pp. 1–14). Dordrecht/Heidelberg/New York/London: Springer.

Baert, F., Scaramagli, T., & Söderbaum, F. (2014b). Conclusion. In F. Baert, T. Scaramagli, & F. Söderbaum (Eds.), *Intersecting interregionalism. Regions, global governance and the EU* (pp. 169–182). Dordrecht/Heidelberg/New York/London: Springer.

Christiansen, T., Jørgensen, K. E., & Wiener, A. (2001). *The social construction of Europe*. London: Sage.

Deutsch, K. W., et al. (1957). *Political community and the North Atlantic area: International organisation in the light of historical experience*. Princeton: Princeton University Press.

Doidge, M. (2014). Interregionalism and the European Union: Conceptualising Group-to-Group relations. In F. Baert, T. Scaramagli, & F. Söderbaum (Eds.), *Intersecting interregionalism. Regions, global governance and the EU* (pp. 37–54). Dordrecht/Heidelberg/New York/London: Springer.

Fioramonti, L. (2012). Building regions from below: Has the time come for regionalism 2.0? *The International Spectator, 47*(1), 151–160.

Fioramonti, L. (2014). Conclusion: The future of regionalism. In L. Fioramonti (Ed.), *Regions and crises. New challenges for contemporary regionalisms* (pp. 220–230). New York: Palgrave MacMillan.

Graham, W. C. (1997). NAFTA vis a vis the E.U. – Similarities and differences and their effects on member countries. *Canada-United States Law Journal, 23*(123).

Habermas, J., & Derrida, J. (2003). What binds European together: A plea for a common foreign policy, beginning in the core of Europe. *Constellations, 10*(3), 291–297.

Haftendorn, H., Keohane, R. O., & Wallander, C. A. (1999). *Imperfect unions. Security institutions over time and space*. Oxford: Oxford University Press.

Hamilton, D. S. (2014). TTIP's geostrategic implications. In D. S. Hamilton (Ed.), *The geopolitics of TTIP* (pp. vii–xxxii). Washington, DC: Center for Transatlantic Relations.

Hamilton, D. S., & Quinlan, J. P. (2016). *The transatlantic economy 2015: Annual survey on jobs, rade and investment between the United States and Europe*. Washington, DC: Center for Transatlantic Relations.

Hettne, B. (2014), Regional actorship: A comparative approach to interregionalism. In F. Baert, T. Scaramagli, & F. Söderbaum (Eds.), *Intersecting interregionalism. Regions, Global Governance and the EU* (pp. 55–57). Dordrecht/Heidelberg/New York/London: Springer

Hill, C., & Smith, M. (2005). Acting for Europe: Reassessing the European Union's place in international relations. In C. Hill & M. Smith (Eds.), *International relations and the European Union* (pp. 458–481). Oxford/New York: Oxford University Press.

Howorth, J. (2014). European security Post-Libya and Post-Ukraine: In search of core leadership. In N. Tocci (Ed.), *Imagining Europe. Towards a more united and effective EU* (pp. 133–162). Nuova Cultura: Rome.

Hurrell, A. (2007). One world? Many worlds? The place of regions in the study of international society. *International Affairs, 83*(1), 127–146.

Kagan, R. (2003). *Of paradise and power. America and Europe in the new world order*. New York: Random House.

Kazal, R. A. (1995). Revisiting assimilation: The rise, fall and reappraisal of a concept in American ethnic history. *The American Historical Review, 100*(2), 437–471.

Keohane, R. O. (1993). Institutionalist theory and the realist challenge after the Cold War. In D. Baldwin (Ed.), *Neorealism and neoliberalism. The contemporary debate* (pp. 269–300). New York: Columbia University Press.

Lake, D. A. (2006). *Hierarchy in international relations: Authority, sovereignty and the new structure of world politics*. San Diego: University of California San Diego.

McCalla, R. B. (1996). NATO's persistence after the Cold War. *International Organisation, 50*(3), 445–475.

McNamara, K. R. (2008). The ties that bind? US-EU economic relations and the institutionalisation of the Atlantic Alliance. In J. Anderson, J. Ikenberry, & T. Risse (Eds.), *The end of the West? crisis and change in the Atlantic order* (p. 157–185). Ithaca/London: Cornell University Press.

Mearsheimer, J. (1990). Back to the future. Instability in Europe after the Cold War. *International Security, 15*(1), 5–56.

Menon, A. (2014). The JCMS annual review lecture: Divided and declining? Europe in a changing world. *Journal of Common Market Studies, 52*(1), 5–24.

Merlingen, M., & Ostrauskaite, R. (2006). *European Union peacebuilding and policing*. Abbingdon/New York: Routledge.

Moravcsik, A. (1993). Preferences and power in the European Community: A liberal intergovernmentalist approach. *Journal of Common Market Studies, 31*(4), 473–524.

Moravcsik, A. (1998). *The choice for Europe: Social purpose and state power from Messina to Maastricht*. Ithaca: Cornell University Press.

Novosseloff, A. (2012). Options for improving UN-EU cooperation in the field of peacekeeping. In J. Krause & N. Ronzitti (Eds.), *The EU, the UN and collective security* (pp. 150–174). London: Routledge.

Nuttall, S. (2000). *European foreign policy*. Oxford: Oxford University Press.

Pastor, R. (2003, June). North America: Three nations, a partnership, or a community? *Jean Monnet/Robert Schuman Paper Series, 5*(13).

Pollack, M. (2012). Realist, intergovernmental and institutionalist approaches. In E. Jones, A. Menon, & S. Weaterhill (Eds.), *The Oxford handbook of the European Union* (pp. 3–17). Oxford: Oxford University Press.

Risse, T. (2012, September). *Determinants and features of international alliances and partnerships* (Transworld Working Paper).

Robberecht, M.J. (2013, October). The European Union external action in time of crisis and change: Impact of the economic and financial crisis. *GREEN European Policy Brief*.

Rosato, S. (2011). *Europe united: Power politics and the making of the European community*. Ithaca: Cornell University Press.

Tocci, N. (2014). *On power and norms: Libya, Syria and the responsibility to protect* (Transatlantic Academy 2013–2014 Paper Series No. 2).

Tull, D. (2012). UN peacekeeping missions during the past two decades. In J. Krause & N. Ronzitti (Eds.), *The EU, the UN and collective security* (pp. 117–149). London: Routledge.

Van Langenhove, L. (2012). Why we need to 'Unpack' regions to compare them more effectively. *The International Spectator, 47*(1), 16–29.

Waltz, K. (1979). *Theory of international politics*. Ithaca: Cornell University Press.

Waltz, K. (1993). The emerging structure of international politics. *International Security, 18*(22), 44–79.

Waltz, K. (2000). Structural realism after the Cold War. *International Security, 25*(1), 5–41.

Wendt, A. (1992). Anarchy is what states make of it: The social construction of power politics. *International Organization, 46*(2), 391–425.

Wendt, A. (1999). *Social theory of international politics*. Cambridge/New York: Cambridge University Press.

Wiener, A., & Diez, T. (2009). *European integration theories*. Oxford: Oxford University Press.

Chapter 9
Latin America's Interregional Reconfiguration: The Beginning or the End of Latin America's Continental Integration?

Paul Isbell and Kimberly Nolan García

Abstract This chapter investigates the development of regionalism and interregionalism in Latin America as pertains to trade relations, one of the key drivers of regional integration in the region. The chapter develops the outlines of the thesis that Latin America or South America no longer provide the optimal geography for constituting an appropriate region. New ocean basin regions offer more promising regional and interregional trajectories to regroup Latin American countries than do their currently conceived land-based trade regions. By 're-mapping' national figures for bilateral commercial trade the chapter provides initial quantitative evidence of new Latin American regional trade dynamics emerging within the continent's two flanking ocean basin regions – the Pacific Basin and the Atlantic Basin – where new forms of non-hegemonic and maritime-centered regionalisms are being articulated and developed. The chapter concludes that new 'ocean basin regionalisms' offer alternative options for regional trade agreements and interregional trade integration which, while remaining complementary to the current sub-continental and continental regionalisms, could become a new guiding frame for Latin American regionalism.

Keywords Atlantic • Interregionalism • Regional organisations • Regionalism • Regions

P. Isbell (✉)
Center for Transatlantic Relations, Johns Hopkins University SAIS, Washington, DC, USA
e-mail: pisbell1@jhu.edu

K.N. García
Centro de Investigación y Docencia Económicas (CIDE), Mexico City, Mexico
e-mail: k.nolan.g@gmail.com

© Springer International Publishing AG 2018   149
F. Mattheis, A. Litsegård (eds.), *Interregionalism across the Atlantic Space*,
United Nations University Series on Regionalism 15,
DOI 10.1007/978-3-319-62908-7_9

9.1 Introduction

The unique construct of Latin America – partly cultural, partly geographical – has been forged and bounded by experiences of conquest and independence, language and history, political movements and economic trends that have unfolded since the Napoleonic age, which prepared the way for Simon Bolivar's *Gran Colombia* – the first union of independent nations in Latin America – some two centuries ago.[1] This 'Latin American history' has been common enough to have long served to designate the countries of the 'continent' of South America, the 'sub-continent' of Central America, and Mexico, along with the islands of the Caribbean basin, as an identifiable *region*[2] – that is, a set of states interconnected by varying forms of state interaction (Alcaro and Reilly in this volume).

The Bolivarian dream was once to unite the Andean states under a single political project. In more contemporary periods, however, the heterogeneity of Latin American states (both between and within them) that remained hidden behind failed regional integration projects are generally viewed to have conspired to leave *political* cooperation less than minimally realized. This in turn channeled regional integration forces toward the potentially more immediate and concrete payoff to be expected from the deepening of fruitful *economic* linkages implied by regional integration.

Certainly from 1960 forward, with the creation of the Latin American Free Trade Association (LAFTA), the Central American Common Market (CACM), and later, the emergence of the Andean Pact in 1969, the motor of 'regionalism' in Latin America has been *regional integration, defined as* the process by which states within a particular region increase their level of interaction with regard to economic, security, political, or social and cultural issues (Van Ginkel and Van Langenhove 2003: 4). More specifically, for this chapter we recognize and prioritize trade as the driver of regional integration, meaning both trade and policy decisions made by states to facilitate the removal of barriers and promote commercial trade in goods and services (following Hurrell [1995: 43]).

By the twenty-first century, those early Latin American trade agreements had transformed into modern and complex regimes: LAFTA into the Latin American Integration Association (ALADI) in 1980; CACM into the Central American Integration System (SICA) in 1993; the signing of NAFTA (North American Free Trade Agreement) with Mexico, the US and Canada by 1994, a modern Mercosur by 1991, and transformation of the Andean pact into the Andean Community by

---

[1] 'Latin America' has historically been used as a cultural category, originating from the European idea to set it apart from the Protestant, Anglophone former British colonies in the North and to tie them to European 'Latin' countries, mainly France (Panlatinism). However, with time the context and framing of its use have changed both in the 'Latin American world' and globally.

[2] Admittedly, to call South America a 'continent' – as we do here – is more in line with the way the English-speaking world tends to see, and to regionalize and label the world map. The 'Latin' or 'Iberoamerican' tendency, at least historically, would have been to view 'South America' as a 'subcontinent' of the 'Americas.' But whether it is labeled in *anglo* or latin terms, South America has served as an aspirational framing for either a regional integration goal or a 'sub/continental stepping stone' to an inclusive Americas regional association. Today, the world's international organizations, like the UN or the Inter-American Development Bank designate Latin America and the Caribbean (or LAC) as a formal categorical region, including all of the non-Latin countries of the region.

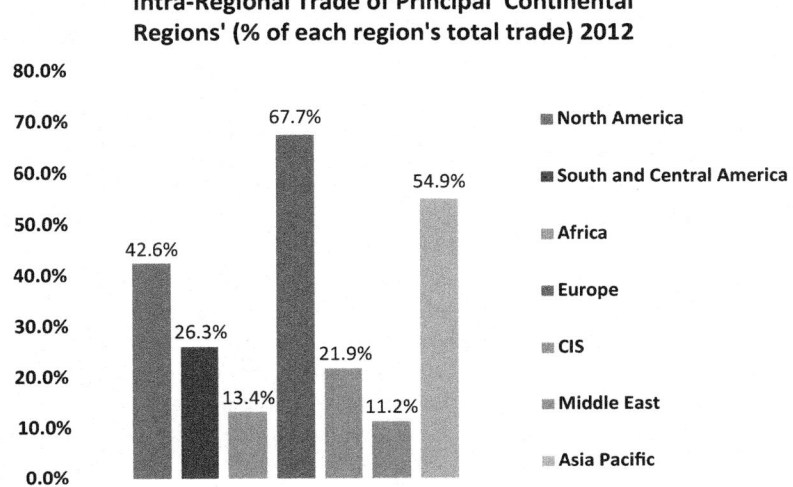

Fig. 9.1 Intraregional trade of principal 'continental regions' as a percentage of each region's total trade (2012) (*Source: WTO and own elaboration*)

1996. Despite this – and together with the emergence of an overlapping sets of new trade agreements, sometimes featuring the same members and sometimes not – 'intra-regional' trade in 'Central and South America' today still lags far behind some other 'continental' regions and regional projects. Using data from the WTO, Fig. 9.1 shows that intraregional trade in Central and South America combined stands at just 27%, compared to Asia-Pacific and broader Europe at 55% and 68% respectively. In terms of regional projects, intraregional trade is 52% in the Asian blocs, 63% in the European Union (EU) and 44% in North America/NAFTA.[3]

Clearly, repeated attempts to unite the Latin American region under the banner of trade integration have not overcome the very real complexities of political cooperation, nor has insertion into world markets through trade resolved questions of uneven economic development within Latin American countries. Although lip service is often paid to geography, most evaluations of LAC's integration failures focus on political factors, like insufficient political will, excessive 'political heterogeneity' or the barriers often unpredictably posed by the various domestic political economies. Only rarely is geography invoked as a force as powerful as politics, even though it favors disaggregation and disunion.[4] Even when some have acknowledged

---

[3] We refer to *intra-regional* trade as the commercial exchange of goods and services within states of the same 'region'. *Extra-regional* trade is therefore trade with a state outside of a chosen region. Individual *inter-regional* trade flows are part of total extra-regional trade (Söderbaum and Van Langenhove, 2013).

[4] Apart from the continuing barriers represented by the Andes, the Amazon and the rest of the vast continental deep interior, analysts also point to the uniqueness of the South American hinterland which, along its Southern Atlantic counterpart in Africa, has never been as porous to global flows, or as accessible to governance, as have the Great Plains of North America, the northern-central plains of the European subcontinent, or even the great Heartland of Eurasia (Botafogo and Oliveira 2013).

the role of Latin American geography, Latin American states have not often looked beyond the horizon bounding the geographic and culturally-defined space of 'Latin America', and certainly not beyond the landmasses of the 'Western Hemisphere', when charting their regional and inter-regional strategic trajectories.[5]

Although geography is somewhat fixed, both technology and political economies continue to shift, changing our relationship with geography and the ecology which it embodies, even if our perceptions of what we consider the relevant geography do not change. This suggests that the many impasses and forced fits of Latin American regionalism today, and those associated with 'trade regionalism' in particular, have been produced by an overly simplistic and outmoded perception of geography. This conceptualization is at the core of the thesis of this chapter: *while geography has not been completely forgotten, it continues to be misread by many Latin Americans, and many others, because we are reading it with increasingly distorted and outmoded maps.*

We argue that 'Latin America' no longer serves as the optimal geography for an appropriate region, whether interpreted narrowly as a trade region, or more broadly as a multi-faceted governance region. Although the vectors of Latin American trade flows continue to overlap to some degree with the currently existing system of formal regional trade agreements (RTAs), these shifting flows may no longer appropriately fit what is an increasingly outmoded system of Latin American trade regionalism. Rather, new Latin American regionalisms based on the spaces of the 'ocean basins' may offer a more appropriate regional horizon for Latin American countries to pursue. This chapter presents the outlines of that new map, arguments for its use (at least as a useful new complement to the typical integration roadmap focused on land-based, 'continental' regions), and its implications for Latin America.

9.2   Regionalism and Latin American Regional Integration

As the editors of the Ashgate Research Companion to Regionalism concluded: "Despite a number of recent analyses [...] that have cogently illustrated new regionalism's promising precepts – drawing our attention to the multiplicity and multilayered character of regions and emphasizing the importance of non-state actors and spaces – the main theoretical implications of 'new' regionalisms still seem to bypass many contemporary (and conventional) studies of regions [...]. The orthodoxy of the state as the principal builder and shaper (or dismantler) of regions remains central in many of these studies [...]." (Shaw et al. 2010: 4).

9.2.1   Trade as Driver and Indicator

In the definitional space between a 'region', understood as a set of states interconnected by forms of state interaction (which does not necessarily require active state *agency,* following Alcaro and Reilly (in this volume), and 'regionalism' as a

---

[5] EU relations is of course is the prominent exception (see Ayuso and Gardini in this volume).

'state-led project' to reorganize regional space along economic or political lines (Payne and Gamble 1996), there is an intermediate and flexible form: 'regional integration.' Van Ginkel and Van Langenhove (2003) define this as a process by which states in a region increase their level of interaction in the economic, security, political, or social and cultural domains, but 'regional integration' *may or may not* imply a proactive state role, particularly at earlier stages, or in more shallow forms. Holding a simultaneous view of regionalism as a *process* as well as an *outcome* – as we do – would imply that a project of creating a 'region' can always be under construction, potentially, regardless of the proactive nature of state involvement (or lack of it), or of the expanding range of transnational protagonists and agents now operating in lieu of, or alongside, states.

Trade takes over nearly from the beginning of the story in Latin America as the most obvious driver of 'South American' or 'Latin American' regionalism. We start with the assumption – which we claim, *prima facie* – that a relatively high degree of 'intra-regional' economic interdependence – or its pursuit – has acted as the key component in the construction of regionalisms, but particularly in Latin America.[6]

In such a context, 'intra-regional' trade (in relation to 'extra-regional,' and 'inter-regional' trade) represent one of the (if not the) key connections between the countries of a region or potential region, and becomes a key indicator of the existence or nascent emergence of a region or potential region, in trade terms in particular, but also of a broader regionalism as well. But because trade is so important among international connections via physical flows, intra-regional trade also serves as a broad but credible proxy for regional connectedness and mutual interdependency in general.

9.3   Post-hegemonic Regionalism and New forms of Regional Integration in Latin America

In the most recent stage of regional integration, which Tussie and Riggirozzi (2012) labeled *post-hegemonic regionalism*, new patterns have begun to emerge. As we will demonstrate more fully below, some of these new patterns play out upon the 'mental map' of Latin America's broadening regional and inter-regional horizons. This includes the widespread perception that the Atlantic has been displaced by the Pacific (and by China in particular) in terms of global economic significance and geopolitical importance, but other dynamics are unfolding in and across the very ocean basins of the Atlantic and the Pacific worlds. The Atlantic and the Pacific basins represent a newly emerging form of open, post-hegemonic,

---

[6] One can make the case that other aspects of global economic activity, including investment balances and flows, corporate and supply-chain structures, and technological advances should also be considered key drivers of regionalisms and regional dynamics, but we do not treat these here, at least not directly, for reasons of space, time and resources. See Ayuso and Gardini in this volume for a discussion of waves of Latin American regional integration.

maritime-centered regionalism. Both are currently experiencing multi-faceted intra-regional-basin deepening, in trade and other flows, and in new forms of transnational cooperation, mutually feeding each other's development with 'inter-basin' Atlantic-Pacific trade – an inter-regional trade flow vector that will grow with the enlarging of the Panama Canal.

The most recent example of this post-hegemonic phase of regionalism has been the movement –both regional and inter-regional at once– toward cooperation and integration among the Pacific Basin states of Latin America, as in the Pacific Alliance of Mexico, Colombia, Peru, and Chile, an initiative that began in April of 2011. While these four partners have, in general terms, liberalized their trade through previous agreements, their objective now is to eliminate 92% of tariffs between them (IISS 2015). The Pacific Alliance also represents a new 'coastal' vector of inter-regionalism within Latin America, as it joins Mexico with three Pacific Andean states. Furthermore, the Pacific Alliance (Chile, Peru, Colombia and Mexico), through its participation[7] in the proposed Trans-Pacific Partnership (TPP),[8] is extending this vector of open, non-hegemonic inter-regionalism across the Pacific Basin to Asia,[9] possibly creating a new form of maritime-centered, ocean basin regionalism, as we propose more thoroughly in the sections that follow.

9.4   The Limits of Latin America's 'Continental' Regionalism

In the end, Bolivar's dream has never been realized, and the history of regional economic integration in Latin America as a whole largely reveals a record of relative failure. While integration seemed the ideal solution early on, sovereignty and heterogeneous policy preferences proved to be important obstacles (Moreira et al.

---

[7] Chile, Peru and Mexico have all signed the TPP (Trans-Pacific Partnership), while Colombia announced interest in signing the TPP back in 2010.

[8] The future of the TPP has been clouded with uncertainty since Donald Trump, President of the US, signed an executive order on January 23, 2017 which withdrew the US from the trade agreement. Nevertheless, it remains more than possible that a transpacific trade agreement will come into being, sooner or later. It could be a TPP which initially does not involve the US. China could also sign the TPP – possibly provoking a future US administration to return to it as well – or it could take advantage of the moment to consolidate the Regional Comprehensive Economic Partnership, a pan-Asian regional trade agreement which is not as deep or as wide-embracing as the TPP and does not include any transpacific partners from the Americas. The TPP includes: Australia, Brunei, Canada, Chile, Japan, Malaysia, Mexico, New Zealand, Peru, Singapore, the United States (until January 23, 2017) and Vietnam. The RCEP includes: the ten member states of the Association of Southeast Asian Nations (ASEAN) (Brunei, Cambodia, Indonesia, Laos, Malaysia, Myanmar, the Philippines, Singapore, Thailand, Vietnam) and the six states with which ASEAN has existing free trade agreements (Australia, China, India, Japan, South Korea and New Zealand).

[9] Non-hegemonic in that a Pacific Basin with both the US and China, along with developing and emerging countries would offset any hegemonic pattern. See "Pacific Alliance Trade Bloc Eyes Global Role," *Strategic Comments*, February 2014, 20(2), pp. ix–x.

2007: 101). For example, even four decades of integration efforts, the Caribbean has not yet achieved the desired results. Other experiments (eg, Mercosur and Andean Community) failed due to the central contradiction between wanting greater integration internationally, while sustaining protectionist policies of import substitution domestically (ISI) (Kaltenthaler and Mora 2002: 72). The 'old regionalism' in Latin America never had a lasting economic impact – independent of what some countries, like Brazil, actually managed to get out its ISI strategy, and was never implemented on a wide scale, although it did generate lively historical and theoretical debates and was emulated in other parts of the developing world, particularly in Africa (Moreira et al. 2007).

During the first two decades (1990s and 2000s) of the globalization era, the economic potential of integration was not fully realized. This has generally been attributed to the fact that states did not implement sufficient domestic policy changes to promote deep integration, or to remove barriers that remain around rules of origin, residual tariffs, technical standards and harmonization and other regulatory standards, infrastructure issues, and other market structure barriers (Mashayekhi et al. 2005: 20). Yet, the 'continental' Latin American dream that has grown from Bolivar and was fed by many others, is not yet quite dead. Inter-regionalisms between intersecting sub-regional agreements with overlapping memberships, and the growing need for harmonized rules of origin and other trade rules imply that 'continental scales' of integration are possible.[10]

We would have expected that the proliferation of regional trade associations (RTAs) in Latin America during the 1990s (undertaken in spite of ongoing political heterogeneities), along with the expansion of bilateral agreements between American states in the post-2000 period, would have generated relatively high, or, in the very least, higher levels of 'intra-regional' trade within these regions, as a percentage of total trade, than in the past. However, this has not necessarily been the case.

Figure 9.1 presents intra-regional trade (as a percentage share of total trade) for the world's principal 'continental' regions. It reveals that intra-regional trade in Latin America – in this particular case meaning, South and Central America plus the Caribbean, but not Mexico – is very low, only 15% of the total trade of the 'region.'[11] This is well below (or, about half) the global intra-continental average (and is dwarfed by the intra-regional trade levels of Europe (68% in broader Europe) and those of Asia (55% in the broader Asia-Pacific).

---

[10] UNASUR, the Union of South American Nations, is one such continental project. Signed in 2008, the agreement intends to unite the already consolidated agreements of Mercosur and the Andean Community into one agreement that features the rules of the regional trade accords of both, within a Mercosur-style overarching political structure for common policies, including regional security issues and a regional development bank. The key to the UNASUR project is overlapping membership by Bolivia and Venezuela. Mexico and Panama serve as outside observers.

[11] Mexico is included in the North American region, as its main source of imports and market for exports remains the US, both through NAFTA.

Extending the regional unit of analysis to embrace the entire 'super-continental' landmass of the Americas would average out the intra-regional trade levels of North and Central/South America, but also now include within the 'intra-regional' trade category all of the 'inter-regional' trade flows between North and South America that would previously not have been included. Nevertheless, this act of 'data cartography' only puts Latin Americans within the much larger context of the old 'Western Hemisphere' at 'intra-regional' trade levels of only 32%, which is still well below the global average, 37%, for the world's 'continental regions'.

Perhaps, as we propose throughout the remainder of this chapter, the missing piece to the puzzle of failed Latin America regionalisms in general, and regional integration in particular, is to be found in their faulty geographies, not only in the nature of the agents and protagonists, as the incipient 'third waves' of regionalism thought and analyses are beginning to suggest (see Shaw 2010).

9.5   Re-mapping Latin America's Trade Regionalisms and Interregional Horizons

Ever since the World Wars and the times of decolonization, the *Atlantic* has generally meant the North Atlantic (i.e., the US, Canada and Europe) and *transatlantic relations* have largely meant relations between the nation-state members of the North Atlantic Treaty Organization (NATO). The Southern Atlantic has been, if not forgotten, then typically split up and distributed into other conceptual or regional categories. In any event, most observers do not yet tend to think of the Atlantic Basin in its entirety, both North and South, as a distinct, coherent and potentially unifying space upon their mental maps.

In large part this is because the emergence of the Pacific Basin in the late 1980s sparked a cyclical global discourse over the decline of the West, giving rise to a conceptual rivalry over whether the new century would ultimately be proclaimed the 'Pacific Century' or rather, the 'Asian Century.' The former might imply that the net effect of post-Cold War globalization would be a long-term shift in the center of gravity of global power from the Atlantic to the Pacific Basin. North America would still remain the dominant protagonist, via its Pacific projection (due to the weight of the US market), but such a shift would imply that Europe would now find itself increasingly irrelevant in geopolitical and geoeconomic terms (Lamo de Espinosa 2010).

An 'Asian Century,' on the other hand, could imply that globalization would produce a structural shift in relative global power and influence from the geographic and historical West to the East, regardless of whether this would be the result of an absolute decline of the West or a relative 'rise of the Rest' (Amsden 2011). In both cases, however, the 'Atlantic' slips out of view, as the focus of attention shifts to 'Asia-Pacific,' the geographical antipodes of the 'West' and its traditional North Atlantic axis.

These recent shifts upon our mental maps of the world have largely followed the global media's portrayal of the rise of Asia and the Pacific during the age of globalization. As we will see below, however, these 'shifts' are more deeply framed by a number of ingrained patterns of perception developed during the Cold War past which continue to obscure from our view both the Pacific and Atlantic Basins, and the oceans and seascapes in general as coherent analytical, strategically significant, and potentially unifying spaces.

9.6   The Emerging 'Ocean basin seascapes': The Blind Spot on Our Global Data Maps

The four major ocean basins –the Atlantic, Pacific, Indian and Arctic Basins, along with their tributary seas and sub-basins (like the Caribbean, Mediterranean and Baltic Basins)– together constitute a global seascape which covers the dominant part of the surface of the planet and constitutes, within its sub-surface depths, 96% of the living space of the biosphere by volume (Borges de Sousa and Lobo Pereira, 2014). This 'global seascape' connects all of the terrestrial continental bodies, and envelops all of the world's islands through its four main ocean basin articulations.

Furthermore, this global (or basin) 'seascape' is on the rise, relative to the landscape, in strategic terms. Transportation and commerce have, and continue to be, far more efficiently undertaken by sea. Over 90% of physical merchandise trade (by volume, and three-quarters by value) takes place via marine transport along the world's sea lanes (Stopford 2010). This maritime traffic includes two-thirds of the global oil trade, one-third of the gas trade, and the large majority of other global material flows, which together are expected to triple by mid-century (Stopford 2010). Total global seaborne trade has increased since 1970 at an average annual rate of 3.1% and is expected to double yet again by 2030 (UNCTAD 2012).

Already some 5% of global GDP – or 3 trillion U.S. dollars annually – is generated from marine and coastal industries, while some 40% of the world's population directly depends upon marine and coastal biodiversity.[12] Some estimates monetize the full economic value of the ocean basins at as high as US$20 trillion per year, (upwards of 20% to 25% of current annual global GDP.[13] Furthermore, the role of the oceans in the maintenance of species diversity and of coastal ecosystem ser-

---

[12] See Marcia Stanton, "The Worth of the Deep Blue," *Namib Times*, April 27, 2013 (http://www.namibtimes.net/forum/topics/the-worth-of-the-deep-blue), and Global Ocean Commission, "Petitioning Ban Ki-moon: Help secure a living ocean, food and prosperity – propose a new agreement for high seas protection" September 2014. (https://www.change.org/en-GB/petitions/ban-ki-moon-help-secure-a-living-ocean-food-and-prosperity-propose-a-new-agreement-for-high-seas-protection-in-september-2014).

[13] According to Pitta e Cunha (2014), a World Bank study undertaken in 2008 estimated that the total annual value of all marine ecosystem services, globally, and for which there already existed a market, was US$20 trillion, equivalent to about 33% of a nominal Global GDP at the time of around US$60 trillion.

vices, and in the absorption of carbon dioxide, is critical, and given the deplorable state of oceans in general and their rapid rate of deterioration it will demand more and more intensive transnational collaboration (Holthus et al. 2012; Holthus 2012).

Even so, most of our historical, existing or aspirational 'regionalisms' and 'regions' remain terrestrial, land-based, 'sub-continental' or 'continental', as opposed to maritime-centered, ocean basin-based-regions and regionalisms. Certainly, the central thrusts of the trade driver of Latin America regionalism in the age of globalization have come primarily from the more traditional, land-based, sub-continental and continental RTAs and regionalisms like Mercosur, the Andean Community, the Central America Common Market, and even NAFTA and the aspirational Free Trade Association of the Americas (FTAA), although there have been some maritime-centered exceptions, like the CARICOM.

9.7   New Data Cartography

Our approach begins by re-categorizing, rearranging and 're-projecting' existing and generally available data. Applying this data cartography to the annual volumes of world trade, we have 'remapped' the intra-regional, inter-regional and other extra-regional trade flows of Latin America countries. To chart these data maps we have used two different cartographic data projections. The first – what we call the 'continental' projection reflects our current land-centered conceptions of regionalism. In this regional projection of the world, the data aggregates (and disaggregates) along national, conventional regional (ie, 'sub-continental' and 'continental') and global lines. We trace a world of individual countries, then an aggregated world community, and then the world organized as 'continental' regions; the result is a vision of regional borders that is nothing more than an exact 'print' of our land-dominated mental maps.

The second, new projection of the global map, we call the 'ocean basin projection.' This projection of the data onto the global trade map allows for a maritime-centered conception of regionalism. Rather than simply see – and analyze – data, trends and projections at the continental level (in additional to the national and global level), this projection organizes the regional categories very differently.

Critically, the conceptual starting point is the sea, as opposed to the land. Rather than start with the island-landmasses and then proceed rapidly to drawing lines around the 'continents', cutting 'Europe' into existence by slicing the supercontinent along a very porous internal border, and leaving the oceans as the marine residue, we take any world map, and set the focus of our attention first on the oceans. An 'ocean basin projection' would incorporate the seascape along with its maritime rimlands and its islands, including 'dual basin islands' that separate one basin from another, mediating between them.

To generate an ocean basin map projection, we cast the data within the frame of a world map which has been then 're-projected' into three major ocean basin regions and a residual land-based region:

1. the Atlantic Basin
2. the Pacific Basin
3. the Indian Basin

Once the ocean basins have been delineated[14] and the continental landmasses split, as a result, along their geographic and political economy continental divides, a new regional unit of analysis is acknowledged:

4. the Great Crescent

This new 'notional region' groups together the 'rest of the world' (ROW) that is 'left over' by such an ocean basin projection of the globe, that is, the Middle East, Central Asia and Russia. Put another way, the so-called 'Great Crescent' is what remains as the residual land-based region of an ocean basin world. The Great Crescent could be viewed not just as a shadow of the former 'pivot of history,' but also as the geopolitical antipode or geopolitical photographic negative of what was once the forgotten South Atlantic.

Ocean basin projections provide a cartographic data tool with which to nudge our currently reigning geopolitical and geo-economic maps away from their over-whelmingly national, land-based, continental regional framings, and towards a more fully-fledged ocean basin projection of our global mental maps, one that we believe is more in line with the emerging strategic realities and global flow vectors.[15]

9.8   The Emerging Outlines of Ocean Basin Regions

To produce an ocean basin projection of the global geopolitical and geo-economic flow map requires 're-cutting' the current data to account for a number of geographical realities of the world's ocean basins. Continental data categories need to be split between the ocean basins on their shores. Among other issues, this analytical need raises the question of how to meaningfully reflect and properly account for the 'intra-basin' and 'extra-basin' trade of the land-locked and dual basin countries

---

[14] The Arctic Basin is one of the inevitable 'blind spots' of this version of the ocean basin projection. However, we have only ignored the Arctic Basin because of very limiting data and methodological constraints. In particular, to build our regional mapping model of global flows to include the Arctic as the 'fourth basin' would require a category for 'tri-basin countries,' and much more complex structures and coding within the model. Given these short-term limitations, together with the fact that the Arctic has not yet truly opened to global flows, it has been sacrificed in this initial version of the projection.

[15] While we believe that this new conceptualization is a more valid and universal construction, we also acknowledge that we are only advocating substituting one paradigm for another.

(ie, those with coastlines on more than one ocean basin, like the US, South Africa or Indonesia).

In order to affect this re-cutting of dual basin and land-locked countries and their trade flow splits, and then to aggregate country trade flows into our new ocean basin regions, we have created an Alternative Regional Mapping Model (ARM). A description of the model, including an explanation of the dual basin adjustment, and a list identifying each country in the world by basin region, can be found in the Annex.

The broad outlines of an ocean basin world emerges in Fig. 9.2, which presents the recent evolution of the share of each basin's intra-regional trade in relation to its total trade. Both the Atlantic Basin and Pacific Basin exhibit very high shares of intra-basin trade at 72% and 65%, respectively. These intra-regional trade shares remain more than twice as high as the corresponding shares for the entire Western Hemisphere and the world's other 'continental' landmasses. The recent evolution has been relatively flat for both, with the expected slight decline in the Atlantic, and the expected slight rise in the Pacific Basin. This suggests that these two ocean basins have regionalized far more in trade terms than have the landmasses of the Americas, Latin America's traditional space for trade regionalism and inter-regionalism.

Furthermore, while the intra-regional trade shares of the Indian Basin and the Great Crescent are much lower, at 23% and 20% respectively, these are still higher than most of the world's continental landmasses, and they have grown faster than any other intra- or inter-regional trade flow vectors possible in an ocean basin world, 10 in all. This suggests that as the ocean basins coalesce as a basic regional structure within the global system, the gravities of trade are pushing the frontiers of regionalisms into the sea.

Figure 9.3 and Table 9.1 broaden the picture of global trade flows by including the six ocean basin inter-regional flow vectors along with the four intra-regional flow vectors shown above in Fig. 9.2. Table 9.1 reveals that the intra-Atlantic trade

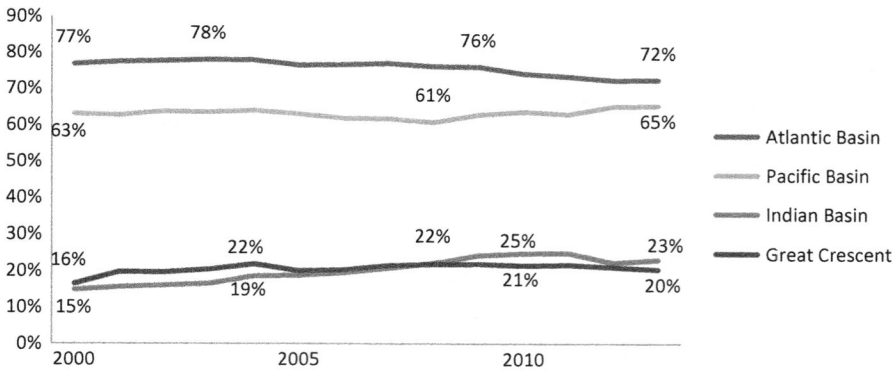

Fig. 9.2 Ocean basin 'Intra-regional' trade in the world's ocean basin regions (*Source: UNCOMTRADE database on total global (bilateral) trade and own elaboration*)

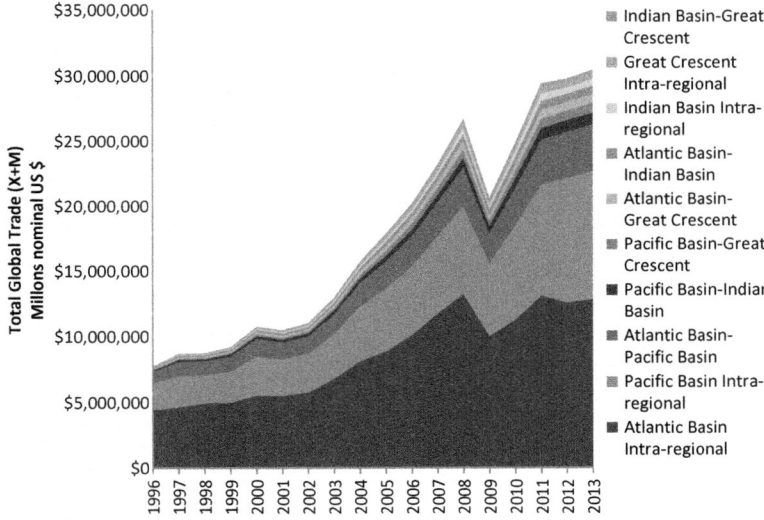

Fig. 9.3 Regional articulation of global trade in a regional ocean basin world, 1996–2013

contributed more to total growth in global trade than any other flow vector at 37.1%, including intra-Pacific Basin trade (35%) and Pacific-Atlantic Basin inter-regional trade (12%). Nevertheless, flow vector growth rates of the period were more or less inverse to the size of relative shares – suggesting 'basin re-balancing' in the context of globalizing growth – with the smallest flow vectors like intra-Indian Basin and intra-Great Crescent trade growing the fastest. In Fig. 9.3, we see the dominant share of intra-Atlantic Basin trade with the total of all global trade flows (nearly half over the entire period); while this share fell to 42% by 2013.

9.9 Testing the 'Ocean Basin' Hypothesis

In light of the above, we propose an 'ocean basin' hypothesis:

> The ocean basins are more densely connected, or 'regionalized' by international, 'intra-regional' flows than are the traditional, land-based continental regions in LAC.

This hypothesis will be tested by *a comparison of 'intra-regional' trade connections* which serve as proxy indicators for regionalization as defined by the density of international flow connections. If this hypothesis can be supported by the data, then it is worth further exploration of our claim that a more logical, if not optimal, space for economic regionalisms, are the ocean basins not the land-based, 'sub-continental' and 'continental' regions which have dominated Latin American (and most other) strategic traditions.

Table 9.1 Intra-basin and Inter-basin Regional Trade Patterns Articulating an Ocean Basin Pattern and Dynamic of On-going Globalization, 1996–2013

Intra-regional (4)/ interregional (6) trade flows	Share of total global trade			Total growth (%) of trade flow vector 2000–13	Contribution of trade flow vector to growth in total global trade 2000–13
	1996	2000	2013		
Atlantic Basin intra-regional/ intra-basin (1)	57%	51%	42%	133%	37.1%
Atlantic Basin-Pacific Basin inter-regional/ inter-basin (1)	11%	13%	12%	168%	11.5%
Atlantic Basin-Indian Basin inter-regional/ inter-basin (5)	1%	2%	2%	275%	2.3%
Atlantic Basin-Great Crescent inter-regional/ inter-basin (4)	1%	1%	2%	345%	2.8%
Pacific Basin Intra-regional intra-regional/ intra-basin (2)	26%	27%	32%	233%	34.9%
Pacific Basin-Indian Basin inter-regional/ inter-basin (2)	1%	2%	3%	293%	3.4%
Pacific Basin-Great Crescent inter-regional/ inter-basin (3)	1%	1%	2%	379%	3.0%
Indian Basin Intra-regional Intra-regional/ intra-basin (3)	0%	1%	2%	569%	2.3%
Indian Basin-Great Crescent inter-regional/ inter-basin (6)	0%	1%	1%	300%	0.9%
Great Crescent intra-regional in (4)	0%	1%	1%	489%	1.8%
Total global trade	*100%*	*100%*	*100%*	*184%*	*100%*

The testing of this hypothesis is underpinned by a few assumptions. The first assumption is that trade is at least a potential driver of regionalism. The second is that intra-regional trade is at least a reasonable for indicating regional connectedness. A related assumption is that the growth of intra-regional trade and its contribution to the growth of total trade indicates, as a proxy, a deepening 'regionalization' of such connectedness. Finally, it is assumed that deepening 'regionalization' and 'connectedness' are reasonable indicators of the possible existence of a justifiable logic for exploring a more formal regionalism, like regional integration in any of its deepest or more shallow forms.

9.9.1   First Indicator Test

The first key indicator used to test the hypothesis is the share of a country's total international trade which is considered to be 'intra-regional', meaning trade with another country that is considered to belong to the same 'region.' This indicator represents the relative intensity of a country's international trade interdependence, or intraregional trade 'connectedness' within a defined region. This indicator is formulated, once the region of comparison has been defined, by dividing the level of a country's intraregional trade by the level of its total global trade. What is not 'intra-regional' trade is considered to be 'extra-regional' trade with the rest of the world, meaning trade with countries outside the defined region. 'Inter-regional' trade, which is a sub-set of 'extra-regional' trade, is considered to be trade outside the defined region with another defined region.

To conduct the test, a country's intra-regional trade share within its corresponding 'ocean basin region' is first compared to that within its existing traditional land-based 'sub-continental' region. Second, a country's intra-regional trade share within its corresponding 'ocean basin region' is then compared to that within its land-based 'continental' region. Finally, a country's intra-regional trade share within its corresponding 'ocean basin region' is compared to that within its land-based 'super-continental' region. In doing so, we provide new maps with comparative trade data across three levels of analysis: the sub regional scale, the midrange scale of continent, and the superregional scale.

Our expectation is that if the traditional, land-based, 'sub-continental' and 'continental' regionalisms of Latin America, driven as they have been by trade, regional integration and RTAs, are to be deemed successful today, then the share of *intra-regional trade* of Latin American countries *within* these RTAs should be higher than their conceptual counterparts, the ocean basin regions, and/or growing.

Table 9.2 summarizes the full range of results for Atlantic and Pacific Latin American countries, and dual basin and land-locked countries, respectively. All of the Atlantic and Pacific countries in our universe of ten Latin America countries passed the hypothesis test at all the levels of regional scale, with the sole exception of Ecuador, which passed the ocean basin test at the 'sub-continental' and 'continental' regional scales, but not at the 'super-continental' scale of the notional FTAA. A completely successful test at all three levels of regional scale is marked by an asterisk (*), while a plus (+) denotes that the test was successful at all but the 'supercontinental' (FTAA) level.

Table 9.2 confirms that all of the dual-basin and land-locked Latin American countries in our universe pass the hypothesis test (when applying the first indicator of intra-regional trade shares) at the 'subcontinental' level of scale. Paraguay, which is land-locked, meets the test on all scales. Bolivia, which is land-locked, and Colombia, which is dual-basin, both meet the test on all but at the scale of the super-continent, meaning that they both trade more within the Atlantic Basin than they do within their sub continental zone, or within South America. In the case of Colombia,

Table 9.2 Trade with Sub-Continental, Continental and Ocean Basin Regions, 2000–2013

Projection:	Sub-continental		Continental			Ocean Basin	
Country/Region	Mercosur	Andean Community	South America	FTAA	Other	Atlantic Basin	Pacific Basin
Atlantic Basin Countries ('Atlantic Latin America')							
Argentina							
% share of trade 2013	35		35	33		57+	30
% contribution to total Argentine trade growth	35		34	45		54+	33
Uruguay							
% trade 2013	36		36	46		59+	27
% contribution to total Uruguayan trade growth	32		31	39		53+	30
Brazil							
% share of trade 2013	15		15	33		49+	38
% contribution to total Brazilian trade growth	15		14	28	27	45+	41
Pacific Basin Countries ('Pacific Latin America')							
Chile							
% share of trade 2013	18		18	40		41	51+
% contribution to total Chilean trade growth	18		16	37		37	55+
Peru							
% share of trade 2013	19	7	19	47		45	50+
% contribution to total Peruvian trade growth	23	7	18	45		43	52+
Ecuador							
% share of trade 2013	22	12	22	65	2	42	53*
% contribution to total Ecuador trade growth	26	12	21	64	–	41	54*
Dual Basin and Landlocked Countries, Trade with Sub-Continental, Continental and Ocean Basin Regions							
Projection:	**Sub-continental**		**Continental**			**Ocean Basin**	
Country/Region	Mercosur	Andean Community	South America	FTAA	Other	Atlantic Basin	Pacific Basin

(continued)

Table 9.2 (continued)

Projection:	Sub-continental		Continental			Ocean Basin	
Country/Region	Mercosur	Andean Community	South America	FTAA	Other	Atlantic Basin	Pacific Basin
Dual Basin Countries							
Colombia							
% share of trade 2013	15	4	15	57		49*	44*
% contribution to total Colombia trade growth	19	3	13	53		47*	45*
Mexico							
% share of trade 2013			3	72	67	46∞	50∞
% contribution to total Mexican trade growth			5	62	54	43∞	54∞
Landlocked Countries							
Paraguay							
% share of trade 2013	46		46	54		61+	31
% contribution to total Paraguayan trade growth	44		44	51		58+	33
Bolivia							
% share of trade 2013	58	10	58	72	3	64*	33
% contribution to total Bolivia trade growth	62	10	60	72	4	64*	33

Source: UNCOMTRADE 2014 and own elaboration. "Other" categories are NAFTA (Mexico) and Alba (Bolivia and Ecuador)

the country trades more within both of its dual basin regions than it does with its own sub-continental zone or the entire South American continent.

Finally, Mexico, a dual-basin country, meets the test at the 'sub-continental' level in both ocean basins, but not at the continental or super-continental scales, as marked with an (∞). Mexico's intra-regional trade within the Pacific Basin is 50% of its total trade, and 46% within the Atlantic Basin. However, its intra-regional trade within the continental North American region to which it belongs (as in NAFTA) is 67%, greater that of its Pacific Basin trade, and within the All-Americas/FTAA notional 'super-continental' region it would be 72%. In the wake of the NAFTA agreement nearly 25 years ago, Mexico has integrated more within its traditional, land-based, continental North American region than with its equivalents in Latin America. However, its integration within the Pacific and Atlantic Basins was just behind its level of 'continental' integration in 2013, suggesting that basin-based 'intra-regional' trade is on the rise.

9.9.2   Atlantic Latin America

Nearly 60% of Argentina's merchandise trade is within the Atlantic Basin, compared to only one third of trade that takes place with countries of the 'continentally-constructed' Western Hemisphere. Half of Brazil's trade is intra-regional Atlantic Basin trade, while again only one-third – the global 'continental average' – is intra-regional 'super-continental trade' within a notional FTAA or Western Hemisphere. Even in Uruguay, where this ocean basin gravity is slightly less pronounced, the maritime-centered region of the Atlantic Basin still captures 15 percentage points more of its trade than does 'the continental region' of the Americas. Of course, in each case, the level of intra-regional trade (as a percentage of total national trade) within 'continental' Latin or South America is even lower than their levels within the super-continental Western Hemisphere (see Table 9.2).

9.9.3   Pacific Latin America

The overarching pattern in Pacific Latin America –Chile, Peru and Ecuador– with respect to the Pacific Basin parallels that of their Atlantic partners in Latin America with respect to their Atlantic Basin. In all three countries, intra-regional trade shares are higher with the maritime-centered Pacific Basin than with their land-based, 'sub-continental' and 'continental' regions – or (except in the case of Ecuador) the notional FTAA, which covers the entire Western Hemisphere. Once again, the ocean basin projection accounts for a higher percentage of trade, than the 'continental projection' (see Table 9.2).

Nevertheless, there are also some important differences between the Pacific and Atlantic Latin American countries, at least with respect to the intra- and inter-regional trade flows on our maps. For example, the former have higher intra-regional trade shares with their (land-based) 'notional' FTAA region than their Atlantic counterparts. On the other hand, the latter have higher intra-regional trade shares with their (land-based) actual 'subcontinental' (Mercosur, Andean Community) and notional 'continental' (South America) regions than do their Pacific counterparts. Furthermore, the Pacific group's trade with the Atlantic Basin is still higher than the Atlantic countries' trade with the Pacific, though the latter is increasing. These differences suggest that the Pacific Latin countries are more integrated with both the dual-basin countries of North America and the broader maritime-centered regions of both the Pacific and Atlantic Basins than with their own land-based sub-continental and continental regions in LAC. Meanwhile, although the Atlantic Latin countries have more intra-regional trade within the 'continental' regions of Latin America, they are still more integrated within their own Atlantic Basin region than are the Pacific Latin countries within their corresponding Pacific Basin.

9.9.4   Dual Basin Latin America

For both Colombia and Mexico – Latin America's two major 'dual-basin' countries – intra-regional trade shares are more or less balanced between their two potential basin regions – as expected, given their dual-basin status. However, Colombia currently inclines slightly to the Pacific Basin, while Mexico inclines slightly to the Atlantic. Again, for both countries, intra-regional trade shares are higher for both of their basins, simultaneously, than for the current land-based sub-continental regions in Latin America (ie, Mercosur, Andean Community). However, Mexico's intra-regional share is higher for its 'continental' region (NAFTA) than for its basin regions, as is its share within a notional FTAA. Within an FTAA, Colombia's intra-regional share is also higher than its basin shares, only not by nearly as much as in the case of Mexico.

9.9.5   Landlocked Latin America

Both land-locked Paraguay and Bolivia incline heavily to the Atlantic, as opposed to the Pacific, on the ocean basin projection of the regional map. Both countries, despite their 'land-locked' realities, are more connected with the Atlantic than with either the Pacific Basin or their respective land-based regions. Bolivia's intra-regional trade within the Alianza Bolivariana para los Pueblos de Nuestra América (ALBA) Accord is only 3%, and only 10% within the Andean Community, but its share within the Atlantic Basin is nearly 65%.

9.9.6   Second Indicator Test

In addition to using three scalable levels of hypothesis testing, we also perform a check by applying the second key indicator, the contribution of 'intra-regional' trade to the growth of total trade over the period 2000–2013, to each sub-continental, continental, super-continental, and ocean basin region for each of the ten Latin American countries in our study universe. This indicator represents an absolute deepening (or erosion) of a country's 'intra-regional' connectedness with any 'region' to which it belongs, or might belong. This indicator is formulated by dividing the total growth in intraregional trade in absolute terms (over the period 2000–13) by the total growth in a country's total global trade, over the same period. This indicator measures the degree of change in trade over time and thus identifies the particular region with which a country has recently most deepened (or weakened) its interdependencies.

This indicator is designed to help account for the very different starting levels of the Atlantic and Pacific Basins in terms of their respective levels of shares within

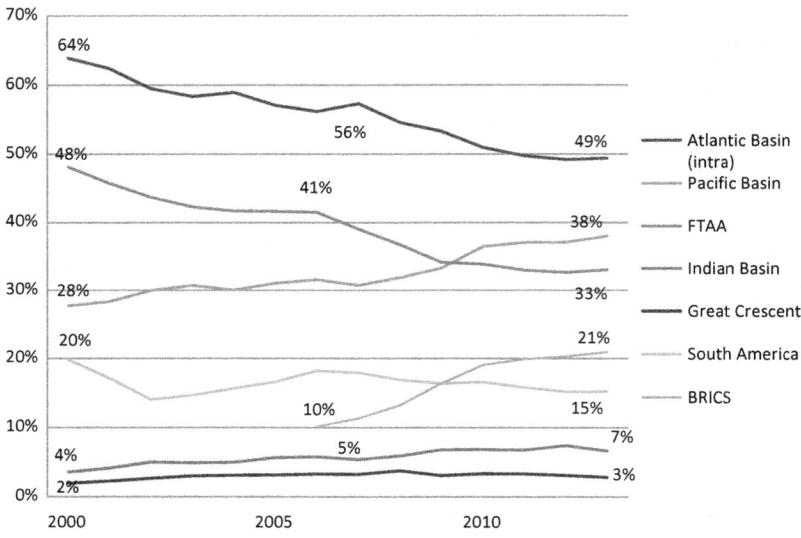

Fig. 9.4 Brazil: 'Intra-regional' Trade, Continental vs. Ocean Basin Projection, 2000–2013 (*Source: UNCOMTRADE 2014 and own elaboration*)

total global trade. As a rule, the 'intra-regional' trade shares of Atlantic Latin America countries within the Atlantic Basin, as a percentage of their global country totals, are very high, both at the end of our study period of 2013, and at our 'original' starting point of 2000. These Atlantic Basin shares are also typically the highest of all Atlantic countries' regional possibilities. However, they have also been declining over the time period of our study, while their shares in the Pacific Basin have been rising, at least as a percentage of the total.

9.9.7   Brazil and Argentina

Brazil (Fig. 9.4) and Argentina (Fig. 9.5) are two of the most – if not the most – emblematic countries of 'Atlantic Latin America.' Not only are they the largest countries of the region's Atlantic littoral, but they are also the two Latin American countries which more than any others, have historically built, or aspired to a trade regionalism at the sub-continental ('Southern Atlantic Cone' Mercosur), continental ('South America') and super-continental (Pan-American) scales.[16]

Of all the intra-regional trade shares possible, Brazil's highest is its intra-regional trade share within the notional/aspirational 'Atlantic Basin' region, which accounts for 49%, or half, of its total trade in 2013. This current Atlantic Basin 'intra-regional trade' share for Brazil is 11 percentage points higher than its trade with the 'Pacific

---

[16] Both states' opposition to the FTAA is a notable exception.

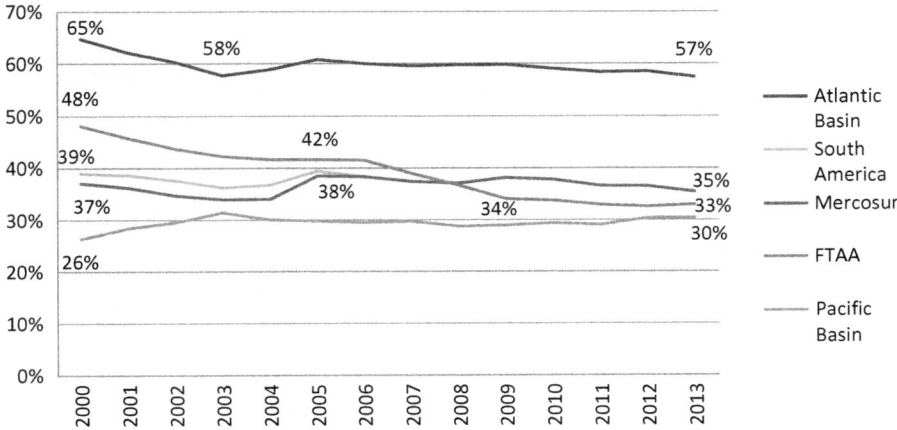

Fig. 9.5 Argentina: 'Intra-regional' Trade, Continental vs. Ocean Basin Projection (*Source: UNCOMTRADE 2014 and own elaboration*)

Basin' region, 16 percentage points higher than with the 'notional FTAA', 28 percentage points higher than with the new alternative 'conceptual region' into which Brazil has inserted itself, the BRICS, and 34 percentage points higher than with its land-based, aspirational 'continental' trade region, 'South America'.

However, over time Brazil's Atlantic share has fallen by 15 percentage points (from 64% to 49%) while its Pacific share has risen by 10 percentage points. Trade diversion here has resulted in faster growth in Brazil's Pacific Basin, Indian Basin and Great Crescent trade, and has crowded out growth in its Atlantic trade. When the increased shares of the Indian Basin and the Great Crescent are factored in, these expanded 'inter-regional' flows more or less mirror the recent decline (in percentage point terms) of Brazil's intra-Atlantic trade over the last decade and more.

Yet, the Atlantic Basin remains an attractive space not only for Brazilian trade but also for the strategic trajectory of Brazil's trade regionalisms and inter-regionalisms, particularly given that the economies that are most obviously set to grow the most in the future are those of Africa, in the Southern Atlantic. A new strategic trajectory of trade regionalism in the Atlantic Basin could place Brazil on the edge of a number of upward moving curves, including African growth and the development of the 'blue economy' in the Southern Atlantic (see Mattheis in this volume).

9.9.8 Argentina

The Argentine case is very similar to that of Brazil, only all of the recent trends have been less pronounced. Both Argentina and Brazil successfully pass the hypothesis test when applying the second indicator (contribution to growth in total trade) in all the cases in which they also passed the first indicator test (current intra-regional trade share of the total). This can be seen in Tables 9.3 and 9.4.

In short, the second test confirms that intra-regional trade creation (or, regional deepening) is taking place for the country and region in question. In the case of Brazil and Argentina, rising Pacific trade is not merely diverting Atlantic trade (see Fig. 9.5). Furthermore, in both cases, intra-regional trade continues not only to be created in the Atlantic Basin, in spite of a recent upsurge in Pacific Basin trade, but to be created still in net terms, given that growth is still greater, in absolute terms, in intra-basin Atlantic trade than in inter-basin trade with the Pacific.

9.10   Conclusion: The Limitations of Land-Based Regionalism

The European Union (along with earlier incarnations of Europe) has long served as a crucial benchmark for regionalism within academic, policy and diplomatic circles worldwide (Biswaro 2011). The traditionally high levels of intra-regional economic interaction among the national economies of the European continent, particularly in the trade and monetary spheres, have played a preponderant role in driving some of our current high water marks in transnational cooperation and integration. These achievements have likewise served as catalysts – and, if not models, then at least as reference horizons – for numerous other attempts at regional cooperation and integration in all of the world's 'continental regions'.

What has not yet been generally acknowledged, however, is that almost all of the regionalisms which have been heavily influenced by the EU model are also 'land-based,' 'sub-continental' and/or 'continental regionalisms.' If Europe has been a successful example of a land-based exception to what is increasingly becoming an ocean basin rule, it has only been replicated in low levels of intra-regional trade in Latin America.

This is not to say that all the maritime-focused, basin-based regionalisms that have more recently developed have been any more successful than their land-based, continental peers. The attempts of the various 'Mediterranean Basin' initiatives have suffered the effects of the very futures they had attempted to avoid on both sides of the basin, and at both of its ends. But this exception to the emerging 'basin rule' only underlines its potential strategic relevance for other emerging and potentially emerging ocean basin (and sub-basin) regional systems. As an increasing share of global trade links are routed by sea, the densities of the entire web of economic and political interactions between countries around each ocean basin continue to intensify at the relative expense of the land-based sub- and continental connections which historically have bound together traditional land-based continental and sub-continental regions.

Before the end of the Cold War, these early coalescing ocean basin dynamics could not yet be seen. In part, this was because they were either only barely nascent, or nearly all-pervasive, as in the case of the 'North Atlantic,' which long dominated all 'categories'. But this was also true simply because existing Cold War-era international data categories did not easily allow for their identification and analysis. Even the International Maritime Organization, a nearly universally acclaimed global international organization, classifies most of its data either along more abstract economically-focused categorizations or along 'continental' regional lines.

However, recall that the most recent age of globalization (late 1980s–late 2000s) dawned with the creation of the 'open regionalism' of the Asia-Pacific Economic Conference (APEC). This emergence of the Pacific Basin as a concrete regional system, first in trade, and then in broader forms of commerce and incipient political cooperation, was an early example of an emerging maritime-centered regionalism on the ocean basin scale. Put another way, it was the first expression of the actual geostrategic articulation of globalization that has evolved since.

As this 'age of globalization' unfolded, the coalescence of the Pacific Basin, deepened today by the recent formation of the Pacific Alliance and the Trans-Pacific Partnership,[17] was followed by the emergence of other early examples of the new maritime-centered regionalism, like the CARICOM and Mediterranean regions, along with the Baltic Sea basin region, another sub-basin sub-system within the Atlantic Basin. This emerging 'basin dynamic' was also apparent in the other basins, visible in the formation of the ZOPACAS in the South Atlantic between the southern cone and West Africa in 1986, the Arctic Council in 1996 and the Indian Ocean Rim Association for Regional Cooperation in 1997. Most recently, the Atlantic Basin Initiative (2014) and the Atlantic Energy Forum (2014) have emerged.

Even within the limitations of our conventional, land-based 'continental' projection of the mental/data map, we were well aware – as early as the late 1980s – of the strong turn-of-the-century gravity being exerted by 'Asia-Pacific' on global trade. A 'Pacific Rim' could at least be perceived through our traditional 'continental' framings and projections of the map. But this continental projection cannot readily reveal anything about the dynamics of flows, and their impact on geopolitics and international strategies, which range beyond the terrestrial landmasses and through the sea, to crisscross the world's ocean basins.

Indeed, each of the emerging ocean basin regions have initially coalesced around certain dominant initial 'issue tracks' of ocean-basin based regional cooperation: merchandise trade in the Pacific Basin (as in APEC and TPP), energy in the Atlantic Basin (as in the Atlantic Energy Forum of the Atlantic Basin Initiative), security in its multi-faceted expression in the South Atlantic (through ZOPACAS) and the Indian Ocean Basin (as in the Indian Ocean Rim Organization), or as ecological and maritime security in the Arctic (as in the agenda of the Arctic Council). An ocean basin projection might shed light on the potential for ocean basin based regional cooperation not only in the Atlantic Basin, but also in the other basin regions, including the Indian Ocean Basin, the Pacific Basin and the Arctic Basin, where new regionalisms are in relatively early stages.

---

[17] See footnote 8, above.

As Latin American 'regionalism' – in the form of RTAs – progressed through the 1990s and 2000s, the global attempt to build workable global governance advanced and then retreated. Over this same period of time, this traditional, land-based continental 'regionalism' in Latin America stalled along the 'stepping-stone path' to 'global governance' and got stuck into an unsatisfactory vision for regional cooperation. Any sober if sympathetic assessment of the track records of MERCOSUR, the Andean Community, and other 'continental' aspirations like the 'South American Community of Nations' would have to at least allow, prima facie, for this claim.

Indeed, Latin America's current or aspirational trade accords derive, overwhelmingly, from Latin America's historically land-based, sub-continental (Mercosur, Andean Community) and continental (South America) traditions of regionalism which now suffer from weakening and increasingly eroded regional trade dynamics, indicated by low and declining relative shares of intraregional trade within Latin American country totals. At the same time, new spaces for regionalisms and interregionalisms are emerging on both flanks of the Americas where the intraregional trade dynamics, in contrast, are strong and accumulating – from the perspective of both Latin American countries and from that of the Pacific and Atlantic 'ocean basin regions' themselves. Indeed, as our tables demonstrate, intra-regional interconnectedness (in terms of the density of intra-regional trade) is now higher in the Atlantic and Pacific Basin regions for most Latin American countries than it is in their traditional, land-based groupings. This is certainly not to say the landmasses lose all significance (if any in absolute terms) on the evolving trade map; Only that the significance of landmasses relative to the sea is declining, and that their dynamics (in terms of flows) are changing, both on the maritime 'rim lands' and in the interior 'continental hinterlands.'

This conclusion has important implications not just for Latin America's existing 'continental' regionalisms but also for its historical inter-regional trajectories. The Pacific coast countries of Latin America that have formed the Pacific Alliance now look forward to the TPP and the broadening and deepening of the Pacific Basin.[18] On the other hand, Atlantic countries might reformulate the equations of existing regionalisms and inter-regionalisms which extend across the Atlantic space – from the Iberoamerican and Lusophone Communities to the EU-CELAC bi-regionalism (See Ayuso and Gardini in the volume), and the nascent post-hegemonic links between Mercosur and the Southern African Development Community (SADC) in the South Atlantic. These overlapping experiences could be rearticulated to create a new pan-Atlantic region for transnational cooperation.

Both the Pacific and Atlantic Basins present Latin American countries with new maritime-centered forms and geographical expressions of 'open regionalism' and other 'post-hegemonic' approaches to international trade accords which could be more advantageous to pursue, now and in the future, than the traditional, land-based, continental trajectories of the past. Signs of this nascent 'ocean basin regionalism' can be identified in both of Latin America's ocean basins where concrete expressions of it either already exist (APEC), are being articulated (TPP, TTIP), or are now

---

[18] See footnote 8, above.

on the horizon in the form of a new Atlantic Community which serves as a flag on the strategic scope of the 'Atlantic Basin Initiative'.

Acknowledgments We thank Frank Mattheis and John McCormack for extensive comments on earlier drafts, and Elsy Gonzalez and Jair Cabrera for research assistance. All errors remain our own.

ANNEX: Data and Methods

The Alternative Regional Mapping Model (ARM)

To produce an 'ocean basin projection' of the global geopolitical and geo-economic flow map requires a 're-cutting' of the current data to account for a number of geographical realities of the world's ocean basins.

To generate such an 'ocean basin projection' of the data, we have constructed an 'alternative regional data mapping model' (ARM). Even though the issue at hand is Latin American trade regionalism, in order to capture ocean basin regional dynamics we map beyond the geographical relief of the 'continental' landmasses of the 'Western Hemisphere'. We acknowledge the distortions that might arise in this projection if it were to neglect a proper treatment of the 'dual basin' issue

The ARM model is used to compare the relative regional trade connectedness of a number of representative Latin American countries since 2000, when the full emergence of China into the global trade arena became clear in the wake of its WTO accession at the peak of the post-Cold War globalization era.

Data and Indicators

The basic data used as inputs into the model are national (ie, country level) 'bilateral' trade figures (ie, total merchandise trade: export plus imports) over the period 2000–2013. This annual bilateral trade data comes from the UNCOMTRADE database. Because UNCOMTRADE's coverage includes all of the world's annual bilateral international trade at the country level, it captures nearly all of world trade each year in a way which allows for national level analysis. Following the appropriate conceptualization and coding, the national figures are aggregated and subsequently 'mapped' from (or in relation to) any scale or perspective (ie. sub-regional, regional, continental, basin, global etc). To test the proposed hypothesis, this annual trade data is compared to chosen the relative intensities of regional and inter-regional connections and dynamics from both the country and the continental/basin regional perspectives.

The first key indicator is the share of a country's total international trade which is considered to be 'intra-regional' – that is, trade with another country that is considered to belong to the same 'region.' This indicator represents the relative intensity of a country's international trade interdependence (or intraregional trade 'connectedness') within a defined region. This indicator is formulated by dividing the level of a country's intraregional trade by the level of its total global trade. What is not 'intra-regional' trade (in relation to any defined region) is considered to be 'extra-regional' trade with the rest of the world – that is, trade with countries outside the defined region. 'Inter-regional' trade – a sub-set of 'extra-regional' trade – is considered to be trade outside the defined region with another defined region.

The second key indicator is the contribution of 'intra-regional' trade to the growth of a country's (or a continental/ocean basin-region's) total trade over the period 2000–2013. This indicator is formulated by dividing the total growth in intra-regional trade (in absolute terms, over the period 2000–13) by the total growth in a country's total global trade, over the same period. This indicator represents an absolute deepening (or erosion) of a country's 'intra-regional' connectedness with any 'region' to which it belongs, or might belong, reveals the particular region with which a country has recently most deepened (or weakened) its interdependences.

Basin Definitions

In this section we delineate which countries of the world belong to which ocean basin regions used in the data projections, including our identification of dual and tri-basin countries.

The Atlantic Basin (AB):

North America Canada (tri-P-A), US (tri-P-A), Mexico (dual-P)

Latin America and the Caribbean (LAC) Mexico (dual-P), Bermuda, Bahamas, Cuba, Jamaica, Haiti, Dominican Republic, Barbados, Trinidad and Tobago, Dominica, Grenada, St. Lucia, *THE REST OF THE Caribbean countries*, Belize, Guatemala (DUAL-P), Colombia (dual-P), Nicaragua (dual-P), Honduras (dual-P), Costa Rica (dual-P), Panama (dual-P), Venezuela, Guyana, Surinam, French Guiana, Paraguay, Brazil, Uruguay, Bolivia, Argentina

Africa South Africa (dual-IO), Lesotho (dual-IO), Namibia, Angola, Botswana (dual-IO), Zaire, Congo, Gabon, Chad, Sudan (dual-IO), Cameroon, Equatorial Guinea, Nigeria, Central African Republic, Togo, Ghana, Burkina Faso, Benin, Ivory Coast, Liberia, Sierra Leone, Guinea, Guinea Bissau, Gambia, Senegal, Mali, Niger, Mauritania, Cape Verde, Morocco, Algeria, Tunisia, Libya, Egypt (dual-IO), Zambia (dual-IO), Zimbabwe (dual-IO)

EU and the remaining Mediterranean Spain, Portugal, France, Italy, Malta, UK, Ireland, Belgium, Netherlands, Germany, Luxemburg, Denmark (dual-A, including Greenland), Sweden (dual-A), Finland (dual-A), Slovenia, Andorra, Croatia, Czech

Republic, Austria, Hungary, Slovakia, Poland, Serbia, Montenegro, Bosnia-Herzegovina, FYR Macedonia, Albania, Greece, Bulgaria, Rumania, Cyrus, Lithuania, Estonia, Latvia, Norway (dual-A), Switzerland, Iceland (dual-A), Turkey (dual-GC), Israel (dual-IO), Lebanon (dual-IO)

The Pacific Basin (P):

Canada (tri-AB-A), United States (tri-AB-A), Mexico (dual-AB), San Salvador, Costa Rica (dual-AB), Panama (dual-AB), Colombia (dual-AB), Peru, Ecuador, Chile, Russia (tri-GC-A), China, Japan, Australia (dual-IO), New Zealand, South Korea, North Korea, Philippines, Indonesia (dual-IO), Vietnam, Thailand (dual-IO), Malaysia (dual-IO), Singapore (dual-IO), Laos, Cambodia, Timor-Leste, Papua New Guinea, New Marshall Islands, Tuvalu, Vanuatu, New Caledonia, Federated States of Micronesia, Salomon Islands

The Indian Ocean Basin (IO):

Israel (dual-AB), Lebanon (dual-AB),Singapore (dual-P), Indonesia (dual-IO), Pakistan, Bangladesh, Burma, Nepal, India, Bhutan, Sri Lanka, Maldives, Thailand (dual-P), Malaysia (dual-P), Australia (dual-P), Saudi Arabia (dual-GC), Iran (dual-GC), Iraq (dual-GC), Kuwait (dual-GC), Mozambique, Malawi, Rwanda, Burundi, Uganda, Tanzania, Kenya, Somalia, Madagascar, Ethiopia, Djibouti, Eritrea, South Africa (dual-AB), Lesotho (dual-AB), Botswana (dual-AB), Sudan (dual-AB), Egypt (dual-AB), Zambia (dual-AB), Zimbabwe (dual-AB) Bahrain (dual-GC), Qatar (dual-GC), United Arab Emirates (dual-GC), Oman, Yemen

The Arctic Basin (A):

Canada (tri-AB-P), United States (tri-AB-P), Russia (tri-P-GC), Denmark (dual-AB, including Greenland), Iceland (dual-AB), Norway (dual-AB), Sweden (dual-AB), Finland (dual-AB)

The Great Crescent (GC):

Moldova (dual-AB), Ukraine (dual-AB), Belarus (dual-AB), Georgia, Armenia, Azerbaijan, Turkmenistan, Uzbekistan, Tajikistan, Kyrgyzstan, Saudi Arabia (dual-IO), Iran (dual-IO), Iraq (dual-IO), Kuwait (dual-IO), Russia (tri-P-A), Afghanistan, Bahrain (dual-IO), Qatar (dual-IO), United Arab Emirates (dual-IO)

References

Amsden, A. (2011). *The rise of the rest? Challenges to the West from late industrializing countries.* New York: Oxford University Press.

Biswaro, J. M. (2011). *The quest for regional integration in Africa, Latina America and beyond in the 21ˢᵗ Century: experience, progress and prospects: rhetoric versus reality? A comparative study.* Brasilia: Alexandre de Gusmao Foundation.

Borges de Sousa, J., & Lobo, F. (2014). On the future of ocean observation. In P. Borges & T. Martins (Eds.), *O mar no futuro do Portugal: ciência e visão estratégica* (pp. 57–67). Lisboa: Centro de Estúdios Estratégicos do Atlântico.

Botafogo, J., & Oliveira, D. (2013). Desenvolvimento e estrutura na América do Sul. In L. Paz (Ed.), *O CEBRI e as Relações Internacionais no Brasil.* Rio de Janeiro: CEBRI.

Holthus, P. (2012). Marine natural resources extraction. In J. Richardson (Ed.), *The fractured ocean: current challenges to maritime policy in the wider Atlantic* (pp. 119–158). Washington, DC/Brussels: German Marshall Fund of the United States and the OCP Foundation.

Holthus, P., de la Gorce, X., & de Saint Salvy, A. (2012). Fisheries: a resource in crisis. In J. Richardson (Ed.), *The fractured ocean: current challenges to maritime policy in the wider Atlantic* (pp. 91–119). Washington, DC/Brussels: German Marshall Fund of the United States and the OCP Foundation.

Hurrell, A. (1995). Regionalism in theoretical perspective. In L. Fawcett & A. Hurrell (Eds.), *Regionalism in World Politics* (pp. 37–73). New York: Oxford University Press.

International Institute for Strategic Studies. (2015). Pacific Alliance Trade Bloc Eyes Global Role. *Strategic Comments, February 2014, 20*(2), ix–x.

Kaltenthaler, K., & Mora, F. O. (2002). Explaining Latin American economic integration: The case of Mercosur. *Review of International Political Economy, 9*(1), 72–97.

Lamo de Espinosa, E. (2010). Un mundo post-europeo. In E. Lamo de Espinosa (Ed.), *Europa después de Europa* (pp. 75–138). Madrid: Academia Europea de Ciencias y Artes.

Mashayekhi, M., Puri, L., & Ito, T. (2005). Multilateralism and regionalism: The new interface. In M. Mashayekhi, & T. Ito (Eds.), *Multilateralism and regionalism: The new Interface* (pp. 1–22). New York/Geneva: UNCTAD. (UNCTAD/DITC/TNCD/2004/7)

Moreira, M. M., Mendoza, E., Meardon, S., & Brambilla, I. (2007). Regional Integration: What Is in It for CARICOM? *Economia, 8*(1), 97–142.

Payne, A., & Gamble, A. (1996). Introduction: the political economy of regionalism and world order. In A. Gamble & A. Payne (Eds.), *Regionalism and world order* (pp. 1–20). London: Macmillan.

Pitta, E., & Cunha, T. (2014). Marine ecosystem services, ocean natural capital and the new blue economy for human well-being. In P. Borges & T. Martins (Eds.), *O Mar no Futuro de Portugal* (pp. 49–55). Lisbon: Centro de Estudios Estrategicos do Atlantico.

Shaw, T. M., Grant, J. A., & Cornelissen, S. (2010). Introduction and overview: the study of new regionalism(s) at the start of the second decade of the Twenty-First Century. In T. Shaw, J. A. Grant, & S. Cornelissen (Eds.), *Ashgate Research Companion to Regionalism* (pp. 3–30). Farnham: Ashgate.

Söderbaum, F., & van Langenhove, L. (2013). Introduction: the EU as the global actor and the role of interregionalism. In F. Söderbaum & L. van Langenhove (Eds.), *The EU as a global player: the politics of interregionalism* (pp. 1–14). New York: Routledge.

Stopford, M. (2010). How shipping has changed the world & the social impact of shipping. Paper for the Global Maritime Environmental Congress, SMM Hamburg, September 7, 2010.

Tussie, D., & Riggirozzi, P. (2012). The rise of the post-hegemonic regionalism in Latin America. In D. Tussie & P. Riggirozzi (Eds.), *The rise of post-hegemonic regionalism in Latin America* (pp. 1–18). London: Springer.

UNCTAD. (2012). *Multilateralism and Regionalism: The New Interface.* New York: UNCTAD.

Van Ginkel, H., & Van Langenhove, L. (2003). Introduction and context. In H. Van Ginkel, J. Court, & L. Van Langenhove (Eds.), *Integrating Africa: perspectives on regional integration and development* (pp. 1–9). Tokyo: United Nations University Press.

Printed by Printforce, the Netherlands